MORBID
MAGIC

Ray Garcia Photography

ABOUT THE AUTHOR

Tomás Prower is a graduate of the University of California: Santa Barbara with degrees in global socioeconomics and Latin American studies. Born and raised in Southern California, his fluency in English, French, and Spanish gave him the opportunity to work for the French government as a cultural liaison throughout South America, with extended assignments in Buenos Aires, Santiago de Chile, and the Amazon jungle. Since then, he has been the External Relations Director for the American Red Cross, LGBT+ Programs Director for entertainment productions in Los Angeles, and a licensed mortuary professional in California and Nevada. Currently, Tomás resides in his hometown of L.A. as a writer and author of popular fiction and nonfiction works.

MORBID MAGIC

DEATH SPIRITUALITY & CULTURE FROM AROUND THE WORLD

TOMÁS PROWER

LLEWELLYN PUBLICATIONS

Woodbury, Minnesota

FIRST EDITION
First Printing, 2019

Cover design by Shannon McKuhen
Book format by Samantha Penn
Editing by Annie Burdick

Llewellyn Publications is a registered trademark of Llewellyn Worldwide Ltd.

Library of Congress Cataloging-in-Publication Data
Names: Prower, Tomás, author.
Title: Morbid magic : death spirituality and culture from around the world
    / by Tomás Prower.
Description: Woodbury : Llewellyn Worldwide, Ltd., 2019. | Includes
    bibliographical references and index.
Identifiers: LCCN 2019021987 (print) | LCCN 2019022255 (ebook) | ISBN
    9780738760612 (alk. paper)
Subjects: LCSH: Death—Religious aspects. | Death. | Magic. | Occultism.
Classification: LCC BL504 .P76 2019 (print) | LCC BL504 (ebook) | DDC
    202/.3—dc23
LC record available at https://lccn.loc.gov/2019021987
LC ebook record available at https://lccn.loc.gov/2019022255

Llewellyn Publications
A Division of Llewellyn Worldwide Ltd.
2143 Wooddale Drive
Woodbury, MN 55125-2989

www.llewellyn.com

Printed in the United States of America

I'd like to dedicate this book to you, yes you, reading this here now. Tomorrow is guaranteed to no one, and there is a finite amount of time each of us has here alive on earth. So I'm honored that you're choosing to spend some of that finite precious time with me exploring the morbid magic of our human tribe around the globe, before your own time inevitably comes …

CONTENTS

Part 2: Europe   59

CONTENTS

CONTENTS

CONTENTS

CONTENTS

CONTENTS

ALL ABOARD

It's not that I'm afraid to die. I just don't
want to be there when it happens.
WOODY ALLEN

What to do with a dead body? I mean, we've got to do *something* with it, right? Should we toss it in a large fire so that only pseudo-recognizable fragments of bone are left? Should we remove its brain and internal organs and anoint it with herbs and oils so that it can hopefully last forever? Should we cut off chunks of flesh and eat it so that its spirit will reside within each of us? Or maybe we should bury it in a hole in the ground?

Then again, if we want to be very modern, we should do what everyone else calls "traditional." And I mean "traditional" in the modern US sense: paying strangers thousands of dollars to take the body away, store it in a refrigerator with other dead bodies, replace all the blood with super toxic carcinogenic chemicals, sew the mouth shut, superglue the eyelids closed, paint the face with stage makeup so that we don't have to be inconvenienced by seeing the visual reality of death, place the body inside a metal container so that it doesn't get dirty when being put in the ground, put that metal container into another container so that the grass above won't shift and thus become more expensive for a cemetery to mow over it, and then affix a small metal plaque on the top with a pithy tagline that summarizes a human being's entire life achievements into a three-second read. Ah, tradition...

Now, I know this might come as a shock, but brace yourself, because I'm about to let you in on a little secret...our modern Western funerals aren't really traditional. So then why do we do them this way? How did

1

we as humans go from leaving our loved ones to decompose back into the earth wherever they fell dead to the bankruptcy-inducing pomp and circumstance that is the modern-day embalmed funeral service? That was the very question that set me off on my global trek around the world, exploring the funerary traditions, beliefs, and afterlife magic of our human tribe throughout millennia.

Working in the US funeral industry as a mortuary professional, I've seen a lot of families come in and try to answer that very first question I asked you at the beginning of this introduction: What to do with a dead body? I always tried my best to help families make the choice most correct for them and their deceased loved one, but at the end of the day, past all the razzle-dazzle of personalized funeral and memorial services, the family really only has two options: pay a lot of money to put their loved one in a Russian nesting doll series of containers that'll be buried in the ground or pay a lot of money to incinerate them and grind their bones in an industrial blender so that the remains look like sand or "ashes." Of course, it also doesn't help that these expensive and permanent decisions are being made in a severe emotional state without much foreplanning and have to be made soon.

But it didn't use to be like this. Before advancements in medicine and the capitalist industrialization of handling the deceased, it was the family and the local village who used to take care of a loved one's corpse. It wasn't just the body they dealt with, either. Creative and participatory rituals were developed to care for the soul of the loved one and ensure their safe passage to the afterlife. There were deities worshiped whose sphere of influence included underworlds, destruction, decay, and the mystery of what happens after we shuffle off this mortal coil. Magical spells were even developed to extinguish the life of an enemy as well as to protect us from the supernatural harm and vengeance that the dead could enact upon us.

We humans used to interact with death every day, physically, emotionally, spiritually, and magically. Nowadays, we are so removed from death that it seems like something unnatural. Then it comes as a complete shock when it does happen, which is ironic because death is *the* most natural and singularly absolute guarantee in life.

Anyway, the more I worked in a mortuary, and the more I tried to help families deal with grief and prepare their loved one's corpse for the great beyond, the more I couldn't help but think of all the ways throughout human history that we have developed to deal with and overcome these saddest and most tragic times of our lives. People have been dying just as long as people have been living, and it was never exclusive to any one creed, color, or corner of the globe. Maybe if I learned about the funerary traditions, spirituality, and magic from our human family all over the world, I could better help the families I serve who come to me at what is undoubtedly one of the worst times in their lives.

This is the accumulation of all that exploration. In these pages are the beliefs and spiritual practices of cultures and religions from every region of the world, from prehistory to the copyright date on this book. You are about to learn the magic and wisdom of the many ways we humans have interacted with death, on both the physical and spiritual planes.

Although this isn't a how-to book on crafting magic spells per se, along our trek we'll meet modern-day living community members from various cultures who'll share some stories and participatory dark rituals from their macabre magical practices and their personal relationships with death. And I'll even share little takeaway challenges/activities for you to implement into your own life and practice, because what good is knowledge if it's not applied? But be warned: These aren't the kind of rituals to pick up and start testing right away. No, dark rituals are very powerful, so very heavy, and sometimes beyond what you could ever bear even at your spiritual peak.

To emphasize this point while our train is loading before we set off on our journey, I'll let the cautionary tragic tale of my friend serve as an example of what I mean. Back in 2016, about a year after my first macabre-themed book, *La Santa Muerte: Unearthing the Magic & Mysticism of Death*, was released, the international rights to the book were bought for it to be translated into Polish and distributed through a Polish publishing company. Well, one of the people instrumental in making that happen was a middle-aged Polish man whom I'll call Dominik. Through his involvement with the Polish version of my book, Dominik and I became friends, and we bonded over our mutual love for the morbid and macabre.

As happens to us all, Dominik eventually started going through a particularly rough patch in his life, and he turned to magic to change things around. He felt his problems were so severe that he enlisted the help of la Santa Muerte (the Mexican folk deity of death and patroness of the desperate, whom we'll explore more when we get to Mexico) to turn things around. Sure, he was familiar with my book and had a magical background of sorts, but he hadn't really ever worked with death magic before, especially not with la Santa Muerte (the spiritual personification of death itself), nor did he truly understand the cultural context in which her morbid magic is rooted.

Well, la Santa Muerte did indeed help my friend, by completely shattering the precious illusions through which he saw his life. Within a week he found out that his wife of twenty-plus years never loved him, only married him for the money, and had been having a regular affair with her real lover. He realized that he was stuck in a personally unfulfilling job wherein, although successful, he had already wasted half his life not pursuing his true passions. And much more.

Without his illusions blinding him, my friend was now free to overcome the difficulties in his life, but in the throes of such unpleasant realizations that were brought into focus by the harsh light of reality, he now saw the world as ugly, unfair, and uncaring. He had gotten what he wanted, but now all he wanted was to see the world through rose-tinted glasses again. He missed the illusions and comforting lies, but once you see past them and into reality, you can never fully believe in the illusions anymore.

My friend killed himself a few months later, around Christmastime. In retrospect, his partnering with a deity of death and the underworld did more harm than good. Yes, Dominik was given the help to change his life around, but in his desperation, he had forgotten that death is a destructive force. Destruction certainly does lead to creation, but you have to be able to withstand the destruction of your current world before you can create a new one. It seems doable when thinking about it, but it's not until the walls come crashing violently down all around you that you realize how difficult and painful a process morbid magic can be.

So take extra care before you go experimenting with morbid magic, especially morbid magic from other cultures. The energy and magic of death is a lot to deal with, let alone the confusion, unfamiliarity, and greater chance of misunderstandings that working with the magic and deities of other cultures can bring.

I'll guide you through this train ride into the morbid nether regions of human spirituality from safe vantage points, but if you *really* want to become proficient in the dark magic of a tradition that calls to you and speaks to your soul, do your research before jumping in headlong. You owe it to the culture, the deities of that culture, and yourself to know what the hell you're doing, lest you become the victim of your own hastiness and lack of respect. Now hop on board; we have quite an adventure ahead of us!

PART I

GREATER MIDDLE EAST

Oh Friend, the cloth from which
your burial shroud will be cut may
have already reached the market
and yet you remain unaware.
IMAM AL-GHAZĀLĪ

Out of the sands of the Middle East have come a good majority of our modern world's most influential and societally powerful religions. Still very much active and influencing our Western lives today, these are humanity's big three monotheistic religions: Judaism, Islam, and Christianity.

When it comes to dark rituals and macabre traditions, these three have very similar practices and beliefs. Eternal paradise is the mutually shared final destination, and it is believed that your entire life should be lived in such a way that you better your chances of getting there. Sure, socially conservative laws/traditions might be restrictive and personally burdensome, but eighty-some years (if you're lucky) of self-denial is a small price to pay for an eternity of unrestricted bliss and happiness. "Suffer in this world, live in the next" is the mentality that dictates daily life.

For our time here, we'll only focus on the two of the big three that are still most prominent here in the region: Judaism and Islam. We'll save Christianity for when we head up north to Europe, where it truly took hold and became the ultraritualized powerhouse it is today.

Nevertheless, there is more in the Greater Middle East than just monotheism. The sun-scorched sands here have seen many cultures and religions come and go. Their grounds are embedded with the dead of humanity's earliest urbanites and the world's first civilizations, whose funerary endeavors still stand the test of time as wonders of the word. So, we'll start here at the very beginning, which, so I've heard, is a very good place to start.

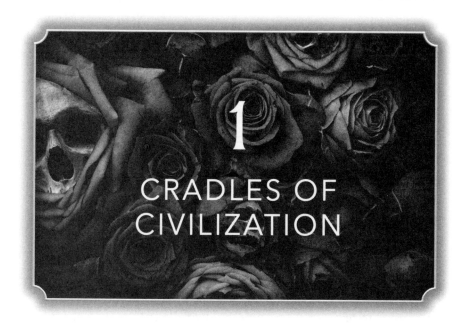

1

CRADLES OF CIVILIZATION

Cultural

MESOPOTAMIA

When our early ancestors began to unlock the secrets of agriculture, the way we interacted with everything, including death, changed forever. Gone were our hunter-gatherer days of traveling here and there to collect ripe vegetation and following migration patterns for meat. The agricultural revolution provided a steady, reliable supply (weather gods permitting) of food and put a stop to our wandering ways, since we now needed to stay in one place to grow, tend, and harvest the fields or pastures of domesticated animals.

With less movement here and there, we developed culture, cities, codified laws to govern those cities, metalworking, architecture, and organized religion. Despite these new agrarian, social, and technological advancements, though, humans kept on dying, and the mortality rate of these new urbanites remained a steady 100 percent (and it still hasn't changed after all these millennia).

In dealing with this assurance of death in the city, the people of Mesopotamia developed their own unique beliefs on the subject. Granted, while Mesopotamia was not a single culture, the various civilizations that rose and fell on the banks of the Tigris and Euphrates Rivers and all along the Fertile Crescent did share a lot of cultural and religious commonalities. Of these civilizations, those most well-known to us today include Sumer, Phoenicia, Akkad, Babylonia, and Assyria.

Location, Location, Location

When it came to what to do with dead bodies, the regional standard was burial. On the practical side, cremation was nonoptimal, because to successfully cremate a human body to completion back then required a lot of wood to burn for a long time, but living in the desert, wood was scarce. Thus, whatever wood was available was too precious and too rare for incinerating corpses. On the religious side, Mesopotamians believed that as the body decays, the soul is set free and can travel to the afterlife. In their cosmology, the afterlife was an underworld located deep beneath the ground, and so by burying the dead, it made sense that the soul of the deceased would have easier access to the underworld, having already been interred in the uppermost regions of that realm.[1]

Being a more urbanized and static society meant there were a growing number of bodies to deal with and less room to bury them all, problems their rolling stone ancestors never had to face. So, these civilizations here in Mesopotamia became some of the earliest to develop communal grounds wherein the deceased could be individually buried, and thus cemeteries came into being. Technically, though, the honor of "world's oldest cemetery" belongs to Taforalt, a cave in modern-day Morocco whose exca-

[Handwritten margin note: Not enough wood for cremation]

---

[1] Joshua J. Mark, "Burial," In *Ancient History Encyclopedia*, Sept. 2, 2009.
https://www.ancient.eu/burial/ (accessed May 5, 2018).

vated skeletons date back 15,000 to 14,000 years (a rarity for the hunter-gatherer peoples of the times).[2]

In terms of Mesopotamia, specifically, the Sumerians were the first to bury their dead in cemeteries, beginning around 5000 BCE. However, just like nowadays, cemetery plots were expensive and difficult to personally maintain (even more expensive if a caretaker needed to be hired to maintain them). Unsurprisingly, the corpses of the upper class became the main inhabitants of Mesopotamian cemeteries. In the case of the common folk, the dead were buried right next to the house (or under the house in the very urban areas) since the land was already theirs and cost and maintenance were much easier.[3]

You've got to understand, maintenance was a *big* issue to the Mesopotamians, because without constant interaction with the resting places of the dead, the ghosts of their deceased loved ones would haunt them like no one's business. You see, despite being dead, it was believed that the souls of the deceased still suffered from hunger and thirst, but they were now unable to procure food and drink (because, y'know, they're dead). That meant their still-living family was expected to offer them regular food and drink at their gravesite. If the living relatives were foolish enough to not offer regular sustenance, it was believed that the disembodied spirits of the dead would become so hangry that they'd purposely terrorize their family through poltergeist activity, human possession, unexplained unfortunate events, and even illness to the point of death.[4]

Epic Underworld

The underworld itself probably contributed to the hostility of the dead toward the living. One of the most thorough descriptions of the afterlife

---

2   Valentina Mariotti, Silvana Condemi, and Maria Giovanna Belcastro, "Iberomaurusian funerary customs: new evidence from unpublished records of the 1950s excavations of the Taforalt necropolis (Morocco)," *Journal of Archaeological Science Vol. 49*, Sept. 2014.

3   Mark, "Bural," In *Ancient History Encyclopedia*.

4   Greg Woolf, *Ancient Civilizations: The Illustrated Guide to Belief, Mythology, and Art* (San Diego: Thunder Bay Press, 2005).

from this region that survives to modern times comes from the *Epic of Gilgamesh*, the world's oldest literary epic. Each Mesopotamian culture had its own translation of the story with its own edits, but in general, the underworld was described as a miserable place. There was no heaven or hell, but rather a singular underground land that was enveloped in shadows, where no sustenance could be found to satiate the dead's hunger and thirst.

In the Sumerian version of the epic (the original version), our hero Gilgamesh ends up going on a quest to obtain the secret of eternal life after being deeply traumatized with existential dread by the death of his best friend and lover, Enkidu. Based on a rumor that the gods had once granted immortality to a man named Utnapishtim, Gilgamesh goes searching everywhere for him to learn how to also be granted immortality.

His search eventually takes him to the underworld, where he learns of the ferryman who takes souls from the gravesite to the underworld, where there is nothing to do; people just spend their time hungry and thirsty in idle tedium surrounded by darkness. Also, if a soul had no living children, they would do nothing but weep and wail in sorrow for all eternity. If a soul's body was not laid to rest and buried, they would be restless and forever unable to relax. The worst fate of all, however, befell those who died by fire. Sumerians didn't believe that the soul was invincible; fire was the only thing that could destroy it. So, if a body was burned to death or cremated, their soul was disintegrated by the flames and simply ceased to exist at all.

The only nonterrible afterlife, however, was reserved for stillborn children. The rationale was that since they were denied a chance to be happy in life, it seemed unfair that they should then spend all eternity without joy. To balance this cosmic injustice, stillborn children were believed to be welcomed by Ereshkigal (queen of the underworld) to reside in a special area of the underworld wherein they could play all the time and there'd always be plenty of food and drink to satiate their needs.[5]

Necromantic Dolls

At the end of his eponymous epic (spoiler alert), Gilgamesh fails in his quest to obtain immortality and dies, the moral being that the pursuit of eternal life is ultimately futile. As a sort of consolation prize, though, Gilgamesh did live on in a roundabout way through the memory of the people, due to his legendary deeds and achievements in the epic. More than just that, though, he was also believed by the people to constantly interact with the living from beyond the grave via necro-magic among the Mesopotamians.

A popular form of Mesopotamian necro-magic involved the use of poppets. By creating a doll that resembled the deceased, the soul of the deceased had a conduit through which it could travel back to the surface world (in a controlled, nondemonic ghost way that was safe for the living) and temporarily reside in the doll. These necromantic dolls had to be treated as if they were a living person, though. They had to have their own space and seat to sit upon in the home, rather than be displayed on a shelf or in the corner of a room like an object.

[handwritten margin note: Already dead]

If death was imminent, poppet necromancy was expected to start while the future corpse was still alive. Specifically, the doll would be prefashioned, and the moment the loved one exhaled his or her last breath, the doll would be given a place of prominence at the table and inundated with food and drink, thereby staving off the soul's hunger and thirst right from the get-go, as well as giving a little more time for the family to say their goodbyes (with focus entirely upon the doll, and not the still-warm cadaver in the room).

[handwritten margin note: made before death]

5   "The Epic of Gilgamesh," *Academy for Ancient Texts*, http://www.ancienttexts .org/library/mesopotamian/gilgamesh/ (accessed Dec. 14, 2018).
Pantera Rider, "*Sumerian Burial Practices/Beliefs*," *Burial Practices of the Ancient World*, Apr. 17, 2012, http://ancientworldburialpractices.blogspot .com/2012/04/sumerian-burial-practicesbeliefs.html (accessed May 8, 2018).

huge thanks to poppets

Gilgamesh himself would become a popular subject of necro-poppets due to his legendary strength and achievements. Since it was believed that proper interaction with poppets of the dead could result in supernatural assistance from the deceased's soul, there was no one from whom the Mesopotamians wanted more help than the mighty Gilgamesh. So popular was posthumous poppetry of him that giant public statues of him were even erected in places of honor (stationary, long-lasting public conduits for magic) where the community as a whole could provide offerings and plead for his assistance. This grand-scale reverence to idols would go on to be admired and respected by the Greeks and demonized by the soon-to-come monotheistic religions that would eventually take over the religious landscape of the Middle East.[6]

Mesopotamian Takeaway:
IN MEMORIAM

Sometime in the future, the very last person to know anything about you will cease to remember you, and then you will disappear forever as if you never existed at all. As Gilgamesh learned, existence on earth, beyond death, is (so far) only objectively possible in the memories of the living. This fear of being forgotten and having one's existence be relegated to the same oblivion as having never existed at all is terrifying.

Because people were motivated to live forever *in memoriam*, many of the world's greatest architectural wonders and artistic achievements have been made as a way to try to leave a lasting impression that will endure beyond flesh, bone, and personal memory (and if you think having children and family will preserve your existence, tell me all about your great-great-grandmother; chances are high that unless she did something of note, her existence has pretty much been forgotten aside from some photographs yellowing with antiquity in a box somewhere in the attic).

The Mesopotamians knew this fear well, and more than that, they *needed* to be remembered so as not to starve for all eternity in the afterlife.

---

6   Sarah Iles Johnston, *Religions of the Ancient World: A Guide* (Cambridge: Belknap Press, 2004).

But what are *you* doing to preserve the memory, nay, the very *existence* of those who have made an impact on your life?

Your Mesopotamian takeaway challenge is to preserve the memory of people who have influenced you to become the person you are today. Use your talents as an artist, writer, storyteller, singer, dancer, craftsperson, etc. to create a lasting homage to someone you feel needs to be remembered for future generations. They *can* be a relative, but they by no means *have* to be. What is remembered never dies. So if you want someone to "live" forever, keep their memory alive (or resurrect the memory of someone seemingly forgotten by everyone).

ANCIENT EGYPT

When seen through modern eyes, the ancient Egyptians seem to be a people obsessed with death. If you think about it, many of the things we'd consider iconic about ancient Egypt involve something to do with death: pyramids, mummies, sarcophagi, the Exodus story in the Bible, and so on.

Lasting Legacy

Much like the Mesopotamian takeaway with which you were just challenged, the Egyptians strongly felt that those who are remembered and spoken of by the living never really die. Thus, by leaving a profound legacy or something by which to be remembered, the Egyptians could attain a form of immortality. The pharaohs of ancient Egypt made sure that they'd be remembered in the form of detailed histories etched in stone and monumental building projects such as the pyramids. These large structures evolved as an exaggeration of the simple burial mounds of the masses, made bigger so as to reflect the pharaohs' greatness and leave something for them to be remembered by (and considering we're still talking about them today, they're definitely achieving their goal).

The pyramids (aka triangular monuments to death) also reflect the very real fears that the Egyptians had toward dying and the afterlife. Infamous are the hoards of treasure found in these ancient wonders of the world, and equally famous are their labyrinthine passageways and deadly traps that lie in wait for intrepid tomb raiders. This was all the result of the

Treasures left in tombs

belief that you, indeed, could take it with you when you died...all the wealth, servants, and luxury accumulated during your time on earth. Naturally, those with more wanted to ensure that they'd still have more in the afterlife, and those with less wanted to steal the entombed treasure to have more during their living years and beyond.[7]

The Soul's Journey

But just because you were a super wealthy Egyptian and buried in the biggest pyramid with the most obscene amount of stuff didn't mean you were guaranteed a smooth journey into the afterlife, or even a good one should you survive that journey. You see, in ancient Egyptian cosmology, there were a couple of things that could happen to your soul after death. In the best of all possible worlds, the soul would eternally reside in a paradisiac land known as *Aaru* ("Field of Reeds"). However, it's worth mentioning that life in Aaru did involve a degree of manual labor for such tasks as managing and harvesting the crops. But if you were rich enough to be buried with servants, slaves, or magical servitor dolls, they could do all that hard work for you. The worst-case scenario would be the eternal void of oblivion and destruction of the soul should you fail the final judgment of the dead by Anubis (the god of embalming, mummification, and escorting the dead through the underworld).

The soul, however, was not a singular spirit, but rather a mix of separate spirits whose whole was greater than the sum of its parts. Regarding the afterlife, the *ka* and the *ba* soul-spirits were particularly important. The ka is more akin to our modern Westerner's idea of a soul; it is the ethereal life energy that leaves our body upon death. The difference is that the Egyptians believed the ka still needed food and drink to survive even after death. This meant the ka relied on the living to constantly offer it sustenance so it could survive, again pointing to the need to be remembered after death.

7   Jeffrey Hays, "Egyptian Book of the Dead and Ancient Egyptian Views of the Afterlife," *Facts and Details*, 2012, http://factsanddetails.com/world/cat56 /sub364/item1949.html (accessed May 8, 2018).

The ba, on the other hand, was eternally attached to the body even after death. If the body disappeared through fire or through natural decomposition, the ba would disappear along with it. This was the impetus for mummification. It was imperative to preserve the body from decay, lest the ba rot away and with it all hope for a good afterlife in Aaru.

Now, supposing the ka kept receiving offerings and the ba was preserved through mummification, the key to getting into Aaru was the fusion of these two spirits into the akh, the reunited soul. The reunion of the ka and the ba was not simple, however, and there were many underworld challenges set in place to determine whether the soul was worthy enough to be reunited. This journey through *Duat* (the realm of the dead) was difficult, but you could receive assistance from the living in the form of magic spells and incantations found in the infamous Egyptian *Book of the Dead* (but more on that later).

The final underworld challenge was your soul's make-or-break moment. It was the "weighing of the heart," wherein the heart (thought by the ancient Egyptians to be the center of thought, memory, and emotion) was weighed against an ostrich feather that represented Ma'at (goddess of truth and justice). All of a person's wrongdoings on earth would stay in the heart, making it heavy, while a pure heart would be free of burden and therefore light. If the heart was lighter than the feather of Ma'at, the ka and ba could be reunited into the akh, but if the heart was heavier than the feather of Ma'at, the heart would be immediately eaten by a chimeric beast who sat in waiting at the base of the gigantic weighing scales. If the heart was eaten, that was it. The eternal void of nonexistence is what would become of you.[8]

Fading away into oblivion by failing the weighing of the heart ceremony or by being forgotten by the living was a fate worse than death, and avoiding the void was an Egyptian's objective in life. Essentially, they lived to die, and through dying correctly, they could attain eternal life, albeit in

---

8   Francesco Carelli, "The book of death: weighing your heart," *London Journal of Primary Care* 4:1, 2011, https://www.ncbi.nlm.nih.gov/pmc/articles /PMC3960665/ (accessed Oct. 24, 2018).

the afterlife. Again, though, dying correctly wasn't just a one-person job. You could do everything right by leaving a memorable legacy and by being a good person, but after death your afterlife was literally in the hands of others. You needed offerings and the ritual of mummification to sustain you through your afterlife journey until you could (hopefully) pass the weighing of the heart ceremony and reside in Aaru.

The Origins of Embalming

The most remembered funerary ritual of the ancient Egyptians is undoubtedly embalmed mummification. Just like nowadays, some embalmers were more reputable, and paying more money meant you got a better embalmer with better techniques and ingredients.

The low-cost option would usually involve injecting cedar tree oil into the abdomen, which would serve the dual purpose of dissolving the internal organs and disinfecting the abdominal cavity. To prevent the liquid from escaping the body through the anal or vaginal orifices, a plug was inserted to cork the holes. *Leakage* is the modern funeral industry term for this, and yes it still happens, and yes we still use plugs, though ours are plastic. Then the body would be covered in natron for about two and a half months to fully dehydrate. When this process was complete, the anal plug was removed to drain the internal sludge mixture of cedar oil and dissolved organs, and voilà, economical mummification.[9]

However, the deluxe mummification procedure was always preferable, if your family had the funds, that is. According to ancient Greek historian Herodotus, this complete process would infamously begin by sticking a hook through the nasal cavity and pulling out the brain through the nose (though modern forensic anthropologists believe the actual brain removal process involved using a rod to pull out only a small portion of the brain, followed by injecting chemicals made from the palm and bamboo family

---

9   Herodotus, "Herodotus on Burial in Egypt," In *Ancient History Encyclopedia*, Jan. 2012, https://www.ancient.eu/article/89/herodotus-on-burial-in-egypt/ (accessed May 9, 2018).

to dissolve the brain, and then rolling the cadaver onto its stomach so that gravity could drain the brain sludge like an intense runny nose).[10]

Now that it was empty, the expensive embalmers rinsed the corpse cranium with an antibacterial solution that not only washed out any bit of brain fragment but also helped prevent internal rot. An incision was then made into the abdominal cavity that allowed for extraction of specific internal organs (lungs, liver, stomach, and intestines, all of which were believed to be needed in the afterlife). These organs were carefully placed in individual containers known as canopic jars, each with a decorative stopper representing one of the four sons of Horus, who were said to protect its contents, along with a corresponding female goddess.

- Lungs: protected by Hapi, baboon-headed god of the north and protector of Osiris's throne, and by Nephthys, goddess of putrefaction and the death experience.

- Liver: protected by Imsety, human-headed god of the south and emotions, and by Isis, mother goddess of the sky, magic, and wisdom.

- Stomach: protected by Duamutef, jackal-headed god of the east and fallen soldiers, and by Neith, goddess of war and hunting, and the creatrix of the universe.

- Intestines: protected by Qebehsenuef, falcon-headed god of the west and closely associated with his father, Horus (who also had a falcon head), and by Serqet, goddess of fertility, nature, healing, and animals (especially venomous animals).[11]

10 Owen Jarus, "Mummy Brain: Gray Matter-Removal Tool Found in Ancient Egyptian Skull," *Huffington Post*, Dec. 15, 2012, https://www.huffingtonpost .com/2012/12/15/mummy-brain-removal-tool-egyptian_n_2301802.html (accessed May 9, 2018).

11 Moustafa Gadalla, *Egyptian Divinities: The All Who Are THE ONE*, 2nd ed. (Greensboro: Tehuti Research Foundation, 2001).

With these four organs safely packed away, the open abdominal cavity was rinsed out with a mix of palm wine and fragrant herbs, and then filled with incense and spices such as myrrh and cassia. After that, the body was covered in natron for no more than seventy days to dehydrate it, and then the whole process was wrapped up (literally) in bandages lined with an antimicrobial gum that acted as a waterproofing agent.[12]

The Last Temptation of the Embalmer

And before we start doing a deep dive into the death deities and legends of these ancient lands, let's close things with one additional morbid detail pervasive throughout ancient Egypt: the suspicion and fears surrounding an embalmer's private access to a dead body. These fears, however, were mostly only relegated to the bodies of the wives of high-ranking officials, royal women, and any female who was deemed to possess above-standard beauty. I'm sure you can guess the reason…and you're right: necrophilia!

Since dead girls never say no, there was a real, pervasive fear throughout ancient Egypt that the embalmers (practically always male) would take advantage of the corpses of women under their private care. Thus the bodies of beautiful and socially well-connected women would be mandated to decompose a bit before they could be embalmed. By doing this, their beauty would rot away and their families would feel more at ease knowing there'd be less temptation on the embalmers to mess around with the women's unresisting corpses.[13]

Ancient Egyptian Takeaway:
BODY PLANNING

A wise practice by the ancient Egyptians, which seems to be an uncomfortable and avoided task in modern society, is planning what will happen to your body after death. Once we die, that's it. No more time to

---

12 Herodotus, "Herodotus on Burial in Egypt," In *Ancient History Encyclopedia*.
13 Herodotus, "Herodotus on Burial in Egypt," In *Ancient History Encyclopedia*.
    Ashley Jellison, "Necrophilia in Ancient and Modern Times," *Out Front*, Jan.
    16, 2017, https://www.outfrontmagazine.com/trending/culture/necrophilia
    -ancient-modern-times/ (accessed Oct. 2, 2018).

sort things out. Thus, all of this morbid planning has to be done while we're alive. But many people can't seem to handle acknowledging their own mortality long enough to get their final disposition plan all set. The ancient Egyptians, however, made it their life mission to plan out what would happen to their body after death, and your ancient Egyptian takeaway challenge is to plan out what you want done with your body.

A lot of people nowadays feel that their family or next of kin "just knows" what they want done with their body upon death. But trust me—I've seen many a family wherein each child has a different idea of "what Mom/Dad would've wanted," and infighting ensues (yes, even in the most picturesque of families). Your ancient Egyptian takeaway challenge is to write down exactly what you do and/or don't want done with your body—a simple and easy way to ease the burden off of everyone, allowing them to grieve with one less hard and permanent decision to make (bonus points if you get it notarized).

This is even more imperative if you're estranged from your family. Common is the story of the LGBT+ person whose body becomes the property of their disapproving next of kin who can technically exclude anyone they like from the funeral (by barring them from the private premises during the services) and/or has them dressed and buried as the gender they did not identify with in life. Legally certified and written plans help prevent this and place your body sovereignty into the hands of someone you trust and love. The ancient Egyptians spent much of their lives preparing for what would happen to them after death; you can at least spend one hour preparing for your own.

Deities & Legends

ANUBIS

Anubis is the ancient Egyptian jackal-headed deity of embalming, mummification, and guiding souls into and through the underworld. Although *Anubis* is his more well-known name, that's actually a Greek translation of his original name, *Anpu* (which is similar to the ancient Egyptian words for "royal child" and "decay").

Also, modern scientists have recently discovered that the African golden jackal, on which his head is modeled, is actually not a jackal at all but rather a species of wolf (I know, po-tay-to/po-tah-to, but it's always good to know facts of a deity with whom you wish to work).[14] The "jackal" representation came about from observation of the natural world. Canines (like jackals and wolves) have scavenger tendencies, so the Egyptians would often see them scrounging up human remains, thereby associating them with the dead.[15]

To the Old Kingdom Egyptians (2686–2181 BCE), Anubis started off as just the god of burial, but this later expanded to him being the official god of the dead (a position later given to Osiris during the Middle Kingdom, 2000–1700 BCE). As god of the dead, he presided over the entire journey from death to final disposition, underworld travels, and final weighing of the heart. However, when Osiris was made god of the dead (which later myths backtrack and justify by saying Anubis voluntarily gave up the position out of respect after Osiris's own death), Anubis kept sovereignty over the hands-on aspects of death (embalming, mummification, burial, weighing the heart).[16]

One of the most interesting and unique things about Anubis is that he has a fiercely independent and "keep to himself" kind of personality and

---

14   Juan Romero, "African golden jackals are actually golden wolves," *Science Magazine*, Jul. 30, 2015, http://www.sciencemag.org/news/2015/07/african-golden-jackals-are-actually-golden-wolves (accessed May 10, 2018).

15   Toby A. H. Wilkinson, *Early Dynastic Egypt* (New York: Routledge, 2001).

16   J. Hill, "Anubis," *Ancient Egypt Online*, 2016, http://ancientegyptonline.co.uk/anubis.html (accessed May 10, 2018).

doesn't really meddle in the affairs of others or participate in social events. This is emphasized in Egyptian mythology by the mere fact that although he is one of the most widely depicted and called upon gods, he hardly appears in or plays any major role in a majority of surviving myths (except for the death of Osiris, which we'll explore more in a second).

EGYPTIAN BOOK OF THE DEAD

The *Book of the Dead* is an infamous ancient Egyptian literary text that contains all the essential information for a soul's journey through the underworld. It can probably best be compared to the *Handbook for the Recently Deceased* from the popular film *Beetlejuice* because it's designed as a practical reference guide to help the recently deceased navigate through the strange, dangerous, and often bureaucratic underworld, complete with tidbits of helpful hints on what to say to whom in the underworld to facilitate the journey.

Aside from being a handbook, the *Book of the Dead* also acted as a communal grimoire that contained a jumble of spells, prayers, and incantations to help give the soul an extra edge on its perilous journey in the afterlife. At present, there are about 192 surviving sections, ranging from protection and necromancy spells to special techniques for wrapping a mummy and character bios of all the major players one would encounter in the underworld.[17]

In addition to being buried with it so that they could have it in the underworld, the dead also had portions of the book inscribed in their tombs and written on their burial shrouds and bandages. The living also had their own copies, which they referenced during embalming, mummification, and funerary ceremonies, as well as had on hand for personal endeavors like helping a loved one in the afterlife and communing with the spirits of the dead.

It should be said, though, that the *Book of the Dead* was not a book in the same sense as this one you're reading now. Really, it was a loose collection

---

17   Dr. Raymond O. Faulkner, *The Egyptian Book of the Dead: The Book of Going Forth by Day* (San Francisco: Chronicle Books, 2008).

of individual spells and passages of postmortem insight that varied from copy to copy. Some copies could share some of the same info, but none of them contained all 192 surviving passages. In fact, physical collections of the book didn't even start to be compiled until the end of the Middle Kingdom (1700 BCE). The text's older incarnations from the Old Kingdom and earlier in the Middle Kingdom were known as the *Pyramid Texts* and the *Coffin Texts*, respectively (and their contents were both eventually absorbed into the *Book of the Dead* as it survives today).[18]

ERESHKIGAL

Goddess queen of the underworld to Sumerians (and to the successive conquering civilizations of Mesopotamia), Ereshkigal plays important roles in many of the region's myths, often as an instigator whose schemes tend to backfire on her, but not before causing lasting harm to others. In one of her most famous myths, she is portrayed as the villain in the "Descent of Inanna into the Underworld" tale, though the modern anthropological community sees her as the tragic hero of the tale.

In brief, the general story goes like this: The goddess Inanna wants to go to the underworld to attend a funeral for Ereshkigal's husband (a death that Inanna technically caused). The widow Ereshkigal tries to prevent Inanna from coming to the funeral and has her remove various accessories and articles of clothing at each checkpoint gate in the underworld. Once Inanna is naked and vulnerable upon reaching the end of the line, Ereshkigal kills her and hangs her corpse on the wall. As tends to happen in myths, though, Inanna's corpse is eventually spirited away by the agents of celestial gods and revived, essentially invalidating Ereshkigal's power and domain over death in that instance.

In modern times, New Age Jungians who worship the ancient gods interpret this to be an *Eat, Pray, Love*-esque story of a woman (Inanna) finding herself and her inner power through hitting rock bottom and confronting the darker aspects of herself. According to modern anthropolo-

---

18   John H. Taylor, *Journey Through the Afterlife: Ancient Egyptian Book of the Dead* (Cambridge: Harvard University Press, 2013).

gists of Mesopotamia, though, the story, in its original reading, clearly shows Inanna as a self-serving and self-centered woman deserving no praise. They go on to point out that Ereshkigal only killed her after the *Annuna* (judges of the dead) declared Inanna guilty of carelessly causing the death of Ereshkigal's husband out of selfishness (the person whose funeral Inanna was crashing by descending to the underworld uninvited).

Because Inanna is revived by the gods and escapes the punishment she is due, anthropologists have come to believe that this myth was actually a way to showcase and explain injustice. If a deity as powerful as Ereshkigal could be invalidated, wrongly overruled, and a victim of injustice, while a selfish, popular, and influential woman with powerful friends could escape punishment for her crimes, then so too could mere humans both be denied justice and not always get their just comeuppance.[19]

OSIRIS

God of regeneration, rebirth, the afterlife, the underworld, and the dead, Osiris is a major deity in the Egyptian pantheon. Like Anubis, the name by which he is well-known today (Osiris) is actually a Latin translation of the Greek translation of his name; modern Egyptologists have various versions of his name, though the most common is *Asar*.[20] In iconography, he was usually depicted in pharaonic clothes, wrapped in mummy bandages from the torso downward, and with either black skin (symbolizing the fertile soil of the Nile floodplain) or green skin (symbolizing rebirth/resurrection).[21]

In earliest Egypt, Osiris was a fertility and agriculture deity living on Earth among humans, while Anubis was the ruler of the underworld and everything postmortem. Osiris was very friendly with humanity and

19   Joshua J. Mark, "Inanna's Descent: A Sumerian Tale of Injustice," *Ancient History Encyclopedia*, Feb. 23, 2011, https://www.ancient.eu/article/215/inannas-descent-a-sumerian-tale-of-injustice/ (accessed Nov. 6, 2018).

20   "Osiris" In *Online Etymology Dictionary*, https://www.etymonline.com/search?q=osiris&source=ds_search (accessed May 13, 2018).

21   Mark Collier, and Bill Manley, *How to Read Egyptian Hieroglyphs: A Step-by-Step Guide to Teach Yourself* (Berkeley, University of California Press, 2003).

taught them how to utilize the Nile to grow and harvest food, as well as how to utilize laws to govern for a more harmonious society. Osiris's brother, Set (god of disorder, violence, the desert, and storms), hated the stability and order that Osiris was bestowing upon humans, and plotted to get rid of him. As the story goes, Set tricked Osiris to lie in a coffin in which Set's minions sealed him and tossed him in the Nile to drown. Isis (Osiris's wife and sister...because ancient Egypt) eventually found the coffin, which had been washed out to sea, but he was already dead by the time she opened it.

The story goes on to tell of how Set found Osiris's recovered corpse while Isis was out looking for a way to revive her late husband, during which time he cut Osiris into pieces, scattering him throughout the land. With help, Isis found (again) and assembled all the body parts (except the penis, so they just fashioned a prosthetic one for him) and revived him.

Having actually experienced death, the gods made Osiris the ruler of the underworld, demoting Anubis to psychopomp and the presider of funerary rituals on the body. Once Egypt came under Greek rule, Osiris began to lose his association with agriculture and become more stiffly aligned with death and the underworld, an alignment that still predominates today in Western consciousness.

2

JUDAISM

Cultural

While the ancient peoples of Mesopotamia and Egypt have left only static evidence of their existence, the Jewish people are still around today and practicing the same faith as their ancestors from millennia ago. This unbroken line of continual practice has made Judaism an exceptionally fascinating faith to explore when it comes to funerary rituals. The continuation of ancient rites in a modern world that has been changed by technology, industry, education, and globalization has often placed Jewish customs of death and dying in positions of contention with the laws and practicalities that dictate life in the twenty-first century.

Ancient Ways vs. Modern Days

Two of the biggest hot-button issues on funerary protocol that cause infighting between the various denominations of Judaism and modernity revolve around cremation and organ donation. In regards to cremation, it is expressly forbidden according to *Halakha* (Jewish religious law) because of the belief that the coming of the Messiah will resurrect the dead from their graves (and you need to still have a body, albeit a dead one, in order to be resurrected).

Your body is a gift from God, so burning it away entirely is seen as highly disrespectful. Some Orthodox denominations are so anti-cremation that cremated remains are prohibited from Orthodox Jewish cemeteries and traditional mourning over those who have been cremated is forbidden (unless, of course, they were cremated against their will as happened in the Holocaust). More progressive Reformist denominations, however, have adopted cremation as an acceptable alternative to burial, but still, the percentage of Jews choosing cremation is one of the lowest in comparison to that of adherents of other religions in the Western world.[22]

Postmortem organ donation is just as touchy, and this is because the standards and qualifications to be declared medically and legally dead are different in Jewish law than they are in the Western medico-legal community. According to the American Medical Association and the American Bar Association, there are two ways you can be declared officially dead: (1) all brain function irreversibly ceases, or (2) both your heart and lungs irreversibly cease to work.[23] According to traditional Jewish law, however, a person is officially dead only if the heart stops beating for at least five minutes straight.

---

22   Naftali Silberberg, "Why Does Jewish Law Forbid Cremation?" *Chabad*, Apr. 2017, https://www.chabad.org/library/article_cdo/aid/510874/jewish/Why -Does-Jewish-Law-Forbid-Cremation.htm#footnote1a510874 (accessed May 11, 2018).

23   National Conference of Commissioners on Uniform State Laws, *Uniform Determination of Death Act*, Aug. 1, 1980, http://www.lchc.ucsd.edu/cogn _150/Readings/death_act.pdf (accessed May 11, 2018).

Therein lies the problem: in most cases, an organ for transplant needs to be harvested while the heart is still pumping, otherwise the stagnation will lead to cellular breakdown of the organ, making it unfit for transplantation. Both sides of this issue are to this day fiercely defended in the Jewish community, with the Orthodox denominations opposing it and the Reform denominations supporting organ donation. Nevertheless, there does exist a group of Orthodox and ultra-Orthodox rabbis, called the Halachic Organ Donor Society, who are currently working to expand Jewish legal and cultural thinking around the practice of organ donation. Still, the general "agree-to-disagree" recommendation from both the Orthodox and the Reform denominations of Judaism is to consult a rabbi on a case-by-case basis.[24]

Assuming cremation has not been selected and regardless of whether there have been organs donated, the strict body-handling procedure in Jewish law again places it in conflict with the majority of modern funeral homes, which are not able to provide Jewish-specific rigorous services. Practicalities are at odds right from the get-go with the washing of the body because, unlike modern mortuaries which wash all the purging blood and body fluids down the drain (the same drainage system your sink and toilets empty into), Jewish adherents believe you need to be buried with all of your fluids, so anything washed away needs to be collected, stored, and eventually buried with the cadaver (which means embalming is out of the question). Then the body has to be purified with a continuous stream of water, followed by ritual drying. Finally, the body is swaddled entirely with a simple, hand-sewn, white burial shroud called *tachrichim*, which is purposely unadorned to symbolically show how all are the same in death (the only exception being that men can choose to also be buried with the iconic prayer shawl called a *tallit*).[25]

24   Aaron Moss, "Organ Donation," *Chabad*, May 2008, https://www.chabad.org/library/article_cdo/aid/635401/jewish/Organ-Donation.htm (accessed May 11, 2018).

25   Richard A. Light, *Guides for Performing Tahara*, May 2005, http://jewish-funerals.org/sites/default/files/spiritweb/cknm.pdf (accessed May 14, 2018).

A Chosen People's Protocol

When it comes time for burial, the Torah (first five books of the Jewish Holy Scriptures) dictates that it be done soon after death, ideally within twenty-four hours, lest the corpse "defile" God's earth.[26] This rush stemmed from a time when human decomposition was thought to spread disease and sickness (which science has since proven untrue, though the smell would have you think otherwise),[27] and so it was thought that the body needed to be buried ASAP in order to keep the community healthy. However, only the strictest Jewish denominations still adhere to that rule, with most denominations allowing a reasonable grace period so far-flung family can come and pay their last respects.

As for burial, caskets should be simple, wooden, and without metal of any sort so that they can decompose naturally in the ground. In Israel (and specialized Jewish cemeteries), the body is buried directly in the ground without a casket. It is even required that Jewish entombments in mausoleums have natural soil entombed with the body in the casket because it's outlined that never should the earth be completely distanced from a corpse.[28] Regardless of burial or entombment, the preferred body position is with the feet facing toward the Temple Mount in Jerusalem to await the coming of the Messiah (though for reasons of economy, Jewish tombstones may not always face the same direction as the bodies beneath them).[29]

Because of these strict protocols of burial (especially *shemira*, the ritual rule wherein a corpse must be accompanied by watchers who say prayers over the body from the moment of death until burial), *Chevra Kadisha*

---

26   Deuteronomy 21:23, *Tanakh*, https://www.mechon-mamre.org/p/pt/pt0521 .htm (accessed May 14, 2018).

27   "Dead Bodies & Disease: The 'Danger' That Doesn't Exist," *Funeral Consumers Alliance*, Jan. 30, 2008, https://funerals.org/embalming-myths-facts/ (accessed May 15, 2018).

28   Rabbi David H. Lincoln, *The Use of Mausoleums for Jewish Burial*, Jun. 7, 1983, https://www.rabbinicalassembly.org/sites/default/files/public/halakhah/ teshuvot/20012004/21.pdf (accessed May 14, 2018).

29   Baruch S. Davidson, "Do Jews Bury the Dead in a Specific Direction?" *Chabat*, Jan. 2017, https://www.chabad.org/library/article_cdo/aid/1672031/jewish/ Are-Bodies-Buried-in-a-Specific-Direction.htm (accessed May 14, 2018).

(which best culturally translates to "volunteer burial societies") are available within most Jewish communities around the world, and they ensure that the deceased are handled and buried in total accordance with Jewish law, often doing much (if not all) of the hands-on work themselves. Though most common in Orthodox Jewish communities, they can be found in all communities of all denominations, and should you like to inquire more about them, check with your local rabbi, who should know the contact information for your local Chevra Kadisha.

The seven days following the funeral is a time of deep mourning called *Shiva*. Mirrors are covered, makeup is not applied, shaving is not done, shoes are not worn indoors, bathing is kept to a bare minimum for hygiene, and the mourners only sit on the floor. Although this austere protocol isn't always so strictly adhered to anymore, the belief behind this was to focus all of one's energy on getting through the grief, facing it head on, and foregoing worldly comforts until you've come to terms with your new loss.

Ideally, the community would pitch in, help pay all the family's bills during this time, and supply them with food like in the olden days, but because modern communities are rarely that communal anymore, this part of the protocol is happening less and less. After the seven-day intense mourning, the next thirty days are a time of less mourning when normal life resumes, but frivolity and social fun is frowned upon. On the thirtieth day, the mourners visit the gravesite for the first time since the funeral, and the period of mandatory mourning is over.[30]

Abstract Afterlife

As to what happens to the soul after death, Judaism doesn't really focus much on it. Bits of the Torah allude to the afterlife being probably located in the center of the earth in a physical place called *Sheol*, but it was never authoritatively described. Around the time of the switch from BCE to CE,

---

30   Greater Lansing Chevra Kadisha, *Timeline for Jewish Traditions in Death and Mourning*, Mar. 28, 2004, http://kehillatisrael.net/docs/chevra_timeline.htm (accessed May 14, 2018).

the idea of an afterlife really began to flourish, but again, the details were kept vague. The only real details about the Jewish afterlife are about how souls will reunite with their loved ones in a world to come (called *Olam Ha-Ba*).

Thus, there certainly is no belief in hell in Judaism, heaven is left to an abstract concept of being with loved ones, and our actions on earth determine whether or not we will experience this reunion. The historic, purposeful de-emphasizing of the afterlife is thought by rabbinic scholars to be a way for Jewish people to focus on the here and now, because if a person does something only in expectation of a reward, then they are not deserving of the reward.[31]

Jewish Takeaway:
ALL IN THE FAMILY

One of the biggest worries from families that I've seen while working in the funeral industry is the anxiety that the deceased is being cared for with dignity (mortuary franchises often capitalize on the idea of "dignity" and even have it as their main selling point). They're scared that mom will become just another object to store in the industrial freezer and prep for final disposition, never being recognized as an individual or treated with loving respect. At best, this "disrespect" would be rough handling of the body and jokes about physical appearance. At worst, it would be something inappropriate done to the body or the stealing of jewelry, wedding rings, and cash left in wallets.

For practical purposes and peace of mind, Jewish societies have historically relied on their local Chevra Kadisha to take care of their loved ones after death. They would guard the bodies twenty-four hours a day to keep them from being "disrespected," handle them with the utmost religious dignity, and even pray for their individual souls. Most modern cultures

---

31   Rabbi Howard Jaffe, "In Judaism what is believed to happen to someone after they die? Is there some idea of an afterlife, or is that purely a Christian invention?" *ReformJudaism.org*, https://reformjudaism.org/judaism-what -believed-happen-someone-after-they-die (accessed May 14, 2018).

don't have something like this, and thus they rely on paying strangers a lot of money to do everything behind closed doors away from the family.

I can assure you that the vast majority of mortuary employees are good people who do try to treat every corpse as if they were family, but the reality is each corpse is still a client. During busy season (winter) a mortuary can be handling twenty-plus new clients every week, making it more difficult to give each corpse special attention. And even with personalization, your loved one is going to be wrapped in a plastic bag and stored on a numbered shelf in a dark, crowded industrial freezer next to all manner of people from bums and criminals to kids and community leaders.

If you're really worried about how you or your loved one will be treated after death, and you don't have a Chevra Kadisha, you can keep it all in the family. You know who's going to be ultrarespectful to the body? Family. In Australia, the UK, the vast majority of US states, and most provinces in Canada, the next of kin has the right to have the body at home so long as they can do all the paperwork and properly care for it (pro tip: dry ice), and there is a growing industry of do-it-yourself funeral assistance services that will help you wade through all the bureaucratic paperwork, care for your loved one, and hold services at home.[32]

So, if this sounds like a better option for you, your Jewish takeaway challenge is to start preparing to bypass the funeral industry and let your loved one be taken care of by family when the time comes. Especially if

---

32   Jaweed Kaleem, "Home Funerals Grow as Americans Skip the Mortician for Do-It-Yourself After-Death Care," *Huffington Post*, Dec. 6, 2017, https://www .huffingtonpost.com/2013/01/25/home-funerals-death-mortician_n_2534934 .html (accessed Oct. 25, 2018).
Karen Laing, "Can You Organise a Funeral Yourself?" *Lady Anne Funerals*, Apr. 7, 2016, https://www.ladyannefunerals.com.au/blog/do-it-yourself -diy-funerals (accessed Oct. 25, 2018).
"What to do when someone dies," *Age UK*, Mar. 23, 2018, https://www .ageuk.org.uk/information-advice/money-legal/legal-issues/what-to-do -when-someone-dies/ (accessed Oct. 25, 2018).
Rochelle Martin, "The handling and transfer of the deceased in Ontario," *Community Deathcare Canada*, Mar. 27, 2016, https://www .communitydeathcare.ca/handling-transfer-deceased-ontario/ (accessed Oct. 25, 2018)

you are a part of a minority faith, this ensures the body can receive any specialized last rights or rituals that a funeral home would never allow for "fringe" belief systems or because they would set off the smoke alarms. By keeping possession of your loved one, you ensure that mom receives the best care from people she loved, is always surrounded by family, and gets to stay in a loving, comfortable, personalized place until her final disposition (plus you save a hell of a lot of money, which mom would probably be happy about, too).

Deities & Legends

LILITH

In Jewish mythic folklore, Lilith is known as the wife of Samael (a Satan-like angel) and co-chief of all evil. Legends of her have varied throughout the centuries to depict her as a demon with various roles including murderer of children and their mothers, vampiric blood-sucker, succubus, mother of demons, queen of hell's angels, and much more. Her legendary origin story tells of how she was the first female human whom God created and the original partner to Adam from the Garden of Eden story arc in the Book of Genesis. As opposed to Eve, who was subsequently created from Adam's rib, Lilith was created as Adam's equal and made from the same source material.

Despite being derived from ancient Mesopotamian legends of "the dark maiden," most of Lilith's Jewish mythology really arose during the Middle Ages when she became the maligned icon of rebellious, sexually assertive, independent women, supposedly from her refusal to be subservient to Adam. Instead, she chose the company of the apple-tempting snake and refused to live in the Garden of Eden (preferring the uncertainty of being alone than the security of living with a man who wanted to control her).

In her loneliness, though, Lilith eventually kept trying to return to Eden by attempting to vocally befriend Eve (whom God created as Lilith's replacement) from the other side of Eden's border wall. Adam, however, feared that Lilith would influence Eve to become just as rebellious and demand equal rights, so he convinced Eve that Lilith was a monster of pure evil who was only trying to trick her.

On one occasion, Lilith got back into Eden by sheer brute force, but Adam ultimately beat her back into exile. Still, Eve saw Lilith during this fight and realized that she was a human just like her. At that moment, Eve became aware that Adam had been lying to her this whole time. From that point on, the couple became somewhat estranged, and Adam was constantly on edge that Eve and Lilith would join forces and take control of Eden away from him (sisterhood unity overthrowing the patriarchy, anyone?).

Lilith's demonic acts and hatred for humanity came later as a response to God murdering her children. As they were the *Rosemary's Baby*-esque spawn of Lilith and her unholy lover (Samael/Satan), God killed her babies when they were still very, very young so as to prevent them from growing strong enough to be a threat. Hurt and outraged, she sought vengeance, taking it out on God's beloved humans by murdering pregnant women, infants, and mothers. So great was the fear people had of Lilith that the wearing of specialized anti-Lilith magic amulets became fashionable and popular since they were their only believed protection against her. And if that wasn't enough, she gained a reputation for seducing men into having sex with her (often under the darkness of night) so as to populate her horde of demon offspring.

Essentially, Lilith was demonized (literally and figuratively) because she represented everything the ruling Jewish patriarchy of the time feared: an unapologetically liberated woman in total control of herself and her desires. Today, these same characteristics have made her something of a feminist icon among many Gentiles.[33]

SAMAEL

Samael is listed in Jewish mystic texts (particularly the Book of Enoch) as one of the angels who rebelled against God. He later played a big part in the Book of Genesis as (depending which texts you read) either the snake in the Garden of Eden who tempts with the apple of knowledge or the being who planted the forbidden apple tree in the garden in the first place. In the Zohar (which is a group of books in the Qabalah tradition that comments on the mystical psychology, cosmogony, and inherit mysticism within the Torah), he and his wife Lilith are described as the leaders of "the other side" (aka: evil).

Samael himself takes on the role of a Satan-like figure who is frequently associated with wickedness, holding the charge of "head of all the devils," "chief of the tempters," and, more commonly, "Angel of Death." Locked in an eternal struggle against Michael the Archangel (God's generalissimo of the heavenly angels), it's believed once Michael triumphs over Samael, the end of days will come. In traditional Jewish scripture, his most notable appearance comes from the Passover story when lambs' blood was smeared on the doorposts of Jewish homes to ward off the Angel of Death from taking their firstborn sons during the infamous final Plague of Egypt.[34]

33   Rabbi Jill Hammer, "Lilith, Lady Flying in Darkness," *My Jewish Learning*, https://www.myjewishlearning.com/article/lilith-lady-flying-in-darkness/ (accessed Nov. 6, 2018).
Kristen E. Kvam, Linda S. Schearing, and Valarie H. Ziegler, *Eve and Adam: Jewish, Christian, and Muslim Readings on Genesis and Gender* (Bloomington, Indiana University Press, 1999). https://books.google.com/books?id=Ux3bSDa2rHkC&pg=PA220#v=onepage&q=Lilith&f=false (accessed Oct. 26, 2018).
"Lilith Demon Goddess," *The Mystica*, https://www.themystica.com/lilith/ (accessed Oct. 26, 2018).
34   "Samael," *Jewish Virtual Library*, https://www.jewishvirtuallibrary.org/samael (accessed Oct. 26, 2018).

3

ISLAM

Cultural

Coming from the same region of the world, Islamic funerary rituals have quite a lot in common with their Jewish neighbors. Both follow strict protocol for the handling of a corpse, both have a specific mourning timeline, they have similar burial mandates, and they have similar death spirits. This isn't surprising since both Islam and Judaism share the same monotheistic supreme deity as well as the same founding father (Ibrahim/Abraham). For Muslims, though, *sharia* (Islamic religious law) predominately dictates what should happen when and who should do what in which manner in regard to death.

Unfriendly Fire

First and foremost, cremation is absolutely forbidden, no exceptions. There are a few reasons for this, but the main one is that it's considered disrespectful because it's classified as mutilation of the bodily vessel gifted to you by Allah (which also means the ultra-invasive process of embalming is *definitely* out of the question).

This prohibition on cremation also comes from a place of playing it safe, as well as serving a psychological healing purpose. You see, Muslims acknowledge that our human understanding of what happens after death is limited, and thus it is best to not destroy a human body after death and err on the side of caution, because Allah only knows if you'll need it later on in eternity. On the psychological side, Islamic mourners are encouraged to be present with the actual dead body because, although difficult, it helps the cognitive process of grief and grants closure (a practice modern science is discovering to be valid).[35]

Sharia Simplicity

According to sharia orthodoxy (still very much in practice by many today), a deceased person must receive a ritual washing (*ghusl*) by a fellow Muslim of the same gender, and because the dead body is considered unclean, all who come in physical contact with it are required to ritually cleanse themselves afterward. The dead body itself is technically required to be cleaned with warm water, ziziphus lotus leaves, and camphor … though household dish soap is mainly utilized nowadays just like in Western mortuaries (if it's good enough to get oil spills off ducklings, it's good enough for our corpse, no?). All in all, the ritual may be repeated as many times as necessary for a complete clean, but the total always has to

35   Candy Kaduce, "Cremation and Islam," *Neptune Society*, Oct. 13, 2015, https://www.neptunesociety.com/cremation-information-articles/cremation-and-islam (accessed May 15, 2018).
      Claire White, Daniel M. T. Fessler, and Pablo S. Gomez, "The effects of corpse viewing and corpse condition on vigilance for deceased loved ones," *Evolution and Human Behavior* 37:6 (2016).

finish on an odd number and be done soon after death (preferably within hours).

Immediately once the corpse is cleaned, it must be layer-wrapped in white burial shrouds (*kafan*) made of inexpensive material and free of stitching. Like in Judaism, the simplicity of the shroud and lack of elaborate embellishments emphasizes the equality of mankind in death and does not give status to the deceased.

In an additional effort to avoid glorifying the dead, burials are kept simple and austere, but have many strict rules. The body itself needs to rest on its right side facing Mecca. It doesn't need to be encased in a casket and can (preferably) be naturally and ecologically placed in a simple hole in the ground (though a sheet of wood should cover the body so dirt is not directly thrown onto it). Paramount to keep in mind during all of this is that only men can take part in the hands-on physicality of burial (and all must abstain from sex the night before), it must not occur at night, and Muslims can only be buried in Muslim-only cemeteries (preferably where the person lived most of his/her life and not transported back "home" or to where surviving family now reside).[36]

Widows in Waiting

The loved ones left behind (particularly women) are allowed to observe a three-day mourning period of grief and sorrow (beyond that, it's interpreted to mean the mourner neither trusts Allah's decision to call the deceased home nor believes Allah made the right decision). It's the widow in particular who has a very special postfuneral ritual. She is allowed (and expected) to follow a greatly extended mourning period of four lunar months and ten days, called *iddah*. During iddah (which is considered an extension of her marriage), the widow must not date, socialize with bachelor men, or engage in any sexual activity. After this period, the widow is

---

36   "The Ghusl Procedure," *Muslim Funeral Services, LTD,* https://www.mfs.asn.au/ ghusl—burial-steps.html (accessed May 15, 2018).

freed from her marital obligations and can resume life as a single woman once more if she so chooses.[37]

This extra stringency on widows served a social purpose for early Muslims (nowadays, strict adherence to the iddah largely depends upon the cultural conservatism/liberalism of the widow, the family, and the community at large). Back before DNA paternity tests were available, it was more difficult to determine who was the father of a child. So, if a widow gave birth around nine months after her husband's death, the community could not be 100 percent certain whether the child was conceived during the last months of the deceased's life or if someone else had gotten the widow pregnant soon after the funeral. Knowing this was important because a child's status and property rights were wholly tied to paternity.[38]

Moreover, the extra waiting period protected the widow from the repercussions of appearing too eager to remarry. Especially back then, married Muslim women were entirely economically and socially dependent upon their husbands, so it was natural that a widow would want to immediately start looking for another husband, even if she was still sincerely grieving, because it was a matter of survival. For better or for worse, the waiting period made certain that the widow would not gather gossip and be marked as unmarriageable (which would render her destitute for life) and protected any newborn from being forever stigmatized as a bastard child.

Also for economic safeguards, the deceased husband had expectations of him, too. The Qur'an dictates that a married man needs to write an official will sometime before his death. In the will, the husband must leave his widow with enough finances (either from direct savings or in premade arrangements with friends and relatives) for her to be sheltered and able to economically survive in modest comfort for at least a whole year

37   Aisha Stacey, "Funeral Rites in Islam," *The Religion of Islam*, Jan. 2, 2012,
        https://www.islamreligion.com/articles/4946/viewall/funeral-rites-in-islam/
        (accessed May 15, 2018).

38   Shehzad Saleem, "The Social Directives of Islam: Distinctive Aspects of
        Ghamidi's Interpretation," *Renaissance Islamic Journal*, Apr. 3, 2017, https://
        web.archive.org/web/20070403024603/http://www.renaissance.com.pk/
        Marislaw2y4.html (accessed May, 15, 2018).

after his death. However, the widow is not obligated to accept any of this should she have other, more favorable options available to her. Still, it's quite amazingly progressive a millennium and a half ago to mandate the preparation for a woman's economic security via a type of life insurance policy, and in a holy text no less.[39]

Waiting for Judgment Day

While not necessarily a "magical" religion in the strict sense, most of the supernatural overtones of Islam occur postmortem in the afterlife. It's Muslim belief that Allah created this world as a testing ground to see if a soul is worthy of a heavenly afterlife, and therefore *real* life begins after death.[40] I'll save a lot of the details and cool mythological stories for later, but for now, we'll just explore the general afterlife in Islam.

Upon death, the ethereal soul is thought to leave the body (very painfully[41]) and enter into a Limbo-esque afterlife to wait for the end of the world, during which they'll either be in peace or perpetually beaten by angels (more on that later). The belief is that the *true* and ultimate paradise will only come about when Allah decides to bring about the end of time. At this point, all people who have ever lived (assuming they weren't cremated, though this is still debated) will be resurrected, and body and soul will reunite and eternally reside in either a Garden of Eden-esque Paradise (*Jannah/Firdaws*) or a fiery Hell (*Jahannam*).

Meanwhile, sometime between death and the end of the world, angels are sent to question and place the recently deceased souls on trial for their goodliness. If they are deemed good, they can enjoy a peaceful waiting time, and if they are deemed wicked, they get to suffer a painful waiting time. Still, there's a very specific way a soul can avoid having to endure a painful purgatory, but we'll explore that when we talk about the angels Munkar and Nakīr coming up in the "Deities & Legends" section. First, though, a takeaway.

---

39   *Quran* 2:240, https://quran.com/2/240 (accessed May 15, 2018).

40   Matt Stefon, *Islamic Beliefs and Practices*, ed. by Hope Lourie Killcoyne (New York: Rosen Publishing Group, 2009).

41   Oliver Leaman, *The Qu'ran: An Encyclopedia* (New York: Routledge, 2005).

Islamic Takeaway:
WITNESSING DEATH

There is something about seeing a dead body that affects you in no way anything else can. To be witness to the severe stillness, quiet, and truth of a human body devoid of life affects your soul. Throughout most of human history, people saw death every day. Times were tougher, life spans were shorter, and the chance of dying from something we'd now consider minor or treatable made death a common sight. Nowadays, hospitals, nursing homes, and the funeral industry do everything in their power to whisk away a dead body and hide it from public view, because seeing death makes people sad and scared (both of which are bad for business). And when given the chance to see the dead body of a loved one, most people reel away because it would be too upsetting.

Yes, it's upsetting, but that's the point. The Islamic community knows this and still encourages it. Witnessing the dead is a sacred act. From very early on, they knew (and, again, modern studies have later confirmed) that one of the best ways to get closure from a death and expedite the grieving process is to witness death face-to-face. By seeing the body, you *have to* acknowledge that the person is gone. The stillness and quietness of death is unmistakable. The mental gymnastics of denial that we play to lessen our pain usually cannot be done if we see the truth with our own eyes. But if we never see death, we can delude ourselves to believe that it never truly happened, and we can never get closure on something that we delude ourselves into thinking hasn't happened.

For modern-day workers of magic, this same delusion is also all too common. Working with spirits of the dead (whether as a necromancer, a psychic medium, in prayer to one's ancestors, or what have you) is very popular. It's edgy and cool, and a lot of people resonate strongly with underworld archetypes and spirits. The delusion comes into play when those of us who are fascinated by underworld magic and deities of death refuse to witness what death actually looks like.

How can you work with ancestral spirits and death gods if you refuse to look death in the face? There's a name for such people who work with death spirits yet are frightened by and abhor an actual corpse...they're called posers. So, for your Islamic takeaway challenge, witness a corpse and be personally present with it for at least a minute or two the next time there is a death in the family.

Ideally, avoid the painted, "sleeping" version of a casketed corpse wearing mortuary makeup. That isn't death, that's a cosmetic and stage-lighting illusion specifically designed to help people avoid seeing the reality of death. Barring some severe accident that truly leaves the body "not suitable for viewing" (though if you think you can stomach it, all power to you), ask to see the body as it truly is without makeup and stage lighting (if you're the legal next of kin or have their written permission, the funeral home cannot refuse this request, and if they do, find another funeral home). It's painful, but shattering illusions and witnessing truth usually is.

Deities & Legends

ANGEL OF DEATH

The Angel of Death in Islamic belief is an agent of Allah, subservient to His will and direction only. He does not know when anyone will die, nor is he tasked with choosing who will die; he's just the messenger and separator of souls from their bodies. Nonetheless, he's classified as one of the four major archangels who has his own charge of lesser angels under his command.

Officially, he's only referred to as "Angel of Death" in the Qur'an, but he's commonly known as Azrā'īl (also spelled "Azrael," though both names come from Jewish interpretations and translations).[42] In Islam, the Angel of Death plays a major role in training prophets. In order to gain the spiritual wisdom and insight it takes to be considered a prophet of Allah, one of the recurring themes is that the Angel of Death is sent down to teach the trainees the secrets of the afterlife and of the magic in mortality.

---

42 Shaykh Muhammad Saalih al-Munajjid, "Name of the Angel of Death," *Islam Question and Answer*, Ju. 13, 2003, https://islamqa.info/en/answers/40671/name-of-the-angel-of-death (accessed Oct. 26, 2018).

One of the more unique encounters between him and a prophet in Islamic lore is the one he had with Moses.

According to the story, the Angel of Death came to separate Moses's soul from his body, but Moses apparently slapped him and refused to die. Never having been in this situation before (let alone with a famous and influential prophet), the Angel of Death recounted Moses's stubbornness to Allah who, in turn, told him that Moses could be granted a special exception.

Specifically, the decree was that Moses place his hand on an ox, and each tiny hair that touched his hand would be an additional year of life that Allah would grant to him. Moses excitedly did this but soon realized that getting what you want isn't always a good thing. Already pretty old and frail, Moses became gravely aware of what hundreds of extra years would actually mean. It would be that much longer before he could be reunited with his deceased loved ones, and everyone he'd meet and form a relationship with would die well before him. In that moment, Moses understood the harsh truth that extended length of life doesn't equal extended quality of life. The story comes to a quick end after that, with Moses asking to die and the Angel of Death dutifully obliging.[43]

MAWT

Mawt is the pre-Islamic Arabian spirit of death and infertility who was believed to be assimilated from the Canaanite god of death, Mot. Rather than a direct deity, the Arabians saw Mawt as the personification of the concept of death. Because of this abstraction, Mawt was not really worshiped directly, although he was often linked to macabre tales involving owls, ghosts, and nighttime.

To the ancient Arabians before the arrival of Islam, the afterlife itself was very similar to that of their Mesopotamian neighbors. After death,

43   Whitney Hopler, "Archangel Azrael," *ThoughtCo.*, Aug. 25, 2018, https://www.thoughtco.com/meet-archangel-azrael-124093 (accessed Oct. 26, 2018).
Imam Muslim ibn al-Hajjaj, *Sahih Muslim*, https://sunnah.com/muslim (accessed May 16, 2018).

a person's spirit would reside in a gloomy, dark, dismal underworld. The only exception would be for socially influential and well-respected people whose souls were believed to ascend to the realm of the gods, where they could help influence human events.[44]

MUNKAR & NAKĪR

Munkar and Nakīr are a pair of angels in Islamic lore who are tasked with being the first-round judges that the recently deceased will encounter, who determine if they will experience a pleasant or painful waiting period afterlife until Allah brings about the end of time. In English, their names best translate to the nonoptimistic "the Denied" and "the Denier," respectively. They are said to carry hammers with which they mercilessly beat the souls of those who fail their judgment.

The judgment's ruling is based on a simple series of questions, and their protocol for reaching a verdict is always the same. Immediately following the burial, Munkar and Nakīr enter the grave, prop the deceased upright, and ask their questions, which can be summarized as "Who is your god? Who is your god's messenger/prophet? What is your religion?" The only correct answers to these questions are "There is no god but Allah, Muhammad is his messenger/prophet, and I am a follower of Islam."

Should the deceased give these answers, Munkar and Nakīr will bring a peaceful purgatorial afterlife into the tomb where the soul can reside until the end of time. However, if any other answers are given, Munkar and Nakīr commence ceaselessly beating the soul with their hammers until the end of the world.[45]

---

[44]   Amr-Athtar Yunajjam, "Mythology and religion of pre-Islamic Arabia: Deities, Spirits, Figures and Locations," *Arabian Paganism*, Nov. 9, 2011, http://wathanism.blogspot.com/2011/11/deities-beings-and-figures-in -arabian.html (May 16, 2018).

[45]   Shaykh Muhammad Saalih al-Munajjid, "Authentic Descriptions of Munkar and Nakeer," *Islam Question and Answer*, Jul. 29, 2005, https://islamqa.info/ en/72400 (accessed May 16, 2018).

And as a side note, scholars for a long time now have believed that Munkar and Nakīr are Islamized versions of Zoroastrian and Mesopotamian deities (especially Nergal) absorbed into folk beliefs after the Muslim conquest of the Middle East. Aiding this belief is the fact that neither Munkar nor Nakīr appear anywhere in the Qur'an.[46]

46 Edward G. Browne, *A year amongst the Persians: Impressions as to the life, character, and thought of the people of Persia, received during twelve month's residence in that country in the years 1887-8* (London, Adam and Charles Black, 1893).

4

GREATER MIDDLE EASTERN MAGICAL COMMUNITY

STEPPING INTO THE GREAT BELOW

To start off the very first community section on our world tour of death, we have my good friend, Dr. Jacob Tupper, joining us all the way from the University of Minnesota to provide an authentic insight into how a modern-day devotee of the Sumerian gods incorporates his religious tradition's teachings of death and the afterlife into his everyday life. And if you're wondering, the "Dr." in his title is because he's a veterinary anesthesiologist who also spends time on the clinic floor teaching students. Outside of work, though, he's an active volunteer at soup kitchens and in local organizations promoting community action and environmental causes. In particular, he's a lifelong devotee of Inanna, Dumuzid, and Ereshkigal, the last of whom helped him out during a particularly dark time in his life, as the personal story and ritual below will explain.

When I first started on my spiritual journey, I never thought I would end up where I am today. I first became acquainted with Lady Ereshkigal through my first patron, her twin sister Inanna. For some time, I honored Ereshkigal as Inanna's dark counterpoint, but otherwise avoided directly engaging Her. That all changed when I got a call in August of 2015 telling me that my beloved cousin had died of a heroin overdose.

In the months that followed, multiple relatives ended up in the hospital with terrible illnesses, and I was subjected to horrific emotional abuse by the people around me in my professional life constantly ripping me apart and sending messages telling me that I was broken and incapable of love and integrity, undeserving of kindness and empathy. In desperation, I turned to Inanna and her husband Dumuzid for help and guidance.

To my great surprise, it was Ereshkigal who answered, asking me to stand on my own and help lay the dead to rest. Using the resources available to me, I constructed a quick ritual taking in the souls of the dead and encouraging them to pass on. Strangely, I actually felt stronger afterwards. In the years since then, I've refined my practice, and now work mostly as a mediator between the two Queens, working to mark both birth and death as sacred acts moving into the next phase of existence. The text for the modern ritual is included below:

(At night, start fully clothed and wearing a pendant or other piece of sacred jewelry. Place candles along a path from your home altar to another room, arranging them to mimic the seven gates of Irkalla. Call the quarters as desired, using an athame, wand, cup, and offering dish as tools to represent air, fire, water, and earth)

"We come on this night to honor the place of the Queen of the Great Below. You who have passed on, be welcome here on this night. Let us pass together through the gates of Irkalla, that you may know peace."

(Step to the first gate, the four tools in hand)

"We come to the first gate. Here, with the blessings of Earth, we relinquish our earthly containers, and thus our sickness, pain, and ills."

(Place the offering dish at the gate, then proceed to the second gate)

"We come to the second gate. Here, with the blessings of Water, we relinquish the bonds of love that bind us and keep us from moving on to our rest."

(Place the cup at the gate, then proceed to the third)

"We come to the third gate. Here, with the blessings of Fire, we relinquish the passions and wills that tie us to our old lives."

(Place the wand at the gate, then proceed to the fourth)

"We come to the fourth gate. Here, with the blessings of Air, we relinquish the thoughts and boundaries that separated us from all others in life."

(Place the athame at the gate, then proceed to the fifth)

"We come to the fifth gate. Here, we relinquish the armor that shielded our souls from the harsh truths of this world."

(Place your upper vestments at the gate, then proceed to the sixth)

"We come to the sixth gate. Here, we relinquish the contracts and graces imposed on us by the world."

(Place your lower vestments at the gate, then proceed to the seventh)

"We come to the seventh and final gate. Here, we relinquish the fears and tribulations that have held us back since birth."

(Place the sacred jewelry at the gate, then proceed beyond)

"We now enter the audience chamber of the Great Below, naked and bowed humbly before mighty Ereshkigal. My Lady, please accept these souls into your care, until the time comes that they may return to the world."

(Sit and take in what wisdom you can in the Great Below. Then, bowing humbly, ascend through the gates in the reverse order, picking up and replacing the articles left therein. Close the ritual as desired)

—Dr. Jacob Tupper

THE TRANSFORMER OF FEAR

Our next community member came very highly recommended by a number of people "in the know" about the death positivity movement. Her name is Danielle Dionne, and she's a psychic medium, Witch, writer, and teacher. I've brought her on board to share her story of how the Egyptian god of death, Anubis, helped her face and overcome her fears. If you're not already a fan, it's amazing to learn just how active she is in the community. She's been connecting to the dead since the age of six, doing psychic readings professionally for over a decade, and even runs Moth and Moon Studio (a spiritual education center located in Bedford, New Hampshire). I could go on about how Danielle's eclectic practice draws upon a vast foundation in mediumship, healing arts, witchcraft, herbalism, and rootwork, but it's probably better if we get right to it and let her tell her story of her lessons from Anubis.

Since childhood, I've been touched by death. Eventually, we would become close friends and partners on my spiritual path as a medium and witch. When I was six years old, we became acquainted after the unexpected death of my best friend. We met again after the death of another childhood friend to brain cancer. I became familiar with what death looked and felt like, lurking in the corner during my Grande Mémère's last days. A quiet air, somber at times, patiently waiting as my family cooked and cared for her. I remember sitting outside her room and could feel the crowding grow as ancestors gathered and she made her transition. Even as a child, I understood what dying meant. I understood the concept that we are not physically "here" anymore and that our bodies stop working. I saw it and I knew it. I had just one slight hang up. Dead bodies.

After the death of my friends, I began having visitations from the dead. Overall, the experiences were comforting and I was happy to connect. While the spirit world drew closer to me, it was around this time that I began having nightmares about the dead. Nightmares about the bodies. I experienced recurring dreams of dead bodies in the basement. I'm not talking zombies, no reanimation, or even gruesome, gory images. Just dead bodies on tables or slabs. In a basement. In the dreams, I would have to go downstairs and tend to the bodies. This immobilized me with fear. This went on for years. And then I met the jackal.

It wasn't until I dreamt of the black, thin-faced dog that my relationship with dead bodies, and, ultimately, my relationship with death, began to change. In my dream, a dog came to me while I was sleeping and stood on my chest and stared into my eyes. The eyes looking at me were yellow and intense and I remember being afraid. It was Anubis, Egyptian god of the underworld, psychopomp, and embalmer. How appropriate that he would show up in dreamtime, as a lot of my fears were perpetuated because of dreams.

At first I did not understand the message. It was about confronting fear to overcome it. It was quite literally about "facing fear" and looking death in the face. I knew that I was pulled to work with the dying, but it scared me. Death wasn't a stranger to me, but to truly know death we have to look death in the eyes. Accept death in its guise of compassion and severity, in its harsh realness. I feared this.

Anubis pointed out to me my role was to be closer to death than I was allowing myself to get. I was in college studying epidemiology, the study of disease in populations. I had chosen a "safer" route than direct care, still studying death but not touching it. Yet I found myself working in an assisted living home to pay the bills and had my first transformative, hands-on experience with death as an adult with my first hospice patient.

Anubis showed up again in dream form in the days before a resident that I had bonded with died. She had no family except for an estranged niece. I picked up extra shifts to stay with her and began to stay late to voluntarily sit vigil. After an intense week of the laboring of death, we reached her final night. I learned so much from this quiet, intimate journey to the end. The experience was profound. And then it happened. It was just me, alone, with this dead woman. After notifying the facility, another caretaker asked if I would stay and help wash her body and assist until the funeral home could pick her up. With love and compassion, we washed and cared for her body. It felt so natural and sacred. I knew I had done this before. And I was not afraid, thanks to Anubis.

Call to Anubis to transform your fears around death. Watch your dreams for the black, thin-faced jackal and listen to the wisdom he brings. What truths need facing when confronting your thoughts and feelings about death? Death comes for us all; do not be afraid.

—DANIELLE DIONNE

SITTING SHIVA

In humankind's curious march toward greater industrial advancements, we have gained the ability to travel far and wide and reside in places that are a great distance away from our hometown. For better or for worse, one effect this has had on many of us in the modern world is that families no longer live all together nor even nearby enough to get together for the good times and for the bad. So, when a death occurs back at home and you're too far away to return for the funeral on such short notice, what do you do?

Our next guest with us here on our world journey found herself in that same dreaded situation. A beloved family member had died and was set to be buried the next day, as per Jewish custom. Now living in a place far from her hometown, though, it was impossible to be there for any funerary services. However, our guest, Stefani Goerlich, had an alternative, an age-old tradition enacted by mourners in the Jewish faith, called *Shiva*, and she's here to give us more insight into this morbid ritual of Judaism that's been handed down for millennia.

I was grocery shopping when the call came. I heard my mother's voice when I answered the phone, listened briefly, then began to sob. Dropping my phone, I reached up and tore a small hole in my t-shirt, just below my left clavicle. Through my tears I whispered, "Baruch Dayan ha'Emet"— Blessed is God, the True Judge—the words Jews say upon receiving news of a death.

My grandmother, the woman who had effectively raised me from age five until I moved out as a young woman, had passed away. By tearing my shirt, symbolically exposing my heart, I was fulfilling the act of Keriah— the rending of garments by those in mourning—which ushers in Aninut, the first and most poignant stage of grieving. Aninut acknowledges the simultaneous existence of both the visceral pain of loss and the mundane necessity of planning and holds space for the one in between.

During the time immediately after a death, we are absolved from observing any other active mitzvot ("commandments") until our loved one is laid to rest. As her granddaughter, I was not technically obligated to fulfill the mourning requirements laid out in Jewish law. These are limited to immediate family: parents, siblings, spouses, children. But my grandmother had lived with us and been my primary caregiver my entire life. Now that I lived hundreds of miles away from the rest of my family, I wanted—I needed—to honor her. She would be buried the next day, according to Jewish tradition, and I had no way to be there at her graveside when we laid her to rest. I could not travel to her, but I could sit Shiva to honor her, this most important person in my life.

Returning home, I took sheets from the linen closet and began to walk through the house, covering each mirror. The time of mourning is not a time to be distracted by vanity. The term "ugly cry" exists for a reason and no one should feel obligated to withhold or contain their grief out of concern for appearances. Thus, the mirrors are hidden away. I removed the cushions from our chairs and furniture and set them on the floor. For the next week, I would sit low, my posture reflecting my emotional state. Grief can feel like a collapse, a crumbling. Forgoing raised chairs allowed my body to follow my heart downward, toward the grave.

My Rabbi called, and I know that word of our loss had begun to spread. She asked me what hours our family would be receiving visitors and let me know she would make the announcement at services that evening. For the next seven days, my community would gather around me to hold sacred space while I grieved.

The next afternoon, shortly after my grandmother was buried five states away, my home had been turned into a House of Mourning. I sat on the floor, wrapped myself in an afghan crocheted by my beloved, now departed, grandmother, and wept. It was less than an hour before the door opened for the first time. Jews are quick to gather in times of crisis.

Three older women from my synagogue let themselves in (a mourner is not expected to play hostess) and removed their shoes. Shoes are symbols of luxury and the mourning period is a time when we need not concern ourselves with fashion, with pride.

Two of the ladies busied themselves in the kitchen. One put a casserole she had brought into the oven to warm. Another put a pot of coffee on. The third came and sat next to me on the floor. She gently rubbed my back. She said nothing. This silence, too, is sacred. Our tradition encourages us to refrain from speaking until those in mourning have spoken first. What can you say to someone who has experienced a great loss? What words could possibly comfort a pain so fresh, so raw? And so, she sat beside me, holding me, while tears fell.

I didn't speak that first night, and the ladies left in silence, just as they arrived. But eventually, over the coming days, I found my voice again. I thanked our visitors. I listened and even laughed as people came in and out of our house, bringing food and sharing stories. For six days, I was held, and fed, and prayed over, and cared for by my community. Close friends and near-strangers; my door was unlocked, and they comforted me. "Hamakom yenachem etchem b'toch sha'ar avlei tzion ve'yerusha-luyim" they would say to me ("May God comfort you, together with all the mourners in Zion and Jerusalem.").

On the seventh day, my Rabbi helped me to stand up. She placed the cushion back on my chair and she handed me a hairbrush. "It's time" she whispered. I washed my face. I brushed my hair. And together with those who had gathered to support me, I walked out my front door. This act signifies my transition from Shiva to Shloshim: the thirty-day period when we begin to return to our "normal" lives, still feeling our loss, but no longer sitting silent in our grief. I exited the House of Mourning and returned to the world and walked around the block surrounded by those who had gathered to support me. I did what my people have done for mil-lennia. We bury our dead, we weep, we mourn, and then? We rise. As Jews have done since the beginning of time, we choose to live.

—Stefani Goerlich

THE DEATH OF ANGER & SADNESS

Families are interesting, aren't they? Parents in particular. At times they're the source of such joy and happiness. At other times they're the source of such pain and hurt. No matter what, though, each of us is born with an innate need to love and be loved by them, whether or not it's the healthiest or best thing for us. Children are just wired that way, and we carry those longings into adulthood, even after our parents' deaths. In fact, our next community contributor has an epic story to tell on exactly those confusing emotions. Her name is Reni Wulandari, a Muslim friend of mine in Indonesia, and the story she is about to share tells of her turbulent history with her father and how in the darkest of depressions and at the edge of ending it all, Islam helped take her back from the point of no return.

Wulandari, my parents named me that. It means "from the Moon." I was born in April 1985, in a very small town in West Java, Indonesia. Before I learned about spirituality, I thought my life was chaos, like totally chaos. I thought that I was born and grew up in hell; everything was dark, melodramatic, and about the abuse that my parents and environment did to me daily. I hated God and my father, I felt like they made me only to be in pain and suffer.

Since I was a kid, learning about my religion as a Muslim was an obligation. I learned to read the Koran, learned to live in such a way that our prophet Muhammad (Sallallahu Alayhi Wa Sallam) lived, and learned many things about Islam. But I didn't take it as an obligation for myself, I took it because as a child I had to do that or my parents would do physical punishment.

I really hated my father for what happened in my childhood that made me have experiences full of abuse, physically, mentally, even sexually, and God didn't do anything to help. Once I screamed to the sky only to declare my hatred on Him and ask Him "Why me?" God and my father, they ruined my life, they were the source of my suffering and made me want to end my life because I didn't see any kind of good thing from my life anymore. So I decided to attempt suicide because things seemed so dark and wrong, I was depressed as a teenager.

One day, a very good friend of mine introduced me to spiritual self-help books, and the more I learned about spiritual self-development, the more I got interested to learn about God. He was so mysterious to me, and my anger toward Him was still big. I blamed my religion; Islam was bad in my eyes. So, I tried learning about different religions, but they didn't help me find God. The more I tried to find Him the more I couldn't find Him at all.

After taking much time to try to find God, I decided to focus on finding myself, another way of saying I gave up. I started to treat myself better from that time, learned English, and actively worked through my anger to try to have a better relationship with my parents. And just like that, I found Him. I found Him when I stopped looking on the outside and focused on the inside. It was one of the best moments of my life. I converted back to Islam again at that moment and declared my Shahada (Islamic creed).

But not too long after that, my father went into a coma. I spent my days waiting and taking care of him in the hospital by myself. He was so skinny, like a skeleton covered with a blanket. I knew my father had not much time to live, but I did my very best effort to make things better despite still being angry at him. I spent my days crying, full of regret.

I felt bad for being so angry at him for so long, and I knew that, for my own sake at least, I had to find forgiveness (for him, not his actions) to be able to move on, just as God forgives us. And for the first time since being in the hospital with him, I talked to him deeply. I said to him that I forgave him for all the bad things that he did to me and my siblings. I cried like a baby that made my throat in such pain while I held and kissed his toes. Then I realized that his toes were cold, but he was still breathing. I whispered to his ear, if he wants to go and leave this world then I will let him go. I promised him to take care of my whole family, not only because I am the eldest but because I wanted him to know that he can count on me.

A few minutes after that promise, he stopped breathing. I knew that he was gone, but I tried to be calm and called the nurse. The nurse confirmed my father had gone, and I cried even more intensely. My father's death made me depressed and sad continuously for almost two years. I kept blaming myself for not finding forgiveness sooner and for not being able to afford a better hospital that might have saved his life. Often, I cried at work, when I drove my car, at night before going to sleep, or when listening to songs.

So, I surrendered to God because I didn't know what to do. I was really at yet another lowest moment of my life with nowhere to hide or run because I lived in the capital city away from family and friends. In my mind the only place that made me feel safe and welcome was in a mosque, so I spent much time in mosques, sometimes to cry, sometimes to take a nap. And regularly I started to discipline myself to do Islamic daily prac-tices like read the Koran, do the daily prayer five times a day, the midnight prayer, daily routine charity, and fasting from 4 a.m. to 6 p.m.

I found it peaceful and released my sadness, and I realized that the relationship I had with my father was the reason I was now getting closer to God and enjoying being a Muslim. I feel like my father loves seeing me be religious and better, so every day I do my best to do things right and do the right things. I dedicated all my kindness to my father and I hope God gives a special place for my father in heaven.

Now in these thirty-three years of my life, I accepted what happened in the past and am able to move on. I miss my father every day, even when I'm writing this right now I can't stop my tears from falling down. Living as a Muslim and doing things in an Islamic direction has saved my life and made me better; I'm thankful every day for being a Muslim.

—*Reni Wulandari*

PART 2

EUROPE

*It is not Death that will come
to fetch me, it is the good God.
Death is no phantom, no horrible
specter, as presented in pictures.*
ST. THÉRÈSE OF LISIEUX

From the fields and highlands of Europe has come the chimeric mélange of what is now the standard Western funeral. Albeit commodified and industrialized, a "typical" funeral or memorial service that you've probably been to in the past (or certainly will go to in the future) is an amalgamation of Christian and pagan European beliefs and traditions.

It was in these colder, greener climates that the Middle Eastern religion of Christianity took hold and forever changed the way Europe (and those it colonized) looked at death. Through his resurrection, Jesus conquered death, and thus death became a taboo. But before the arrival of ancient evangelists, Europe was already a hotbed of cultures, faiths, and magic with beautiful and frightening ideas of what happens to us after death.

From the deadly portals into the underworld in ancient Greece, to the rowdy Viking feasts in Valhalla, to the chilling fears that Satan is coming for your soul, these are the macabre rituals and mythologies of Europe. So prepare yourself, because our trip north will be noticeably darker and more classically macabre than what we've seen so far. But there's no going back now!

5

ANCIENT GREECE & ROME

Cultural

The Greek Cycle of Death

When we look at ancient Greece's funerary rituals and the way they interacted with their dead from about 800 BCE onward, we can see a noticeable cycle that parallels the rise and fall of Greek democracy. During the Archaic period (800–480 BCE) when the seeds of the philosophical democratic revolution were just beginning to sprout, the lavishness of goods, food, and drink that were once buried along with the dead diminished. As the Classical period came into full bloom (510–323 BCE) the égalité of man (not women because, well, patriarchy of the times) made for the preference for simple, understated funerals, while excessive showiness was frowned upon. However, as the Classical period began to wane and the Greek city-states became subjugated under hereditary, Macedonian rule (via Philip II and his more famous son, Alexander). The bougie-ness of wanting to be like the upper classes took over Greek culture, and the desire to be buried with lavish items and offerings became popular all over again.[47]

A Hero's Death

During this time, all over the Hellenic world, burial was the norm, but two powerhouse city-states in particular had their own version of normal and bucked regional tradition: Athens and Sparta. In Athens, cremation was the popular standard. Originally, cremation was associated with valor and greatness due to it being the common final disposition for brave warriors who died in battle (arising from the only practical way to transport deceased soldiers back to their hometowns) and also due to it being the prominent funerary disposition in the Homeric epics of the *Iliad* and the *Odyssey* (how the legendary heroes had *their* funerals). Mixed with the burgeoning Athenian ideals of the égalité of man, this hero's funeral via flaming pyre caught fashion and quickly became the norm there.[48]

The people of Sparta, on the other hand, saw cremation as a non-optimal final disposition and preferred anonymous burial. Naturally, death in battle was the ultimate and most heroic way to go, but unlike the Athenians, they didn't think individually cremating the bodies and bringing the remains back home was an efficient use of their military's time. Rather, it was seen as a labor-intensive, unnecessary, and sentimental gesture. Those who died on the battlefield were quickly buried without much ritual or pomp; only a small stone marker reading "In War" was placed on their grave.

The female equivalent of this was bestowed upon mothers who died giving birth. These women were also honored with a stone marker (though

---

47   Peter Toohey, "Death and Burial in the Ancient World," In *The Oxford Encyclopedia of Ancient Greece and Rome* (Oxford: Oxford University Press, 2010).

48   Alexandra Donnison, *The Appropriation of Death in Classical Athens* (Wellington: Victoria University of Wellington, 2009), http://researcharchive.vuw.ac.nz/xmlui/bitstream/handle/10063/1153/thesis.pdf?sequence=1 (accessed May 16, 2018).

it's currently debated whether or not the epitaph "In Childbirth" was carved into it). Men and women who died of natural causes were buried near their home in unmarked graves, wrapped in a red robe with only olive leaves to accompany them to the afterlife.[49]

Into the Underworld

The ancient Greek afterlife itself was called *Hades* (named after its eponymous ruling deity, and I'll keep it in italics when referring to the place). *Hades* was thought to be a gloomy underground world of darkness. Originally, it was envisioned to be a place of lugubrious monotony since the belief was that only the physical body could experience pleasure and pain, not the spirit. Later on, *Hades* became a three-tiered afterlife of good, neutral, and bad destinations based not on your morality, but rather on how extraordinary you were.

Regardless of final destination, though, everyone who died had to first cross the river Styx ("Acheron" in some myths) through the help of a frightening ferryman named Charon. Just like in the living world, however, there ain't nothin' for free, and Charon demanded money to take you to the other side. This is why the ancient Greeks placed a coin in the mouth of the deceased before burial/cremation, to take with them to pay the ferryman. But those who were desperately poor or died without proper rites simply had to stay on the banks of the river anywhere from one hundred years to eternity (during which time they could haunt the living).

Once across, the soul next had to face the ferocious three-headed guard dog, Cerberus. Getting past him into *Hades* was not really the issue, though. You see, Cerberus was not there to keep people from entering *Hades*, he was there to keep people from leaving it, thus explaining why the dead could never return to the land of the living. Still, the ancient Greeks didn't like to take any chances, and so, just in case, sweet treats

---

49   Scott Manning, "Spartan Burial Practices and Honoring Fallen Soldiers," *Historian on the Warpath*, Apr. 11, 2011, https://scottmanning.com/content/spartan-burial-practices/ (accessed May 16, 2018).

and meat were sometimes buried/burned with the deceased to give to Cerberus to let them enter *Hades*.

Oh, the Places You'll Go in Hades

Once past Cerberus, the three final destination locations within *Hades* were the Elysian Fields, the Asphodel Meadows, and Tartarus. The Elysian Fields were the best place to go. All the pleasures of life on earth could be experienced here free of both labor and suffering, but you had to prove yourself exceptionally worthy of getting access here by living an extraordinary life of merit. Usually, only legendary heroes and extremely influential people got in here.

The worst place to go was Tartarus, which acted as an abysmal holding cell of darkness for those who were deemed personally offensive to the gods; this included those who proved a physical threat to them (like the Titans) or repeatedly outsmarted them (like King Sisyphus, whom we'll talk about later).

But if you lived a normal life that was neither extraordinarily influential nor heroic and you weren't seen as offensive to the gods, you went to the Asphodel Meadows (named for the ghostly white flowers of the *Asphodel* genus of plants that grow there). The specifics of what this realm was like changed throughout the years, but all descriptions tend to paint it as a monotonous, jaded blandness of neither highs nor lows, just shadowy wistlessness. Naturally, this is where most people went.[50]

The change in *Hades* from a universally melancholic, blasé shadow realm to a multitiered realm of three extremely different lands is believed by some to be an evolution for militaristic reasons. You see, if your nation is on the warpath, it's tough to electrify the spirit of your warriors who are risking their lives if the consequence of death is inescapable gloom and monotonous darkness. Such an afterlife would make your warriors more cautious and less gung ho in battle. However, if the story was changed, and fatal heroism on the battlefield ensured the possibility of an after-

---

50   Abel, *Death Gods: An Encyclopedia of the Rulers, Evil Spirits, and Geographies of the Dead.*

life of pleasures, then your warriors would be much more dangerous and deadly in action. This tactic is definitely not exclusive to ancient Greece, as many other cultures and spiritual traditions after the ancient Greeks have also found great militaristic success in promising afterlife rewards to those who give their lives in defense of the homeland/faith.

Roman Death, aka Greek Death Version 2.0

The ancient Romans loved everything Greek, so much so that their spirituality and culture are essentially Greek appropriations with Roman characteristics, and this included their funerary practices and macabre deities. Much of what happens to a Roman soul after death is, for all intents and purposes, about the same as what the Greeks believed happened, except with different names for the people and places, so our time here in ancient Rome will be relatively brief. The actual handling of a dead body, however, is where the Romans really differed, and they practiced rituals that were both more restrictively regulated and more ostentatiously showy.

A Morbid Thing Happened
on the Way to the Forum

A good example of this is the funeral procession out of the city, the forbearer to our modern funeral cortège. The dead body was thought to be an impure contaminant, and so all corpses had to be dealt with outside of city limits for perceived health reasons. Despite this strict mandate, the Romans turned this dour procession into a show of pomp and status (because why not?).

The deceased were washed, anointed with oils, dressed in their best clothes, and carried along with symbols of their life's accomplishments on their way to their final resting place. Those in the procession (whether actual or paid mourners) wore either special funerary togas or their darkest, most somber-colored clothes. The procession would stop at the forum, where eulogies and words of praise for the deceased were publicly voiced by the mourners, before heading out of the city to the nearby cemetery or funeral pyre.[51]

Except for early Rome (and a few upper class Romans who wanted to continue being ostentatious even in death, via a mausoleum), cremation was the preferred choice of disposal. You see, burial was something the uncivilized savages outside the empire did, and not wanting to be like these "barbarians," Romans looked to mimic the practice of a people seen as the antithesis of barbarism, the Athenians. The greats of Athens were cremated, so wealthy Romans paid to have the same done to them. Then once it had become en vogue among the aristocracy, the masses (in an attempt to be like the upper classes) followed suit, and cremation became the de facto way to go across the empire.

Still, cremations during the empire's glory days always had to take place outside of city limits due to zoning ordinances put in place to prevent fires from burning down the city.[52] However, as the Roman Empire began to destabilize and the population became less urbanized, burial would make a comeback, and cremations wouldn't become popular again in Europe until the late twentieth century when the Catholic Church finally gave its permission to it as a tolerable alternative to being laid to rest six feet underground.

Ancient Greek & Roman Takeaway:
ODE TO THE LIVING

Public discourse was a hallmark of classical Greece and Rome. These cultures would debate and proclaim the greatness of each other so that the many could hear and know how grand someone was. Even upon death, the Greeks wrote poetic odes to the deceased and the Romans made sure to eulogize the greatness of the departed along the funeral procession. Too often nowadays we keep our feelings and sentiments inside of us. We never tell people how much we appreciate them or how great/important

---

51 J. M. C. Toynbee, *Death and Burial in the Roman World* (Baltimore: Johns Hopkins University Press, 1996).

52 Steven Fife, "The Roman Funeral," In *Ancient History Encyclopedia*, Jan. 18, 2012, https://www.ancient.eu/article/96/the-roman-funeral/ (accessed May 21, 2018).

they are to us. Not until someone is dead do we have that gushing regret of words that were left unsaid.

We can learn from the Greek and Roman penchant for public declarations and be more inclined to sing someone's praises while they're still alive. So, your ancient Greek and Roman takeaway challenge is to pick someone close to you whom you respect and write an ode to their greatness with the intention to show them. It'll help you express yourself, and it'll make their day. If anyone gets a little weirded out as to why you're writing a eulogy of praise, just tell 'em I challenged you to do so (and show them this page in the book in case they go "Thomas Power, who?").

But if you're *really* shy about showing it to someone (or just don't know anyone personally who is worthy of such praise), write one for someone you admire who has passed on already (contemporary or historical). You don't have to know them personally, so long as they affected your life in some meaningful way. Too often we communicate with the spirits of the dead for help, advice, or magical ends, but when do we just sing their praises and tell them thanks? If you go this route, let the spirits of the dead know how much you appreciate them and how they are still remembered and cherished for their greatness. They'll appreciate it.

Deities & Legends

HADES/PLUTO

Hades (Pluto to the Romans) is the accidental lord of the underworld who was greatly despised and feared by the people of ancient Greece and Rome. The disgust toward him, however, was not for any personal or mean-spirited reason. To mortals, Hades was just the bureaucratic administrator of the underworld, always swamped with work because people kept on dying, and just doing the best he could in a job that even he didn't necessarily want. In certain respects, he's probably one of the most relatable gods.

As the legend goes, Hades and his siblings had just defeated the Titans and were now in control of the universe. The three male siblings (because, again, patriarchy of ancient times) were deciding which of them should rule each of the three realms: sky, sea, underworld. Despite Hades being the eldest brother, they decided to draw lots so as to make things fair. Zeus drew the sky, Poseidon the seas, and Hades was left with the underworld, about which he was pretty upset. But he knew he couldn't do anything about it since it had all been fair and square.[53]

Whether always stressed about work, harboring anger over his unlucky draw, or influenced by his surroundings, Hades is depicted as a dour yet regal individual. He's strong-bodied with black, partially unkempt hair and a full beard, often accompanied by animals (especially dogs), and rarely leaves the underworld (though if he did, you wouldn't notice since he wears a helmet of invisibility when above ground).

People didn't like thinking about him and his domain very much because it reminded them of their own mortality. Even saying his name was considered bad luck, so they used euphemisms such as *Pluton* (from which "Pluto" is derived), meaning "wealth" since, as ruler of the land below, all underground resources, minerals, and jewels belonged to his realm.[54]

Above ground, cypress trees and asphodel flowers were associated with him and understood to be botanical symbols of mourning. Sacrifices to him were preferred to be black-colored animals, and their blood had to be spilled in such a way that it would drip down into crevices in the ground so as to reach him. His sacred sites were caves where humans and animals would inexplicably die, a real phenomenon that science later attributed to the noxious, invisible gases seeping out of crevices in the caves' floors.[55]

53   Homer, *Iliad*, translated by Robert Fagles (New York: Penguin Classics, 1991).

54   "Hades" *Theoi*, http://www.theoi.com/Khthonios/Haides.html (accessed May 21, 2018).

55   Rachel Tepper Paley, "Animals Dropped Dead Inside Roman 'Gate to Hell.' Scientists Just Figured Out Why," *Time.com*, Feb. 22, 2018, http://time.com/5171047/turkey-gate-to-hell-pamukkale-hierapolis/ (accessed May 21, 2018).

HEKATE/TRIVIA

Hekate (Trivia, or Trivius Dea to the Romans) is a dark underworld goddess of, among many things, ghosts, magic, witchcraft, poisonous plants, thresholds, and the crossroads (one reason for her Roman name, which translates to "Goddess of the Three Ways"). In mythology, she is often described as a particularly powerful deity, but in magic, she was largely invoked for protection both supernatural and physical. Because the crossroads are sacred to her, offerings and spellwork would often be done at crossroads, especially in the darkness of night, even more so during the new moon.[56]

She was depicted usually in one of two ways depending upon the medium. In statuary, she was shown as a triple goddess with three women standing back to back (again, "three-way"), each holding either a snake, a dagger, and/or a torch. Sometimes in her triple goddess form, she had the heads of a horse, a canine, and a snake. In 2-D art, though, she is often depicted as one woman holding a torch in each hand and dressed in a knee-length skirt with hunting boots, giving her Artemis/Diana similarities.[57]

In folklore, Hekate is said to grant favors of all kinds to her devotees and was respected by the Olympian gods as being a primordial deity even older than themselves. However, the Greek epics insist that one must not look upon her when making an offering and must never glance back at the offering while walking away from it.[58]

PERSEPHONE/PROSERPINA

Persephone (Proserpina to the Romans) is the goddess of the dead and Queen of the Underworld. Originally a pastel goddess of flowers and springtime, her most famous myth revolves around her abduction by Hades and the subsequent custody battle for her, waged between him and

56   "Hekate Cult," *Theoi.com*, http://www.theoi.com/Cult/HekateCult.html (accessed May 21, 2018).

57   "Hekate," *Theoi.com*, http://www.theoi.com/Khthonios/Hekate.html (accessed May 21, 2018).

58   Apollonios Rhodios, *The Argonautika*, translated by Peter Green (Berkeley: University of California Press, 2007).

her mother (Demeter, goddess of agriculture), which served to explain the phenomenon of nature's seasonal changes.

Long story short, Hades kidnaps Persephone (though some versions argue she willingly runs away with him) and takes her to the underworld to be his queen. Demeter falls into a profound depression and refuses to let the crops grow until her daughter is returned. The gods intervene and make Hades return Persephone to her mother, but since Persephone already ate fruit of the underworld (pomegranate), she was technically bound there for eternity. Thus a deal is struck wherein Persephone lives half the year with her mother (spring and summer) and half the year with Hades (autumn and winter).

Her ability to walk between the physical and spiritual worlds became a main focus in the immortality-seeking Eleusinian Mysteries and a partial focus in the death-transcending Orphic Mysteries. For everyone else, Persephone was seen as a more approachable and sympathetic underworld deity, especially in comparison to her stern husband.[59]

SISYPHUS

Sisyphus was the king of the Greek city-state of Ephyra (later renamed Corinth) and played the leading role in two of the most god-offending death myths of the underworld. You see, Sisyphus was a very intelligent yet very deceitfully greedy person, but he was eventually singled out as personally offensive to the gods, mainly because he ratted Zeus out for one of his (many) extramarital affairs. So, when Sisyphus was on his deathbed, he became extremely anxious because he knew Zeus would ensure his soul must forever reside in the most hellish realm of *Hades*, Tartarus.

As the myth goes, when the gods sent Thanatos (deific personification of Death) to come escort Sisyphus to Tartarus in chains, Sisyphus came up with a plan. Ever so slyly, he asked Thanatos to demonstrate how the chains went on, at which point, he trapped Thanatos in his own chains and escaped Death (literally). With Thanatos chained up, all death became

---

59 "Persephone," *Theoi.com*, http://www.theoi.com/Khthonios/Persephone.html (accessed May 21, 2018).

impossible on earth, which made Sisyphus happy since, if he could never die, he'd never go to Tartarus.

But immortality began to cause problematic side effects. Those with terminal illnesses suffered endlessly, and sacrifices could no longer be made to the gods. No one was more upset by all of this than Ares, since without death, war became pointless, so he personally put an end to things by freeing Thanatos and bringing Sisyphus back into custody.

Sisyphus's misadventures at cheating death didn't end there, though. As a backup plan before being found by Ares, Sisyphus had instructed his wife to throw his corpse into a public street, leaving it to rot and be eaten by scavenger animals. She did as she was told, and so while in the underworld, Sisyphus complained to Persephone that his wife had been so disrespectful in denying him proper funerary rites that he should be able to briefly return to the surface world and punish her. Persephone agreed; Sisyphus returned to the land of the living, and once there, he refused to return to *Hades*.

The gods were not having it this time, though, and Hermes was sent to drag him down to Tartarus wherein he would forever suffer having to roll a boulder up a hill, with the boulder rolling back down right upon reaching the summit. From this, we get the term "Sisyphean task," meaning an exhaustive effort that is foreseeably pointless.[60]

---

60   "Sisyphus," *Greek Mythology.com*, https://www.greekmythology.com/
    Myths/Mortals/Sisyphus/sisyphus.html (accessed Nov. 28, 2018).
    Bernard Evslin, *Gods, Demigods and Demons: A Handbook of Greek Mythology*
    (New York: I.B. Tauris, 2007).

6

PAGAN EUROPE

Cultural

For our purposes here, "Pagan Europe" refers to the native spirituality of the peoples of Europe outside of Classical Greece and Rome. While these peoples were eventually Christianized, their complete conversion was not instantaneous, with pagans and Christians living side by side for centuries amid varying levels of hostility and cooperation. On this leg of our European trek, we'll focus particularly on the Celtic contemporaries of the Romans as well as the ever-popular and often-romanticized Vikings.

Celtic Grave Goods

The Celts (pronounced "kelts") were a warlike people (though most written accounts of them come from the Romans who encountered them usually through battle, so take that as you will), and as such, death on the battlefield was the most glorious one could hope for. However, "Celts" is a very broad term for a large number of peoples who lived throughout Western and Eastern Europe and shared close linguistic, cultural, and ethnic similarities. Today, "Celts" refers mainly to the people of Ireland, Scotland, Wales, and French Brittany where their traditional culture lasted the longest due to Rome's inability to ever fully subdue their customs and eradicate their cultural identity.

The Celtic peoples located in modern-day France were called Gauls, and like other Celtic tribes, they practiced animism, which is the belief that all things in the natural world are alive and divine. For death rituals, they practiced burial, and archeological finds have uncovered many graves filled with goods ranging from jewelry and weaponry to clothes and foodstuffs. Although there were no designated cemeteries per se, they did tend to bury their dead all in one general area near the village.

When the Romans conquered Gaul, cremation became popular as per Roman preference, and so the Gauls began burning their dead along with all of the deceased's grave goods that they would've been buried with had the Romans not taken over. Then as Rome Christianized (due to Rome's official state conversion to the new religion), the Gauls did too, and burial become the standard again (as mandated by Christian belief). Nevertheless, the crumbling Roman Empire didn't bury their dead in a traditional Christian way. Influenced by the Gauls' traditional practice of burying their dead with grave goods, Romans throughout the empire also began burying their dead with grave goods in the Celtic fashion (despite traditional Christianity's disapproval of it).[61]

In fact, the Celts' neighbors in what is now northern Germany were also well-known for their grave goods, particularly their burial mounds filled with supplies for the afterlife. These Germanic burial mounds could

---

61   Frans Theuws, "Grave goods, ethnicity, and the rhetoric of burial rites in late antique northern Gaul," *Ethnic Constructs in Antiquity: The Role of Power and Tradition*, ed. by Ton Derks and Nico Roymans (Amsterdam: Amsterdam University Press, 2009).

be quite large (towering well over human height) in order to accommodate all the riches of the wealthy, which could include chariots, wagons, animal sacrifices (especially horses), and an arsenal of weapons. This practice of grave goods is pervasive throughout continental European tribes, though a notable exception comes from the native tribes of what is modern-day Spain, wherein the most honored death was not to be buried with a massive amount of luxury items, but rather to be consumed by scavenger animals so that the spirit could travel to a paradisiacal afterlife.[62]

Even in the pre-Roman British Isles, the practice of burial mounds was very popular, and some were even communal mounds, which were ridiculously large to accommodate the growing number of bodies and grave goods being added to the pile daily. The objects buried with the dead included everyday ones they'd need in the next world, magical amulets, and items that were specifically designed for and only had logical/practical use in the afterlife. Those tribes who lived close to peat bogs would even mummify their dead in the acidic, poorly oxygenated soil and then bring the preserved corpse back to the clan home.[63]

Dead Men's Party

Some surviving accounts of funerary rituals that we have from Celtic Ireland outline that the body is washed, dressed in a death shirt (*esléne*), and then carried to the gravesite on a cushion of leafy birch branches (or a bier if they had the wealth). In preparation for the grave, a Druid priest would use a rod of aspen called a *fé* to measure how big the grave needed to be. Aside from being a practical device, the fé was believed to be magical. According to legends, the fé was said to measure the grave of anyone

62   M. Sentia Figula, "Pagan Funeral Rites," *Neo Polytheist*, Nov. 8, 2015, http://romanpagan.blogspot.com/2015/11/pagan-funeral-rites_8.html (accessed May 22, 2018).

63   "Funeral Rites and the Afterlife," *The Druid Network*, https://druidnetwork.org/what-is-druidry/learning-resources/polytheist/lesson-twelve/ (accessed May 22, 2018).

who looked at it (except for the Druid priest) and bring about their death in the very near future.[64]

Nowadays, the Irish wake is the most famous Celtic funeral rite to survive into modern times. While not *traditionally* Celtic, the wake is actually an adaptation of the Catholic funerary rite of the vigil, a practice in which friends and family of the deceased stand guard over the body to ensure a proper burial while saying prayers for the soul of the deceased (definitely not raucous parties to "awaken" the dead person nor an up-all-night watch to see if the deceased will "wake up" from being misdiagnosed as dead).[65]

In Celtic Wales, the belief was that the next world was somewhere underground and that it was pretty much a place of perennial partying where one could drink and feast and fight and have fun forever. Though Welsh legends never call it such, modern neo-pagan practice calls this land of the dead *Annwn* (after the general "otherworldly" lands mentioned in various myths), and it is ruled over by the huntsman Arawn and his fellow chieftains. Other than all the partying, the Welsh afterlife was seen as pretty similar to life on earth except with more adventures and excitement.[66]

Druids vs. the System

In fact, it was a Welsh Druid priest named William Price who brought about the legality of cremation in late-Victorian Britain. It was his personal belief that the earth was sacred, and that burying a human in it would pollute its sacredness. So, when his child died, he naturally chose to cremate the body on a funeral pyre, which caused him to be arrested for illegal disposal of a corpse. During the court proceedings, his defense was essentially that although cremation wasn't legal, it technically wasn't

---

64 P. W. Joyce, *A Social History of Ancient Ireland: Treating of the Government, Military System, and Law; Religion, Learning, and Art; Trades, Industries, and Commerce; Manners, Customs, and Domestic Life, of the Ancient Irish People* (Provo: Repressed Publishing, 2014), (original edition: New York: Longsman, Green, and Co., 1903).

65 David Wilton, *Word Myths: Debunking Linguistic Urban Legends,* (New York: Oxford University Press, 2008).

66 *The Druid Network,* "Funeral Rites and the Afterlife."

illegal either. Acquitted on this technicality, Price's case set a precedent in the legal system upon which the newly formed Cremation Society of Great Britain piggybacked to force the government to legalize cremation so long as it was done in a professional establishment and not out in the open on a pyre.[67]

Viking Send-Offs

Of all the European pagans, however, the Vikings are arguably the most famous in modern-day pop culture when it comes to funerary send-offs. The image of a Viking longboat sailing out into a misty fjord carrying the corpse of a dead warrior and being suddenly lit ablaze by flaming arrows shot from the shoreline while on open water is often used in movies, TV, and video games, but did that ever really happen? The realistic answer is probably not, but the more fun answer is that we cannot be 100 percent certain since those types of send-offs leave little in the way of archaeological evidence.

Longboat funerals, however, *were* a real thing, just not in the way Hollywood makes you imagine. From a mortuary standpoint, a human body needs to burn much more intensely for a much longer period of time than what a fiery sinking ship on the water could provide...otherwise the charred cadaver would just wash back onto shore. So, logistically, it doesn't really get the job done. Add into that the sheer value of a longboat and how often warriors die, and you can see how only those rare individuals with great status could be granted such an expensive and resource-intensive send-off (in which case they were buried with the longboat or cremated on land with it).[68]

---

67   Tim Harris, "Druid doc with a bee in his bonnet," *The Age*, Sept. 16, 2002, https://www.theage.com.au/articles/2002/09/15/1032054710047 .html?oneclick=true (accessed May 22, 2018).

68   Caitlin Doughty, "Wherein I Mercilessly Slaughter Your Dreams of a Viking Funeral," *The Order of the Good Death*, Oct. 22, 2012, http://www .orderofthegooddeath.com/wherein-i-mercilessly-slaughter-your-dreams -of-a-viking-funeral (accessed May 2, 2018).

Regardless of burial or cremation, Viking funerals could be deadly events. When burying objects or throwing them into a pyre for the deceased to take with them to the afterlife, these "objects" could sometimes include people. Servants, the deceased's widow, and sex slaves would be buried or burned alive so that the deceased could continue to "enjoy" them in death.[69] However, the deceased was not socio-legally declared officially dead until a week after the day of death. After this week, though, special funeral ale (*sjaund*) would be made and ritually drunk during a final feast, and the inheritances could finally be distributed.[70]

Riding with the Valkyries

As to the Norse afterlife itself, the sagas and surviving literature talk about several different places, sometimes contradicting each other and rarely consistent among the various stories. Nonetheless, the four most consistent destinations were Valhalla, Fólkvangr, Hel, and Náströnd. The determining factor on which of these you ended up in was a mix of morality and cause of death.

Valhalla was the best place to end up. It was often described as an endless grand hall where food, drink, fun, and carousing never ceased. Only those who died in battle could be eligible, and the god Odin would send Valkyries (which translates to "ones who choose the slain") to the battlefield in order to escort the fallen warriors to his realm of paradise.[71]

Only half of the heroic dead would enter Valhalla, though. The other half would be escorted to Fólkvangr, which was exactly the same as Valhalla except presided over by Freyja (goddess of love, sex, beauty, fertility, and war) instead of Odin. It's unknown why half of those killed in battle went to Valhalla and half to Fólkvangr, but scholars have come up with a

69   Gunnel Friberg, *Myth, Might and Man: Ten Essays on Gamla Uppsala* (Besöksadress: Riksantikvarieämbetets Förl, 2000).

70   Jenny Goldade, "Cultural Spotlight: Viking Funeral Traditions," *Frazer Consultants*, Mar. 24, 2017, http://www.frazerconsultants.com/2017/03/cultural-spotlight-viking-funeral-traditions/ (accessed May 23, 2018).

71   Snorri Sturluson, *The Poetic Edda*, translated by Lee M. Hollander (Austin: University of Texas Press, 1986).

number of various theories such as the differences in initiation rites when becoming a warrior and others, though this still remains a mystery.[72]

Boring as Hel

The majority of people who didn't die in the throes of battle ended up in *Hel* (not to be confused with the Christian "Hell," and I'll italicize it when referring to the place as opposed to the eponymous ruler). *Hel* was similar to *Hades* in that it was perceived as a very neutral, blah place without any suffering but also without any excitement, where both the good and bad alike went. Scholarly contradictions still arise as to whether it was dark and dreary or just bland and unimpressive. Afraid of missing out on the eternal fun of Valhalla and Fólkvangr for the eternal monotony of *Hel*, people on their deathbed would sometimes lacerate their body with axe and sword cuts so as to try and fool the Valkyries into thinking that they had died from battle wounds and thus get to avoid *Hel*.[73]

However, the absolute worst place to go was Náströnd, a subdivision of *Hel*. Náströnd (which translates to "Corpse Shore") was a place of eternal torment by means of having your blood sucked out and being chewed on by the giant serpentine dragon, *Níðhöggr* (which translates to the awesomely metal name "Malice Striker"). Regular bad and immoral people went to *Hel* like everyone else, but Náströnd was reserved for the baddest of the bad. The only way to secure a one-way ticket to Náströnd was by having been an adulterer, a murder, or (worst of all) an oath-breaker.[74]

Pagan European Takeaway:
YOU CAN'T TAKE IT ALL WITH YOU

Regardless of whether or not you believe, like many of the pagan cultures of Europe, that possessions buried/cremated with you can be taken

---

72 Britt-Mari Näsström, *Freyja: The Great Goddess of the North*, 2nd ed. (Harwich Port, Clock & Rose Press, 2003).

73 Gro Steinsland, and Preben Meulengracht Sørensen, *Humans and Powers in the Viking World*, (Stockholm, Ordfront, 1998).

74 "Náströnd," *Encyclopedia Mythica*, Jul. 2, 2003, https://pantheon.org/ articles/n/nastrond.html (accessed May 23, 2018).

into the next life, you can't take it *all* with you. Times have changed, and people just have a lot more stuff nowadays. Back then, the necessities of survival and maybe a small number of luxury goods were all anyone had, but now we all have so much stuff that we don't really need. So, when it comes time to bury/cremate you, there just isn't enough space to take it *all* with you. Caskets and cremation chambers (called "retorts") are only so big, and cemetery/environmental laws restrict what can be buried or burned into the atmosphere.

If you accomplished the ancient Egyptian takeaway challenge from earlier, you've already made a death plan to help alleviate your family from making the difficult decisions on what to do with your body. But what about all the stuff you left behind? All the things that you can't take with you to the grave? You're gonna make your grieving family go through and fight over all the clothes, knickknacks, and random possessions cluttering your home? If you want to really help your surviving loved ones from beyond the grave, make a written plan of what to do with all your stuff, too. Trust me, this helps allow them to grieve more easily and prevents countless in-family fights over senseless yet sentimental tchotchkes.

But let's step back for a second and understand why this is actually a big deal. Hypothetically, let's say you die tomorrow (to make it nice, we'll imagine you died in your sleep). What happens to all your stuff? All those important papers, passwords, and account numbers filed away God knows where. Are any of these things easy for your family to access? Remember, they'll be in the depths of grief, and having them blindly rummage through all your unorganized stuff really isn't helping them. It's only adding an additional burden to their suffering.

If you *know* you don't have much longer to live (or you're getting up there in years) yet don't know who'd want/need what, start asking people. If an argument breaks out, you're still alive to hear everyone's reasoning for wanting a certain thing and to give the final say. Yes, there'll be some awkward moments, but even with the awkward moments, it's still better than having the people you leave behind fight over your stuff without your arbitration. This also has the added benefit of forcing your family to acknowledge your mortality in your living years and start thinking about death before it suddenly blindsides everybody.

In a more metaphysical sense, this helps take stock of where you're spending useless energy. Is that treadmill actually being used, or is it just taking up space? Why are you attached to that sweater you never wear? Could someone else use that specialty cookware you've used once in the last three years? Free yourself and your energy from stagnant things. Give them to family, donate them to those in need, etc. Keep the energy of life in motion, flowing through you. Don't be an energetic graveyard where things come to rest forever undisturbed.

So, your Pagan European takeaway challenge is to make a plan for the things you can't take with you into the hereafter, organize your important documents (letting some people you trust know where they are), and just sort all your stuff out ahead of time so those grieving don't have to.

Deities & Legends

BANSHEES

In Celtic Irish mythology, banshees were ghostly female heralds of doom who would appear to the living when they or someone they loved were soon to die or had just died. They're iconic for their loud, woeful wailing and shrieking that, in and of itself, was known to be hideously unsettling. They would also rock back and forth inconsolably all while sobbing laments to the soon-to-be deceased (a Gaelic funerary custom called *keening*).

The appearance of banshees varied in legends and among people who claimed to have seen one. In general, though, they're pallid women in loose, flowing clothing with long, unkempt hair and intensely red eyes from their incessant, profound weeping. The Irish Celts rarely invoked banshees or worked with them in magic because if one came to you, it meant your death or the death of a loved one.[75]

---

75   Clifton D. Bryant, and Dennis L. Peck, *Encyclopedia of Death and the Human Experience* (Thousand Oaks: SAGE Publications, 2009).

DONN

Donn is a Celtic god of death and a legendary ancestor of the Gaelic Irish. It's tricky to define him in any concrete way because folklore on him varies throughout the ages, and in Ireland, different counties even have their own different interpretation of Donn. In general, though, he's always seen as a death deity who resides in an afterlife realm called *Tech Duinn* ("house of the dark one"). This place was not the underworld itself, but rather a place at the furthest southwestern point of Ireland where the souls of the deceased would stop for a while on their westward journey to the underworld.[76]

In the mythologized medieval pseudo-history of the conquest of Ireland by the Milesians (the ancestral people of the modern Irish), Donn was originally a mortal human, one of the chiefs of the Milesians, and the first to die during their invasion of the Emerald Isle. After their conquest victory, the Milesians honored him by burying him where he died (believed to be Dursey Island off the Beara Peninsula), and his spirit stayed there ever since. The "history" goes on to say that he would sound his horn every year during the end of Samhain (Halloween) to help guide the souls of the dead back to the underworld via its entry point near Tech Duinn.[77]

HEL

Goddess of the Norse land of the dead (also called *Hel*, as mentioned prior) and daughter of the trickster god, Loki, Hel is sometimes depicted as a beautiful woman, though mostly as a rotting corpse, and always somber and gloomy. She rules the afterlife destination of those who have not died a hero's death in battle but rather a "regular" death by old age or disease. Her name and her eponymous realm of the dead were adopted by

---

76 Dáithí Ó hÓgáin, *Myth, Legend & Romance: An Encyclopaedia of the Irish Folk Tradition* (Upper Saddle River: Prentice Hall General, 1991).

77 Ali Isaac, "Donn, the Mysterious Irish Lord of the Dead," *Irish Central*, Jun. 27, 2017, https://www.irishcentral.com/roots/history/donn-the-mysterious -irish-lord-of-the-dead (accessed May 25, 2018).

Germanic-language Christians as "Hell," the place of eternal torment after death.[78]

The scholarly community is mixed as to whether or not the Vikings actually believed Hel was an actual deity. With only ambiguous archeological evidence and lack of mention of her until near the end of the Viking age, the modern consensus seems to be that Hel was a poetic personification of the underworld (thus the deity was named after the location, and not the other way around) and that Christian missionaries who converted Scandinavia during the late Viking age emphasized her existence as a Satan-like evil figure who presided over a frightening afterlife.[79]

Still, the minority of scholars who defend that she was, indeed, a separate deity and not a poetic personification of *Hel* believe that she was originally a more majestic goddess who only started to get a bad rap during the Christianization of the Vikings because the missionaries needed a satanic local counterpart to God and a way to vilify strong, unrelenting women in power.[80]

THE MORRIGAN

Celtic goddess of war, battle, strife, death, regeneration, and the underworld, the Morrigan is known as a triple goddess, often being depicted as three women simultaneously. On October 31 (Samhain/Halloween), she is believed to straddle both the physical world and the spiritual world, allowing contact between the lands of the living and the dead. In her affairs with humans, she is known for her ambivalence, sometimes helping them and sometimes harming them. Occasionally thought of as a Celtic equivalent to the Norse Valkyries, the Morrigan is more popularly known

---

78   Snorri Sturlson, *The Prose Edda*, trans. Jesse Byock (New York: Penguin Books, 2006).

79   Hilda Roderick Ellis, *The Road to Hel: A Study of the Conception of the Dead in Old Norse Literature* (Santa Barbara: Praeger, 1968).

80   Rudolf Simek, *Dictionary of Northern Mythology*, trans. by Angela Hall (Rochester: Boydell & Brewer, 2008).

in modern times through the legends of King Arthur, in which she is characterized as Morgan le Fay.[81]

However, it was Gaelic Ireland wherein she became more prominently associated with darkness, death, and warfare (but not in an evil way since darkness, death, and warfare weren't considered evil in and of themselves, just unavoidable aspects of life). Back over in continental Europe, she still retained stronger ties as an earth goddess and was thought to facilitate the cycles of life, such as birth and death, the phases of the moon, the seasons, war and peace, and so on. When in triple goddess form, she is accompanied by her sisters, Badb (Madness) and Neiman (Violence).[82]

81   Christopher Penczak, *Gay Witchcraft: Empowering the Tribe* (San Francisco: Red Wheel/Weiser, 2003).

82   Honor Johnson, "Morrigan," *The Order of Bards, Ovates & Druids*, https://www.druidry.org/library/gods-goddesses/morrigan (accessed May 24, 2018).

CHRISTIANITY

Cultural

Christianity is currently the largest, most widespread religion on the planet, with about a third of all people on earth identifying as Christian.[83] Although originating in the Middle East as an offshoot of Judaism, it didn't really take off until the Roman Empire began converting to, promoting, and mandating it. Rome's influence over all of Europe helped Christianity take strong root and blossom throughout the continent, and the

---

[83] Conrad Hackett, and David McClendon, "Christians remain world's largest religious group, but they are declining in Europe," *Pew Research Center*, Apr. 5, 2017, http://www.pewresearch.org/fact-tank/2017/04/05/christians-remain -worlds-largest-religious-group-but-they-are-declining-in-europe/ (accessed May 25, 2018).

Europeans' colonial quest for wealth, resources, and land helped spread it (forcibly) throughout the globe.

Conquering Death

Of all the world's major religions, Christianity is arguably one of the most theologically reliant upon death. You see, despite the popularity of Christmas, Easter is the holiest day in the Christian calendar, and it's the feast day of Jesus Christ's resurrection from the dead. If Jesus hadn't risen from the dead, then there really wouldn't have been Christianity. Jesus's resurrection was the ultimate miracle performed by Christ, which once and for all proved his divinity to his still-skeptical followers, empowering them to go out and spread the Good News. Lack of resurrection would've cemented in his followers' minds all the doubts they had about Jesus and made them write him off as just another eccentric guy who believed himself to be special and divine.

The story of the resurrection of Christ goes further than just Jesus coming back from the dead. Jesus is said to have *conquered* death and been *victorious* over it, which paints the picture of death and dying as a kind of antagonist to the holy goodness of God. Thus came into being the idea that death was a villain of sorts.

The softer side of this is that Jesus also is said to have died for the sins of humanity because his death allowed God to forgive the natural wickedness of humans and start allowing souls into Heaven again. So, essentially, without the death of Jesus, Heaven would've been unattainable for everyone, and the angry God of the Old Testament would never have become the loving God of the New Testament.[84]

Still, just because Jesus died for you doesn't mean you automatically get a pass into Heaven; your final afterlife destination is determined by whether or not you were a morally good person. Technically, every denom-

---

84 "Christ's resurrection conquered 'wall' of spiritual death, Pope explains," *Catholic News Agency*, Apr. 10, 2011, https://www.catholicnewsagency.com/news/christs-resurrection-conquered-wall-of-spiritual-death-pope-explains (Accessed May 25, 2018).

ination of Christianity has its own set of extra rules for who goes where after death. However, because going over every denomination's spiritual relationship with death would be a multivolume series on its own, we'll stick to the oldest, largest, most powerful denomination (and the O.G. one in which I grew up and know intimately), Catholicism.

Evolving Views of Heaven

Historically, all of Christianity was what we'd now call Catholicism until 1054 CE when what is now the Eastern Orthodox Church broke away over irreconcilable theological differences and created precedent for the numerous other breaks thereafter. But in the early days when all Christians were Catholic, entry to Heaven was very strict. Only baptized Christians who were free of sin could go to Heaven, and the only way to ensure that you'd be free of sin before death was to confess all your sins to a priest who could absolve you of them. Thus, regularly confessing your sins ensured against not getting into Heaven should you have a premature, unexpected death (which was much more common before the modern era).

Nowadays, the Catholic Church takes a much more relaxed view on who can go to Heaven; so long as you're a good person, you get in. The dogmatic justification for this viewpoint is that Jesus died for everyone's sins, including those who hated him or didn't believe in his message, so therefore everyone is automatically destined for paradise unless they themselves choose to forego paradise by engaging (via their own free will) in earthly sin. It's only really the conservative Protestant denominations nowadays who take the Bible literally and continue on the fearmongering tactics of hell sermons and preaching that everyone who doesn't believe in Jesus is damned. Catholics believe the Bible to be *inspired* by the Holy Spirit yet written by fallible humans and therefore not meant to be taken literally.[85]

---

85   U.S. Catholic Conference, *Catechism of the Catholic Church*, 2nd ed. (New York: Doubleday, 2003).

Burial vs. Cremation

The Catholic Church has also become more progressive on what can be done to a Catholic corpse, and their views on the matter have historically influenced final disposition trends around the world. As Christianity was originally an offshoot of Judaism, burial was the only acceptable final disposition from the religion's inception. Christians believe that Jesus will return and bring about the end of days, at which time God will raise the dead for reunification with the spirit and have both the body and soul of all people reside eternally in Heaven or Hell.

Because of this, any form of cremation was absolutely out of the question. If you chose to burn away your body, it was seen as an act of protest against God and that you didn't believe in the return of the Messiah and the resurrection of the dead. Making cremation even more taboo was that final disposition by fire was favored by the evil Romans during the persecution era and thus labeled not only a pagan practice, but also a practice of the oppressors of the faith.

Because of Christianity's influence on Europe and Europe's subsequent influence on much of the rest of the world, burial was the predominant practice of final disposition throughout the Western, industrialized, and colonized world for about the past 2,000 years. Everything changed, however, in 1963 when Pope Paul VI announced that it was now okay to cremate a Catholic corpse (though officially they'd prefer you still not). Since then, cremation rates have skyrocketed in the Western world, especially in Europe and the former British colonies of the United States, Canada, Australia, and New Zealand wherein it's now statistically the preferred option over burial.[86]

Nonetheless, with the overbearing popularity of cremation in spite of their disapproving consent, the Vatican recently had somewhat of a change of heart whereby the Holy See put restrictions on what good Catholics could do with a family member's cremated remains. Specifically, you are no longer allowed to scatter them, divvy them up amongst family mem-

---

86   http://www.cremationpedia.org/cremationrate.html (accessed May 25, 2018).

bers, or keep them at home; as of 2016, if you're cremated, your cremated remains must remain all together and stored in a consecrated place (like a Catholic cemetery, columbarium, or mausoleum ... all of which you have to pay for, unsurprisingly). All in all, the Vatican felt that cremated remains were being treated too much like personal property and that scattering them was too much like "pantheism, naturalism, or nihilism."[87]

All Souls Don't Go to Heaven

As for the Catholic soul, it could wind up in one of three different afterlife realms. Good people go to Heaven, bad people go to Hell, and the morally ambiguous or those who aren't good enough for Heaven or bad enough for Hell go to Purgatory. Obviously, Heaven is the ideal place to go, and though it's not really described in much official detail, it is thought of as being with God.

And that's the big thing to remember: all the joy and happiness that is associated with Heaven is the by-product of being close to God. Conversely, the sorrow and the suffering that is associated with Hell is the by-product of being far away from God. Hell itself is not seen as a place of horrific tortures; Hell is only torturous because you are excluded from God's loving presence down there. Also, don't think Hell is all fire and brimstone. For most of Christian history, Hell was considered a cold and frigid place because it was far from God's loving warmth (see the ninth circle of Hell in Dante's *Inferno*).

Purgatory is the unique one. It was seen as a kind of afterlife detox center wherein you'd purify yourself through bland monotony so as to be pure enough again to be able to enter Heaven. Still, it was better than Hell because everyone who went to Purgatory would eventually end up in Heaven. Until recently, it was assumed that most people went to Purgatory, because of the pessimistic view that humans aren't pure enough to enter Heaven straight off the bat from death. However, the idea of

---

87 Associated Press, "Vatican issues new rules on Catholic cremation," *Canadian Broadcasting Corporation*, Oct. 25, 2016, http://www.cbc.ca/news/world/vatican-catholic-cremation-1.3820336 (accessed May 25, 2018).

Purgatory is becoming more of a relic of olden-times Catholicism, and the dichotomous destinations of Heaven and Hell are the only real two places modern Catholics see their souls headed.[88]

For better or for worse, the deciding factor for which afterlife realm you'll go to after death in the Catholic tradition isn't based on the ratio of goodliness to wickedness throughout your entire life as one would think, but rather it's based on your level of purity upon the moment of death. The more you sin and do wicked things, the more impure you'd become, but through the sacrament of Reconciliation (confessing your sins to a priest), you could wipe the slate clean and start over again.

However, humans are imperfect and have a tendency to sin, so you'd have to regularly seek Reconciliation to keep yourself in tip-top shape soul-wise (like house cleaning, it's an ongoing process because the house *will* get dirty again simply because you reside in it). Theoretically, this provides a loophole to Heaven since you could be wicked all your life and confess your sins to a priest while on your deathbed, but the caveat is that you have to *truly be sorry* for your sins in order to reconcile them with God ... so, if you were truly sorry at the end of your life, you were allowed that loophole, but if it was just done out of fear of going to Hell, then you're pretty much S.O.L.

How Limbo Went Out of Fashion

Oh, and one last thing we must explore before moving on, the infamous Limbo. No, not the Caribbean dance testing how low you can go; I'm talking about the afterlife destination for infants and the unbaptized. This realm was the explanation to olden-time Catholicism's theological conundrum of what happened to good people who were either too young to be baptized and/or were never exposed to the teachings of Jesus due to living before he existed or living in a part of the world where Christianity was not a known practice.

---

88   Nick Rabiipour, "What Do Catholics Really Believe About Purgatory?," *The Catholic Company*, Nov. 1, 2017, https://www.catholiccompany.com/getfed/what-catholics-really-believe-purgatory/ (accessed May 27, 2018).

It was thought unjust for them to suffer in Hell since their ignorance of Christ and lack of baptism was through no fault of their own. So, all these people and infants were believed to go to a compromise place called Limbo (meaning "edge"), which was not joyous like Heaven, but less arduously boring than Purgatory. It should be said that the Catholic Church itself no longer supports the idea of Limbo, believing it to be an "unfounded" hypothesis. It's really just Heaven and Hell now, with some hard-core Catholics keeping Purgatory in the mix.[89]

Christian Takeaway:
ABSOLUTION

We affect many people throughout our lives, not all of them positively. Though some are inadvertently negatively affected by us due to their own issues and baggage from the past causing collateral damage, some are truly affected negatively through our willful direct action or inaction.

We are to blame for the hurt many others feel. This acceptance of blame, this mea culpa, is not enough in the Christian faith to be forgiven. To be forgiven, one has to not only accept that it's their fault and want forgiveness, but they have to actually ask for forgiveness. Through the sacrament of Reconciliation, Catholics ask God's forgiveness using the intervention of a priest, a crucial act of purification needed to enter Heaven. And that is all well and good for your own soul, but what about all the people whom you've hurt? What if you die without making amends with the souls you've negatively affected?

A very difficult Christian takeaway challenge before you now is to seek absolution for sins of the past. Tomorrow is not guaranteed, and if something tragic happens to you, all those you've hurt will have their hurt seethe and slowly corrode inside of them since they can never get closure from you. Yes, it's ultimately their own duty to move on with life, but

89   John Thavis, "Vatican commission: Limbo reflects 'restrictive view of salvation'," *Catholic News Service*, Apr. 20, 2007, http://webarchive.loc .gov/all/20070508193238/http://www.catholicnews.com/data/stories/ cns/0702216.htm (accessed May 27, 2018).

helping to ease the pain you've caused before it's too late is the least you can do (and it's also pretty disgraceful to say that others "just need to get over" damage you've instigated without you attempting to help out at all). So, ask for their forgiveness. Do it sincerely, and be ready to accept the probability that you won't be forgiven or given the chance to talk with them. Either way, be sure to follow up with real-world action to help reverse the damage you've caused and help those whom you've harmed.

Deities & Legends

BEELZEBUB

Sometimes used as an alternate name for Satan, Beelzebub is more officially known in Christian demonology as Satan's top lieutenant and right-hand general in commanding the armies of Hell. His name is a derivation from the Canaanite god Baal (meaning "Lord") and the Hebrew word for fly. From this, he is given the title "Lord of the Flies."[90]

In the Philistine religion, Beelzebub was a good deity with patronage over healing and flying insects, but in the Christian tradition, since flies and their maggot larvae are strongly associated with rotting corpses, Beelzebub was given associations with death. He is often depicted with large wings and having immediate supervision over Satan's flying demons.[91]

Aside from being the chief general of the deathly armies of Hell, Beelzebub is also the demon who is most responsible for human possession. Back in the days before modern science and medicine, whenever a person began acting oddly or displayed visually disturbing fits, the Christian assumption was that the person was being possessed by Beelzebub, and if not him, then a demon specifically under his command. As the years went on, Beelzebub became the demon associated with witches and witchcraft, giving humans magical powers in exchange for their immortal soul. Most infamously, Beelzebub was the name that was frequently mentioned as

---

90   https://www.etymonline.com/word/beelzebub (accessed May 28, 2018).

91   David Noel Freedman, *Eerdmans Dictionary of the Bible* (Grand Rapids: William B. Eerdmans Publishing Company, 2000).

the instigator of all the evil goings-on in Salem, Massachusetts, during the infamous witch trials.[92]

SAINT MICHAEL THE ARCHANGEL

Saint Michael the Archangel is the good-guy version of Beelzebub. He is a winged angel and God's top general who commands the armies of Heaven. Often depicted as a strong, blond, human-shaped angel with two feathery wings protruding from his shoulder blades, he's easily identified in iconography by his battle armor and having a flaming sword in hand.

Most of what is officially written about St. Michael is in the ultracryptic and poetic Book of Revelation all about the impending apocalypse (a Book of the Bible that even the Vatican admittedly takes with many grains of salt).[93] In this artistic codified text, St. Michael leads Heaven's angels against Satan's demons in an epic celestial war wherein he slays Satan (depicted as a red dragon) once and for all with his sword and heralds the Second Coming of Jesus Christ.[94]

St. Michael is also the designated psychopomp who leads the deceased's soul to Heaven. More than a guide, St. Michael was given this charge to act as a bodyguard (soulguard?) and protect the soul until it was safe in Heaven. Before the trip, though, St. Michael would be the judge of whether the soul was good enough to go Heaven, okay enough to go to Purgatory, or wicked enough to be sent to Hell. If deemed wicked, he would personally cast the soul down into the pits of Hell and prevent any escapes along the way.[95]

The more well-known scenario of St. Peter at the pearly gates being the official enforcement judge of entry into Heaven isn't officially Christian

92 Rev. Cotton Mather, "Of Beelzebub and His Plot," *Original Sources*, 1693, http://originalsources.com/Document.aspx?DocID=5DDGZ6LDDLS5NMR (accessed May 28, 2018).

93 "The Book of Revelation," *United States Conference of Catholic Bishops*, http://www.usccb.org/bible/revelation/0 (accessed May 28, 2018).

94 "Revelation," *The Holy Bible* (via *Catholic Online*), https://www.catholic.org/bible/book.php?id=73 (accessed May 28, 2018).

95 Mirabai Starr, *Saint Michael the Archangel: Devotion, Prayers & Living Wisdom* (Surry Hills: ReadHowYouWant, 2012).

canon, but rather, it's a pop culture imagining that caught trend based on Jesus metaphorically giving Peter "the keys to the Kingdom (of Heaven)." Keys thus became symbolic of St. Peter (and all popes succeeding him), and since St. Peter held the keys to Heaven, he became artistically depicted as the one letting souls into Heaven by personally unlocking it for them. Nevertheless, officially, St. Michael the Archangel is Catholicism's judge, enforcer, and psychopomp to all after-death destinations.

SATAN

Satan (also known as the "Devil" and "Lucifer," though the latter is a literary misinterpretation of the planet Venus) [96] is the ruler of Hell and the most supreme evil being antithetical to God in the Christian faith. Although Satan is rarely mentioned in the Bible, when he *is* mentioned in authentic sources, he's described as more of an intellectual instigator who tests humans' allegiance to God. Interpretations vary, however, as to whether this is done on behalf of God or if he does it out of personal schadenfreude.

Ironically, most ideas and lore about Satan don't come from the Bible, but rather artistic interpretations of Christian teachings (mainly Milton's *Paradise Lost*, wherein he's a beautiful fallen angel and Dante's *Inferno*, wherein he's a giant demon frozen up to his torso in a lake of ice). In fact, Satan is barely mentioned directly in the Bible at all, and thus all nameless evil antagonists are assumed by many throughout history to be him (like the snake in the Garden of Eden and "the wicked one" mentioned in the Gospels).

The main place Satan is directly named is in the Book of Revelation (which the Catholic Church takes with a grain of salt, understanding it was written to be poetic and metaphorical, not taken literally). The other well-known major mention of him is in the Book of Job (again, a parable the Church doesn't take literally) in which he makes a friendly wager with

96   Lynn Hayes, "Lucifer: Satan or Venus?" *Beliefnet*, http://www.beliefnet
      .com/columnists/astrologicalmusings/2009/07/lucifer-satan-or-venus
      .html (accessed May 28, 2018).

God as to whether or not Job would still love God if his life wasn't so rosy and life was harder for him, and so Satan, under the direction and permission of God, makes Job's life miserable by irreversibly taking his possessions, health, and loved ones away from him.[97]

Going back to earliest Christian times, Satan (whose name means "adversary/opposer")[98] was originally thought of as a neutral character who'd act as the prosecution in a postmortem trial to decide whether a soul was good or evil.[99] In this way, he could be metaphorically likened to a district attorney of sorts whose job it is to find you guilty and convince the judge/jury (God) that you are bad even if he himself doesn't necessarily believe it since he's just doing his job, which God tasked to him.

Nowadays, progressive Protestant denominations and the Catholic Church regard Satan to be a mythological metaphor for evil and not an actual being, since, according to Catholic doctrine, even if there was such a being, he and his actions would have to then be permitted under God's divine providence (like in the Book of Job), and a loving God would never allow such a thing. Still, though, conservative Protestant groups strongly assert his existence and power.[100] To those who revere Satan (such as in the Church of Satan or the Satanic Temple), he is seen as a role model of rebellion, rationalism, and personal freedom and symbolizes knowledge, wisdom, self-assertion, and self-respect (albeit they also understand him as a narrative construct, not an actual being).

Since Satan's appearance isn't really described in the Bible (except for, perhaps, the cryptically poetic and not-meant-to-be-taken-literally Book of Revelation), all of his modern pop culture symbolism comes from litera-

97 Timothy Mackie, "The Book of Job: What's Going On Here?" *The Bible Project*, https://thebibleproject.com/blog/book-job-whats-going/ (accessed May 28, 2018).

98 https://www.etymonline.com/word/satan (accessed May 28, 2018).

99 M.J.L., "Do Jews Believe in Satan?" *My Jewish Learning*, https://www.myjewishlearning.com/article/satan-the-adversary/ (accessed May 28, 2018).

100 John Switzer, "What do Catholics believe about the Devil?" *U.S. Catholic*, Sept. 2014, http://www.uscatholic.org/articles/201408/what-do-catholics-believe-about-devil-29310 (accessed May 28, 2018).

ture and art. Usually, these symbols were invented as a way to associate pagan gods with evil (goat legs with Pan, pitchfork with Poseidon's trident, etc.). Other artistic mainstays, like his red skin, were invented as a way to make Satan stand out as a recognizable stock character during medieval productions of morality plays. And as for his horns and tail, those come from the Book of Revelation, which describes "the evil one" as a dragon.[101]

101 Philip Kosloski, "Why is Satan depicted with horns, red tights and a pitchfork?" *Aleteia*, Oct. 17, 2017, https://aleteia.org/2017/10/17/ why-is-satan-depicted-with-horns-red-tights-and-a-pitchfork/ (accessed Oct. 27, 2018).

8

EUROPEAN MAGICAL COMMUNITY

KEYS TO THE DARK GODDESS

I met our next community member, Anthony Lucero, at Phoenix Pagan Pride a few years ago and have remained in touch with him ever since. Knowing his close relationship to Hekate (the epitome of dark goddesses in the Greek pantheon), it was a no-brainer that I invite him to share something about her with you all. So now, taking time out of his eclectic schedule as a Phoenician drag queen and a cofounder of the magic shop Toad and Broom (which you can find at toadandbroom.com), Anthony is going to give us a magical ritual on how to establish a relationship with ancient Greece's original dark lady.

*I just want to begin by stating that I do not take any liability for those
who wish undertake the work to be presented or any of the results thereof.
Hekate has been my patron since I began studying and practicing Witchcraft in my preteen years. I first encountered her in a dream in which I
could hear her name whispered lightly as though it were from shadows
in the darkened woods of my mind.*

*Hekate is an amazing goddess to work with; there is so much to learn
from her on the pathways she can present to us, though we may, at times,
be forced to deal with a lesson head-on. Hekate is often seen as a crone
goddess. To me, yes, she is a goddess of great wisdom, but she has never
appeared as a goddess of old age; she has always appeared as a beautiful
maiden full of life with a strong, and dare I say intimidating, presence
about her. She is a goddess whom I am proud to say is my patron, and I
wouldn't have it any other way.*

*If you wish to work with her, the following ritual is very similar to my
original offering ritual to Hekate, asking that she teach me her mysteries.
I must say as a word of caution that she is not a goddess who will guide
you as a child learning to swim, but rather as the beneficial force of nature
pushing you to your limits to test and strengthen them.*

*To set up a devotional shrine and establish rapport with the Goddess
Hekate, you will need an image (statue or photo), an iron key, two red
candles, dirt from a crossroads, Hekate incense and oil, as well as offerings
(wine, flowers, honey, etc.).*

*Begin by cleansing the area and laying down a black altar cloth. Place
her image at the back of the altar in the center and place the anointed
candles at either side of her image. Place the crossroads dirt in front of
her image with the offerings and incense. Anoint the key to unlock the
mysteries Hekate has to teach. Perform your usual opening rituals and go
into a meditative state while holding the key. See yourself at a three-way
crossroads where the only light about you is from the stars. In the distance,
hear the barking of dogs. The path before you almost seems to glow from
beneath it.*

Now you may call out to Hekate:

"Cthonia! Enodia! Nocticula!" [epithets of Hekate, meaning, Of the Earth, Of the Crossroads, and Light of the Night, respectively, and pronounced "kuh-THO-nee-uh," "eh-NO-dee-uh," and "nok-TIK-you-luh."]

Hekate, mighty key-bearing mistress at the Crossroads! Hear me O' mighty Queen of Sorcery! Teacher of the mysteries of life, death, birth, and rebirth! I call out into the night and ask that you come forth and attend this rite! Receive these offerings I place before you at this shrine I have erected in your honor! With this key unlock the mysteries in the darkness of the universe! Unlock my mind that I may learn your secrets of Witchery! Impart to me your mysteries as I lie resting nightly! Bestow unto me your kiss of truth, envelop me in your embrace, and show me the path that lies beyond the fog of doubt!

Hold your key aloft and say:
"In the name of Hekate Kleidophoros [Key-Bearer], with this key I unlock your mysteries!"

Hold the key to your mind's eye and turn it as though unlocking a lock. Repeat at the solar plexus and root chakras. See your energy centers glowing and radiating. Now begin chanting:
"Cthonia, Enodia, Nocticula!"

Go back into the meditative state with Hekate at the crossroads standing before you. See her embrace you and place a kiss upon your lips. See the bones within the earth rise to the surface and surround the crossroads. See serpents entwine and hear the owls hooting in the air around you. Smell the sweet scents of the earth, yet also the scents of death and decay in the night about you. Listen to any secrets she may divulge to you. Thank Hekate for her presence and bring your ritual to a close. Sleep with a key under your pillow. Repeat this ritual every Saturday until a connection is made or you are given a sign.

—ANTHONY LUCERO

IN THE REAPER'S SERVICE

Coming all the way from the Isle of Anglesey in Wales is our next community member, Kristoffer Hughes. Aside from being an award-winning author (definitely check out his death and Celtic works) and BAFTA-winning television personality, he's the head of the Anglesey Druid Order. He and I share a special bond in that we're both licensed death industry professionals, although he definitely has the cooler title of Anatomical Pathology Technician & Bereavement Officer. So now, as a practicing Celtic Pagan and a Welsh death services professional for Her Majesty's Coroner performing autopsies on the dead of Great Britain, he's here to talk about how those two aspects of his life intertwine while in the reaper's service.

I have given my life in service to the Reaper. This is, I think, quite a statement to make, but one I use with genuine affection and pride. For thirty years I have served the dead and bereaved as an Autopsy Technologist and Bereavement Officer in the UK, but little did I know that the Reaper rarely rewards those that serve it; death is not one for the issuing of favours, death does only what is in its nature to do. Being a death service professional and a Druid affords me no immunity when death knocks at the doors of my loved ones, and for years I had no reason to prepare for the consuming price of love, which is the pain of loss. The integration of my spiritual and professional life would be initially jarring, but ultimately cathartic and deeply transformative.

My little sister was twenty-two when she died suddenly, leaving behind an eight-month-old child and a family reeling in shock. I could taste the iron of my own blood as my heart burst into a cloud of red mist, my own screams deafened me. How could I endure such a loss? What did my tradition, my Druidry teach me about dealing with loss?

Druidry encompasses many philosophies and techniques for exploring the spiritual and the divine, but one word frequents the lips of Druids more than many—honour. It struck me, as a Druid and a death professional, that society often seeks to vanquish that which blights us: illness, mental health issues, addictions, and emotions. Take this pill and it will go away. But why not honour something for what it is, and its potentiality to transform? Grief is a natural response to the pain of loss, and hid within it is the transformative quality of emotional relocation, but this takes time, and deserves to be honoured as an essential aspect of the human condition.

Whilst dealing with my own grief I turned to the Welsh horse Goddess Rhiannon, calumniated wife, a mother who loses her child, twice. Divine queen and the epitome of sovereignty. How could I find my own sovereignty within the maelstrom of my personal grief, and what on earth did it all mean? I longed for the pain to go away, for my sister to come back. In the pain of loss I fell to my knees and screamed imprecations at the Reaper: "How dare you, why have you done this to me? I have given you my life and you take my sister!" The Reaper's silence was punctuated only by a neighing horse in the field opposite, who stopped its leisurely ambling and stared intently at me. Rhiannon...

"Rhiannon—Great Queen, I am your child. Rhiannon, great mother, I am your son."

Rhiannon endured her loss with humility and grace, even when others chose to humiliate her. Her lesson as the mourning mother is the essential nature of grief, and that vanquishing a natural emotional response is never the answer—assimilation is. Grief does truly transform, and eventually it settles somewhere within us and finds its home there. But we are never the same afterwards. Perhaps I believed in some hopeful, whimsical part of myself that I was immune, and that to be surrounded by death, and to tread a spiritual path would afford me my immunity, but no, on the contrary. My Druidry, my relationship with Rhiannon, great Goddess and Queen, taught me the power of "not coping." I hear these words so often in my work—"I can't cope!"—and now I afford the bereaved this retort: "Don't cope, stop coping, this is not a time for coping." There is power in surrender, there is magic in not coping, for when one stops trying to cope, grief floods the heart and breaks it through the metamorphic power of love.

Honour your pain, your loss, and give it voice, and when you stop coping, do you know what will happen to you? You will cope. Grief is punctuated by question marks, but it need not be; it embodies so much of our humanity. I have since learned to honour the Reaper for what is only in its nature to do.

I continue to be in service to the Reaper.

—Kristoffer Hughes

EASING THE PASSAGE

Death is inevitable. Sure, we have medicines, prayers, magic, and miracles that can extend life, but that doesn't mean it'll extend on forever. It's an uncomfortable and scary reality. However, it can be even scarier and much more real to the terminally ill and those on their death beds. There comes a time when we just have to admit reality and prepare for it as best we can, no matter how difficult that may be. Nevertheless, this difficult time can be eased, and to help teach us a Nordic ritual on how to help ease the passage of the dying into what lies beyond the realm of the living, I've invited my friend Abbie Plouff. You can find more of her Scandinavian magic via her shop, Northern Lights Witch (www.northernlightswitch .com), but first take time to really take in this ritual of how to help not only the terminally ill, but also those who are left behind in grief.

Last summer, my ninety-four-year-old grandmother died. She was the matriarch, the one who carried on the traditions of our Norwegian immigrant family. I was struck with how the loss of such a powerful figure left the rest of the family adrift. Right after passage, there is a flurry of activity. The people who are most impacted also need to manage details and logistics for the funeral.

What can we do to ease the passing—for both the deceased, and for the family left behind to pick up the pieces? It doesn't need to be anything big. In my case, my family doesn't practice the Norse pagan ways, so it needs to be discreet and respectful. I just needed something small to give strength.

This is a simple spell, to create bind runes to ease the passage for your family. A bind rune is a glyph combining two or more runes for specific purposes. For this spell, you will want wooden or clay discs.

Step One:

Create sacred space.

If you are so called, create an altar for the deceased. Place mementos of the deceased on the altar—photographs, gifts they gave you. You can also place anything that you think would help them in their passage to the afterlife.

Light the center candle and carry it around your sacred space. Chant the runes as you go. Call your gods into the space. Odin the Allfather, Freyja who watches over Valhalla, and Hel are all fantastic gods to call for the death rites. Bless the discs you will be using for the bind runes.

Step Two:

Create a bind rune to ease the passage of the deceased. You can get creative with how these three runes fit together.

ᛟ *OTHILA: a rune for legacy, for family, for ancestry. Othila is your connection beyond the grave, and the signal to your ancestors to welcome the deceased into the fold.*

ᛜ *INGWAZ: a rune for birth and for death, a portal and transition between realms. Ingwaz connects our life and our death, to ease the transition for the deceased, and to understand death as a necessary part and continuation of life.*

ᛚ *LAGUZ: a rune for the deep waters of mystery, to ease the passage of the soul. Laguz is the water itself, and our protection from the water.*

Carve or burn this bind rune into the disc. Concentrate on the ease of passage between the worlds as you do this.

Step Three:

Create a bind rune to ease the stress of the grieving.

ᛟ OTHILA: *the connection to those recently passed and to the long line of ancestors who show support.*

ᚾ NAUTHIZ: *rune of needful things, to give inner strength in difficult times to do what is necessary. Nauthiz will protect those who remain, and guide them to their new places in the family.*

ᛇ EIHWAZ: *rune of strength, to provide aid and resilience when times are tough. Eihwaz represents the yew, a tree that connects the living and the dead, and lends strength to those in grief.*

Carve or burn this bind rune onto your disc. You will give this to those who are in mourning, who are responsible for the funerary preparations. You can make as many discs as you need, or just one to place on your own altar.

Step Four:

Place your first bind rune in the coffin with the deceased. You can even tuck it into their pocket. It will protect them in the other realm. Next, give the second set of bind runes to those who need to manage the logistics of death. You can place your own bind rune on an altar to the ancestors.

Your spell is complete.

—ABBIE PLOUFF

LOSS

Here now with us, I've invited one of my cousins, Santiago, to come share his story on loss. Loss is universal, and Santiago's is the loss of a parent while still being relatively young himself. I remember this particular story well because I was there at the hospital during visits with all the extended family as the news from the doctors just kept getting worse and worse. Santiago's father was also my godfather, so there was yet another level of loss that I personally had from his death. Of course, the loss of a godfather isn't at all the same as the loss of a father, but the loss of any family member is always something dreadful. Anyway, before I ramble on,

I'll let my cousin tell the story of how the loss of his dad almost lead to the loss of his Catholic faith.

In the darkest of times we turn to "faith," something so strong we have never physically seen but have so much trust in. My dad was diagnosed with stage three colon cancer in spring of 2015. I remember my mom struggling with the idea of having to tell her three sons and husband of twenty-five-plus years. My mom pulled me and my brothers into an empty waiting room, and with tears in her eyes she gave us the heartbreaking news.

The first words out of my mouth were, "This is not a death sentence. God will help. All we need to do is pray." With those words my rituals started. Every night I would pray for the healing of my dad. As time moved on, my prayers turned to "mandas" (direct requests/pleas to God in Mexican Catholic culture) making promises and deals with the Almighty. Things like "I won't miss church this month." Things I know I should already be doing as a Catholic but promising to try and be more diligent on them in exchange for getting help for my dad.

Some time passes. Fear and anger are now in the mix as I see what chemotherapy is doing to his body. It breaks my heart. It took a 6'2" 300-plus pound man and turned him into a frail 6'2" man of 225 pounds. I turn to the Lord and ask, "Why? Why him? He is one of the kindest, most giving gentlemen out there. There are worse people you can take from here. Not him. Not now."

I look at my prayer pattern and think to myself, "Time to step it up." I start to light candles and say prayers to different saints for healing and comfort for my dad. I start to notice my dad sleeping more, but this isn't normal. Why?

In one of my visits I told him, "You don't have to entertain me. I'm just here to see how you're doing and hang around the house."

He turns and says, "I'm tired of sleeping but it's the only time I don't feel pain." With that, I told him that today is a good day for him. He looks at me with a half-smile and says, "I'm here." He lies back and takes a nap. At that time, I start to think it's not what I wanted, but my prayers seem to be answered in that he is finding comfort.

The prayers and talks with a priest become more frequent. We question why my dad is not getting better. The prayers are now "Please give him comfort. Please take his pain away." The prayers then turn from comfort for my dad to prayers of guidance. "What do we do? Keep him on life support and see what happens or keep him hooked up in a coma-like state?"

Over the last weekend of January 2016, we get the news the cancer has spread all over. There is nothing else the doctors or chemotherapy can do. In a morbid way, that was our answer we prayed for. The doctor explained it would be best for him to take him off life support because of the stress being put on his body. God made the decision for us. We took him off later that week; he fought for over twelve hours. On February 3, at the stroke of midnight, Santiago Campos Salceda took his last breath.

It wasn't until I sat down again with a priest one-on-one that I found some comfort. He explained to me that in the Catholic faith, God hears all prayers but answers in a way that he sees fit. My dad wasn't being taken because he was a bad man. There is another reason, but it has to play out before we can see why. In this conversation, he also showed me that all throughout the time I prayed for my dad, my prayers had been answered … from taking the pain away, to finding comfort, to the decision of taking him off life support.

Every February 3 is hard in our family. It's the day we celebrate my daughter's birthday and celebrate the day my dad became our guardian angel. I know my faith will continue to help me push forward. I still pray for my dad, but now the prayers are geared toward asking God to send my dad to watch over the family.

—Santiago Salceda

PART 3
SUB-SAHARAN AFRICA & LANDS OF THE AFRICAN DIASPORA

Praise a person after his death.
Many secret things may yet come
out about a person while alive.
SWAHILI PROVERB

The continent of Africa, south of the Sahara Desert, is comprised of numerous cultures, tribes, and ways of life. Some have changed very little since humankind's earliest days, but most have been greatly influenced (forcibly) by Europe and the Middle East. Nowadays, most of sub-Saharan Africa is fervently Christian and/or Muslim. Some of the world's most extreme Christian and Islamic zealotry thrives strongly in these lands, and their outlook on death, dying, and what happens to us after death has been profoundly shaped by these beliefs.

Likewise, the lands of the African diaspora in the Americas have been profoundly affected and influenced by colonial Christianity. The horrendous slave trade broke apart families from cultures throughout Africa, mixing them together as strangers in strange lands, yet they persisted. Hidden under the mask of Christianity, the slave population maintained their own traditional ways of magic, mysticism, and spiritual communication. Through the centuries, the masks had blended into the faces they were hiding, thereby creating unique Afro-Caribbean faiths whose ancestor worship has made them some of the most infamously macabre in practice, as you're about to find out.

9

SUB-SAHARAN AFRICA

Cultural

Though there are numerous peoples and cultures throughout Africa, a grand commonality between many of them is that "life" and "death" are not seen as separate individual stages that a soul experiences. Rather, everything is seen as a simultaneous oneness wherein being alive and being dead are not mutually exclusive. Because of this, communing with the dead and ancestor worship are highly prevalent. The dead are easily accessible. They can help us out, and we can help them out. And though we in the West often use grief-comforting, clichéd expressions like "they will always be with you" and "they will live on in spirit," many African cultures mean this literally.

Outside Forces

Primarily, deceased ancestors in sub-Saharan Africa take on the role of protectors of the family. They help prevent and mitigate the effects of misfortune that come from outside forces. This is profoundly important in many traditional African societies because pretty much all misfortune is believed to come from some supernatural, outside force. You become sick? Outside force. Earning less money than usual? Outside force. Everyone is more argumentative with you? Outside force. That's where the ancestors come into play: they help protect you from such outside forces of misfortune.

An important thing to keep in mind, though, is that general misfortune is regarded as something serious in much of Africa. Not seen as just a temporary inconvenience, misfortune is believed to deal permanent blows to one's life vitality. You see, here it's believed every human has a finite, set amount of life vitality in them, and each sickness, depressive event, or other misfortune takes a bit of vitality out of you. You can heal your vitality through magic and medicine, but it's a constant back-n-forth depending on how "unfortunate" you are. Death is said to be the result of running out of life vitality. (Video game aficionados can relate to this concept, which is essentially the same as a player's "HP" health bar. You only lose HP when an outside agent inflicts damage to you, and though you can heal your HP, if your HP ever hits zero, you lose.)[102]

The belief in the supernatural having the capability to diminish one's life vitality is interestingly evident in the way sub-Saharan African peoples handle a dead body. Now, because of the sheer amount of native African traditions and beliefs on death, there's just not enough time or space in this book to go over them all. So instead what I'll do is take you on a tour of *general* body handling and funeral traditions that are applicable throughout a good majority of cultures on the continent (though the strict adherence to it naturally varies from culture to culture). After that, we'll backtrack and I'll give some tribal and regional specifics that will add cul-

---

102 Allan Anderson, "African Religions," *Encyclopedia of Death and Dying*, http://www .deathreference.com/A-Bi/African-Religions.html (accessed May 29, 2018).

tural personalization to these morbid rituals. Sound good? Okay, so here's what generally happens.

Corpse Handling Protocol

Immediately upon death, the home is prepared to receive guests from the community to pay their last respects for a wake. Friends and family of the deceased often arrive with food to share so as to help lighten the burden on the hosts. Because the soul doesn't immediately leave the body upon death, it's the responsibility of the family that two things be ensured during the wake. First, all reflective surfaces (including the windows) are covered so the deceased's spirit will not be frightened by seeing itself dead, and second, the bed of the deceased is taken out of the home since it's spiritually contaminated by the death (assuming, of course, they had the luxury of dying in bed).

When it comes time to transport a body out of the home, four specific rituals are adhered to for the protection of the surviving family. These protection rituals are done with the intention to confuse the spirit of the deceased just in case it ends up as a wandering ghost wanting to exact revenge on the family due to any funerary indiscretions or unfinished business. You see, it's often believed that only angry, malicious souls stay behind here on earth. If the soul was happy, they'd move on to the next world, and so these specific protocols were taken in the event that the soul was still lingering here on earth to harm people (especially family due to unresolved family drama).

First, a hole is cut out of the outermost wall of the home, through which the body must exit. It's believed that the spirit will remember how it left the home, so if the hole through which it exited is repaired, then it won't know how to re-enter the home. Second, the corpse must exit the home feet first so the spirit cannot look back at the location of the house. Third, the corpse needs to travel in a zigzag pattern or indirect route to their next location (usually the gravesite or a mortuary) so as to further confuse the spirit on how to get back to the home. Lastly, an obstacle course of branches, holes, thorns, etc. must be placed along the route (behind the body) to act as a final hindrance should the spirit remember its way back.[103]

It used to be that the body would be taken immediately to the gravesite for burial, but as sub-Saharan Africa urbanizes, it's becoming more and more common to transport the body to a morgue or refrigerated holding facility (like a mortuary) so as to allow extra time for far-flung family to be in attendance and for fundraising so that the deceased can have a lavish burial (more on that in a bit). Cremation is highly frowned upon due to the triple threat of conservative Christianity being against it, Islam being very against it, and burial being the traditional practice of most African cultures for millennia.[104]

The burial itself preferably takes place near the family home rather than in a cemetery, though always away from crops since it's believed nothing grows near death. In the regions of Africa where Islam is more pervasive, the body is dressed in simple white linen shrouds, but in the regions where Christianity is more pervasive, the body is dressed in the deceased's favorite clothes, sometimes then wrapped in animal skins. People gather tightly around the gravesite, chanting, singing, drumming, and wailing as loud as they can, all done as an emotional catharsis as well as to protect the body from wandering ghosts who'd love to possess a new, empty human vessel.

The cadaver is finally placed in the bare ground after being washed; males are generally placed facing east since they will continue to rise with morning sun and labor in the afterlife, while females are placed facing west since they will continue to do the domestic work in preparation for the men's return home at sunset. In the subsistence economies throughout rural Africa, though, the funeral may be postponed months until after

103   Dr. Vilma Ruddock, "Death Rituals in Africa," *LoveToKnow*, https://dying
        .lovetoknow.com/Death_Rituals_in_Africa (accessed May 29, 2018).

104   Rodney Muhumuza, "Africa slowly turning to cremations, though long
        taboo," *Associated Press*, May 26, 2018, https://www.apnews.com/
        e4d90cbae6b84d2d95e74e357f2b8c16 (accessed Nov. 14, 2018).

the village's agricultural work is done, otherwise there'd be a lot more funerals in the upcoming year.[105]

Fantasy Coffins

Nowadays, especially in West Africa, funerals are big business. They're large social events to display wealth and prestige and can cost around US $20,000 on average (which is really saying something given the economic hardships of many West African nations). Nowhere is this more so than in Ghana, where being a funeral director can garner an impressive income.

Billboards throughout the country's most congested areas advertise the deceased's funeral arrangements as a community call to come and join in on the revelry. People (including strangers) come from far away to attend these random funerals wearing the traditional mourning colors of black and red, and the family of the deceased (who already paid for the arrangements and advertising) is expected to provide food and drink for all who show up. But the pièce de résistance of a Ghanaian funeral is the casket.

Caskets in Ghana are the ultimate personal statement. The best ones show off wealth, are completely unique, and help express who you are as an individual (much like a custom designer dress). These "fantasy coffins" as they're called, can, at times, seem comical but are wholly symbolic of the deceased. A pilot might have a casket shaped and painted like an airplane, a fan of Coca-Cola might have one shaped and painted like a Coke bottle, a gynecologist might have one shaped and painted like a uterus and ovaries, and the list goes on and gets more whimsical. As a Christian-majority country, though, Ghana's political and religious leaders frown on what they see as debt-inducing worship of the dead, but their party-pooper concerns summarily fall on deaf ears as the funeral industry continues to be big business.[106]

---

105 Karen Story, "A Burial in West Africa," *The Order of the Good Death*, Apr. 20, 2016, http://www.orderofthegooddeath.com/a-burial-in-west-africa (accessed May 29, 2018).

106 Paula Newton, "The long goodbye: Why funerals are big business in Ghana," *CNN*, Mar. 11, 2014, http://www.cnn.com/2014/03/11/world/africa/on-the -road-ghana-funerals/index.html (accessed May 29, 2018).

Radio Free Zambia

In Zambia, radio and television announcements are preferred over billboards. Every day, the nationalized Zambian National Broadcasting Corporation publicly announces the names of the newly deceased as well as when and where the funeral will be for anyone wishing to attend. Male mourners cry out the *kukhuza* (traditional mourning wail) that sounds like "Mayi—baba-bee!" while female mourners cry out the *chitengelo* that sounds like "Ye-e—e-e-e-egh!" Those attending the funeral are to refrain from doing their hair or applying makeup and jewelry and are encouraged to wear old, worn-out clothing. When it comes time for burial, though, Zambians prefer to be buried in village cemeteries unlike the practice of West African cultures for whom burial close to the home is the most ideal.[107]

Home Sweet South Africa

As for the Xhosa down in South Africa, they believe that all human remains must be buried together in their homeland for their spirit to be at peace (specifically, where their umbilical cord was buried shortly after their birth). On the return journey home (whether from elsewhere in the country or from death abroad), the caretaker of the remains is expected to talk to the corpse, giving them detailed accounts of the town they just passed, the river they just crossed, etc. To keep the spirit happy during uneventful parts of the trip, songs of praise (*izibongo*) for the family line are often sung all throughout the escort journey.

At the burial site, cattle are slaughtered with a family-owned traditional spear, and if the bovine don't scream in pain as they die, more animals are slaughtered until one screams from the fear and pain (this scream is what will supposedly please the spirit). When Xhosa native, former president, and civil rights leader Nelson Mandela died in 2013, South Africa put on a

---

107   Mwizenge S. Tembo, PhD, "Funeral and Burial Customs in Zambia," *Bridgewater College Wordpress*, https://wp.bridgewater.edu/mtembo/culture-of-zambia/funerals-and-burials/ (accessed May 29, 2018).

114

special dual state/traditional Xhosa funeral so as to maintain his people's traditions and publicly let the world mourn along with the nation.[108]

Communal Condemnations

When it comes to the afterlife and what happens after death, however, most African cultures don't go into too much detail. In general, it's seen as not really much different than this life, except maybe a little better than here. The one "known" positive about death is that you would join your ancestors and thus always be surrounded by a loving community, a "heaven" of sorts in its own right. However, entrance to this communal and familial afterlife was not guaranteed.

Being an earth-bound wandering ghost was the worst possible thing that could happen after death. Because a lot of the spiritual transition into the afterlife relied heavily on funerary and burial rites, it was the community who could condemn you to this fate. If you were seen as a bad person (or just generally disliked), the community could very well refuse to assist in your burial, thus knowingly ensuring that you'd be doomed to restlessly wander the earth.

Witches, those assumed to be practitioners of harmful magic, and un-Christian people are particularly singled out still to this day as people routinely denied these proper funerary rites. If you're particularly hated and loathed to such a passionate degree, the community could prevent even your family and friends from giving you a proper funeral and burial by stealing your corpse and chopping it up so as to more easily cremate it or feed it to scavenger animals. Getting them eternally barred from reuniting with their ancestors is seen as the worst thing you could ever do to someone, and such personal vendettas against the recently deceased continue on to this day.[109]

---

108 "Nelson Mandela death: How a Xhosa chief is buried," *British Broadcasting Corporation*, Dec. 14, 2013, http://www.bbc.com/news/world-africa-25355245 (accessed May 29, 2018).

109 Anderson, *Encyclopedia of Death and Dying*

Sub-Saharan African Takeaway:
IT TAKES A VILLAGE

In our modern, hyperconnected world, this African maxim is still very apt. It truly does take a village to get something done. In terms of death, peoples throughout Sub-Saharan Africa often try to shoulder the burden of expensive, exhaustive funerals for their community members. They provide food, help pay bills, do general chores, etc.

You can do the same. For this Sub-Saharan African takeaway challenge, if you know someone who has just experienced the death of someone close to them, do what you can to help them out. They could be a friend, a neighbor, or a total stranger. What's stopping you from making an anonymous donation (however small) to a crowdfunding campaign trying to raise the funds for funeral costs and/or hospital bills (which don't go away just because the patient died or surgery was unsuccessful)?

And there are many ways to do this besides donating money. You can babysit, petsit, deliver food, mow their lawn, shovel their driveway, etc. It doesn't take much imagination to help someone in grief, someone in need of a little extra help right now. In fact, chances are that someone you'll meet today will be going through a loss. Be patient, be kind, be of help.

Deities & Legends

ALA

To the Igbo people in modern-day southern Nigeria, there is only one god, but they also believe in a pantheon of deities who are all seen as aspects of this singular god. The deity of Ala is considered the most powerful aspect of the one god, and she is the goddess of the earth, fertility, creativity, morality, rule of law, and the underworld. Because humans live on earth (and her name literally means "earth/land"), they fall under her jurisdiction, and thus she is the afterlife judge and jury for all their earthly crimes.

Her rulership over death and the underworld also comes about as a result of her dominion over the earth. As a "mother earth" goddess, she is believed to bring about widespread death via famine and poor harvests if angered by the people's wickedness. Her womb is the spiritual nexus of all beginnings and endings. It's from there that all life originates, and it is to there where all souls of the dead shall return.

She is usually depicted as a regal figure on a throne with a noticeably long neck and torso (features considered particularly beautiful in Igbo culture). Temples to her tend to be in the village's core center and usually contain a mud figure of Ala enthroned and holding a child.[110]

GAMAB & GAUNAB

Gamab and Gaunab are both deities to the San peoples throughout southern Africa. They are deities in polar opposition to one another, with some people believing they're two aspects of the same being and others believing they're two separate beings entirely. In either case, they're each regarded as a deity of death in their own way.

Regarding Gamab, he's the benevolent supreme sky god who rules and supports all living things via his life-giving rain. However, as the supreme god, he is the one who decides when you will die, and when your time comes, he shoots a celestial arrow into you, causing you to become terminally ill.[111]

Gaunab, in contrast, is the god of all evil who lives beyond the night sky where there are no more stars, a realm called "Dark Heaven." He would reward the most wicked men and women after their death to become his immortal followers and invite them to feast upon the flesh of the dead (believed to be why bodies are reduced to bone after burial). Some tribes regard him as the god of death or a personification of death itself.[112]

110   Don Jaide, "Ani the Mother of the Igbos: The Many Manifestations of Isthar," *Rasta Livewire*, Apr. 7, 2012, https://www.africaresource.com/rasta/sesostris -the-great-the-egyptian-hercules/ani-the-mother-of-the-igbos-the-many -manifestations-of-ishtar/ (accessed May 31, 2018).

111   Patricia Ann Lynch, *African Mythology A to Z*, 2nd ed. (New York: Chelsea House Publishers, 2010).

112   Charles Russell Coulter, and Patricia Turner, *Encyclopedia of Ancient Deities* (New York: Routledge, 2000).

According to legends, though, Gaunab didn't use to be all bad. In fact, he created the rainbow in an attempt to do away with his fearful reputation and be loved by humans, but the other gods deemed that the rain god was technically more responsible for creating the rainbow, giving him all the credit instead of Gaunab. Being overlooked for his act of trying to create more beauty for humans ultimately only contributed in making Gaunab the embittered and hateful deity he is today.[113]

OGBUNABALI

Ogbunabali (whose name translates to "Night Killer") is the Nigerian Igbo deity of the act of dying. He is said to wantonly and randomly select people to murder, thus explaining the undeniable mystery as to why even the young, healthy, and benevolent die unexpectedly. The exceptions to the rule of Ogbunabali's random selection are criminals and those who commit unspeakable taboos. He purposely goes after these people, thus explaining why those of us who are involved in illicit activity are more at risk for death. As his name indicates, he primarily hunts his victims at night, though his appearance is not fully known due to being a supremely skilled and stealthy night hunter.[114]

---

113 Charles G. Dyer, *Abatwa: A Little African Mythology* (Seattle: CreateSpace Independent Publishing, 2013).

114 Adah Mazi, "African Gods: Igbo Deities," *Nairaland*, Jun. 6, 2017, http://www .nairaland.com/3844529/african-gods-igbo-deities (accessed May 31, 2018).

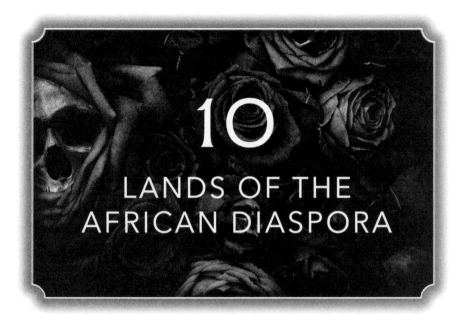

10

LANDS OF THE AFRICAN DIASPORA

Cultural

The horrors of the slave trade are well known. In search of profits and increasing their bottom line, European capitalists (with the assistance of interfighting African tribes) tore apart families, kidnapped, and forcibly removed peoples from Sub-Saharan Africa so that they could labor and toil on the various plantations and serve the upper classes throughout the Americas. With the profits "earned" by utilizing slave labor, investors would purchase more land for more crops and enslave more Africans to work these ever-larger plots of land for ever more profit.

This displacement created a hodgepodge jumble of African cultures on any given plantation, which in turn created unique blends of cultures, traditions, and spiritual beliefs. Over time, as memory faded away, these mixed traditions became the slaves' only link to their past and to their ancestral lands. To this day, a number of these mixed religions born from slave days still thrive, attract, and flourish throughout the New World. For the purposes here in our global trek, we'll look at the big morbid three: Candomblé, Santería, and Vodou.

Candomblé Cortège

Since Brazil was, by far, the most common destination for slaves to the Americas (around one out of every three slaves was taken to Brazil),[115] we'll start our sullen journey here, the birthplace of Candomblé. Candomblé developed as a mix of Fon, Bantu, and Yoruba traditional beliefs from Africa that mixed together with the forcible infusion of Portuguese Catholicism and a bit of indigenous Brazilian spiritualism. Uniquely, there is no set belief in the duality of good and evil; instead, it is believed that everyone has a personal destiny to fulfill regardless of the morality of that destiny.[116]

Candomblé's funerary rites (axexê) have long been noted to be festive spectacles. The eighteenth century bishops of Brazil wrote (with a bit of holier-than-thou disdain) about how the African slaves who practiced Candomblé would gather on the night of a burial, make loud music, and have a huge feast, throwing their leftovers into the grave of the recently deceased. Earlier in the day, the funeral cortège on the way to the burial would be filled with rhythmic drumming and dancing. Even the pallbearers would stop to do synchronized twirls, spins, and dips while still supporting the corpse on a platform above their heads. The actual funerals themselves

115 Dr. Neil A. Frankel, "Facts and Figures," *The Atlantic Slave Trade and Slavery in America*, Jun. 13, 2009, http://www.slaverysite.com/Body/facts%20and%20 figures.htm (accessed May 31, 2018).

116 "Candomblé Beliefs," *British Broadcasting Corporation*, Feb. 2, 2007, http:// www.bbc.co.uk/religion/religions/candomble/beliefs/beliefs.shtml (accessed May 31, 2018).

were attended solely by women (with the exception of the musicians, pall-bearers, and master of ceremonies).[117]

Sisterhood of Our Lady of the Good Death

Candomblé also has the distinction of being the faith from which the oldest sororal organization for women of African descent in the Americas came, the *Irmandade de Nossa Senhora da Boa Morte* ("Sisterhood of Our Lady of the Good Death"). Over a century and a half old, the Irmandade originated as an all-female secret society of freed slaves who would purchase the freedom of other female slaves throughout Brazil.

As the name suggests, this sisterhood has heavy Catholic influences in it (being first funded by the Catholic Church, which was then making an about-face toward abolitionism around the early 1800s), but it also has morbid aspects to it, as the "Good Death" part of the name implies. Officially, the "Lady of the Good Death" was considered to be the Virgin Mary, whose death was "good" because she allegedly died free from sin and was assumed body and soul into heaven. More than a name, though, this sororal society took their Lady's example and made it their mission to give other ladies a good death. Since the abolition of slavery, the funds that they still continue to accumulate and raise now go toward paying the funeral costs for economically downtrodden women of African descent throughout Brazil.[118]

Santería Secrets

Santería grew out of a mix of Spanish Catholicism, Yoruba traditions of imported African slaves, and the indigenous beliefs of the native peoples of the Caribbean islands, especially Cuba, Puerto Rico, and the Dominican

---

117   João José Reis, *Death Is a Festival: Funeral Rites and Rebellion in Nineteenth Century Brazil*, trans. by H. Sabrina Gledhill (Chapel Hill, University of North Carolina Press, 2003).

118   Kwekudee, "Afro-Brazilian Boa Morte Festival: A Unique Testament of Strength and Endurance of African Women in Diaspora," *Trip Down Memory Lane*, Sept. 21, 2012, https://kwekudee-tripdownmemorylane.blogspot.com/2012/09/afro-brazilian-boa-morte-festival.html (accessed Jun. 1, 2018).

Republic. Opposite from the axexê of Candomblé, the funeral ritual of Santería (*Ituto*) is more of a private affair.

Much of the exact details of the rites and practices of Santería are not shared openly with non-initiates (and since it's not an organized religion, there is much internal variance), but here's what we outsiders do know about modern Santería death rites. Rather than the immediate family, the godparents take charge of all the arrangements straightaway upon the day of death. The first arrangement is for a traditional Catholic-esque visitation when friends and family can come, grieve, pray, and share stories together about the deceased.

The second arrangement is the Ituto ceremony, which is required to take place in the decedent's (or a godparent's) home behind closed doors. Guided by a religious elder, only fully initiated members of the faith can be in attendance. It doesn't matter whether you're a best friend or a blood relative; if you aren't officially initiated into Santería, you cannot be in attendance during the Ituto. At the ceremony, those in attendance are encouraged to wear white, and the deceased is dressed in the same white garments in which they were first initiated into the faith, with the addition of a garland crown placed on the head.

Informing the Orishas

The main purpose of the Ituto ceremony is to resolve what to do with the decedent's Orishas (the spiritual intermediaries between God and humans, sometimes alternatively spelled "Orichas"). The attendees sit in a circle in the same room with the casketed corpse and announce to the deceased's Orishas that the person with whom they've been working is now dead. Then the leader of the ritual asks each Orisha one by one if they would like to leave with the soul of the departed or if they would like to stay with the body and be interred in the earth. It's believed that the decedent's soul lingers around the body for seven to nine days following death, and so this gives each Orisha time to decide what they want to do. After this, the attendees begin to sever all of the spiritual ties the deceased's soul might have to this world, allowing it to freely depart to the next life unhindered.

A week after death, the burial takes place, at which time Orishas are known to possess the attendees into wailing and loud mourning. Aside from the burial clothes and garland crown, the same scissors used and lock of hair that was cut from the decedent during their initiation into Santería are buried along with them. As to the decedent's important personal property, shells are cast ahead of time to find out if they should also be buried with the decedent or given to the surviving family.[119]

Initiates of Santería are always buried, never cremated, since the corpse is believed to nourish the sacred earth from which we all came (a belief proven scientifically true: non-embalmed and non-casketed decomposing bodies help provide nourishment for soil ecosystems, while cremated remains are inorganic material that contribute relatively nothing back to the earth if buried or scattered, and embalmed bodies just end up oozing out all that carcinogenic embalming fluid, toxifying the soil).[120]

Heaven Is a Place in the Earth

As for the human soul in Santería, the earth is regarded to be the best afterlife realm. There is no hell, and there is a heaven of sorts, but nowhere is more heavenly for the human soul than the earth. That is why having the body be recycled back into the earth is so important, and the soul too gets recycled via a form of reincarnation. Not the reincarnation of an entire singular soul, but rather bits of the soul can return and be reborn again in newborn blood relatives after our death.

From this Santería perspective, all of us are essentially simultaneous reincarnations of our ancestors and our own unique beings. We are both

---

119 "Ituto," *EcuRed*, https://www.ecured.cu/Ituto (accessed Jun. 1, 2018).
"Ituto," *Religión y Santería*, 2010, https://religionysanteria.blogspot
.com/2009/11/ituto.html (accessed Jun. 1, 2018).
Oshun Koidde, "El Ituto: La ceremonia posterior a la muerte del Santero,"
Iworos, Dec. 21, 2017, https://iworos.com/osha/2017/12/721/el-ituto-la
-ceremonia-posterior-a-la-muerte-del-santero/ (accessed Jun. 1, 2018).
120 J. Niziolomski, J. Rickson, N. Marquez-Grant, and M. Pawlett, "Soil science
related to the human body after death," *The Corpse Project*, Mar. 2016, http://
www.thecorpseproject.net/wp-content/uploads/2016/06/Corpse-and-Soils
-literature-review-March-2016.pdf (accessed Jun. 1, 2018).

the old and the new, something never seen before in history yet very familiar to the earth upon which we walk.[121]

Much Ado About Vodou

Perceived by outsiders as arguably the most morbid and macabre belief system in existence today, Vodou (alternatively spelled "Voodoo," "Vudú," and "Vodun") is infamous for zombies, cemetery magic, voodoo dolls, and its emphatic focus on the dead. Being steeped in macabre mystery, it's often labeled as evil or malicious. In reality, Vodou is a syncretic faith forged from the forcible blending of French Catholicism, traditional beliefs of African slaves (mostly from the Fon, Ewe, Yoruba, and Kongo tribes), and the indigenous beliefs of the Taíno Caribbean natives.

One of the main reasons why Vodou is often labeled as excessively death-focused is because of the faith's emphasis on ancestor worship. Since most of our ancestors are dead, it's natural that death and the afterlife play a big part in our interactions with them. All this unabashed interaction with the dead helped to morbidly malign Vodou as "creepy" and "macabre."

Angels & Zombies

Like Candomblé and Santería, Vodou is not a heavily organized religion, so there's much variance as to how to specifically perform a number of rituals as well as exact afterlife beliefs, but in general, it's believed that the soul is actually comprised of two separate souls: the *gros bon ange* ("large good angel," which is a portion of the grand cosmic soul of the universe) and the *ti bon ange* ("little good angel," which is the personalized, individual soul unique to each person).

Upon the death of a *vodouisant* (an adherent of Vodou), it's believed that the soul lingers around the body for about a week. During this time, the *ti bon ange* is particularly vulnerable to sorcery intended to capture and turn

---

121   Dr. Eñi Achó Iyá, "When a Santero/a Dies ...," *About Santería*, Jan. 19, 2014, http://www.aboutsanteria.com/santeras-blog/when-a-santeroa-dies (accessed Jun. 1, 2018).

it into an ethereal zombie, a spiritual slave. To protect the soul, the family participates in the *dernier priye*. This involves seven days of prayers to help the soul fully separate from the body and go to the underwater afterlife realm of "dark waters" for a year and a day, where it can rest and recover from its experiences on earth.

After this year and a day resting period, a follow-up ritual called the "Rite of Reclamation" is performed to call the soul into a clay jar (*govi*) where it can be worshiped and honored by its living relatives. Through human possession, the soul can communicate its lifetime of wisdom to the family as well as give any special words of advice or warnings.[122]

When it's time to let the soul continue on its afterlife journey, a ritual known as the *boule-zen* is performed. Much singing, dancing, and music-making is involved, interspersed with solemn moments of reflection and liturgy. The climax is the burning of the govi in a great fire, which effectively allows the *gros bon ange* to reunite with the greater ancestral cosmic whole and the *ti bon ange* to able to be reincarnated into a newborn relative.

Prior to the boule-zen, the body of a vodouisant is never to be cremated. The body must be buried completely intact with all its organs, otherwise the soul cannot transition properly and is doomed to roam the earth as a wandering ghost, susceptible to malicious magic such as becoming a spirit zombie doing the supernatural bidding of its master.[123]

---

122   Yvonne Perry, "Haitian Vodoun Perspectives on Death and Dying," *Ezine Articles*, Oct. 28, 2009, http://ezinearticles.com/?Haitian-Vodoun -Perspectives-on-Death-and-Dying&id=3172822 (accessed Jun. 1, 2018). "Death And Funeral Rituals In Haitian Culture," *Haiti Observer*, Jun. 29, 2013, http://www.haitiobserver.com/blog/tag/zombie/death-and-funeral-rituals-in -haitian-culture.html (accessed Jun. 1, 2018). "After Life Beliefs In Voodoo Religion," *Haiti Observer*, Jan. 25, 2012, http:// www.haitiobserver.com/blog/tag/voodoo/after-life-beliefts-in-voodoo -religion.html (accessed Jun. 1, 2018). Amanda MacFarland, "Death In Haiti," *The Crudem Foundation*, http://crudem .org/death-haiti/ (accessed Jun. 1, 2018).

123   Marie José Alcide Saint-Lot, *Vodou, a Sacred Theatre: The African Heritage in Haiti* (Pompano Beach: Educa Visions, 2004).

And All That Jazz

While predominantly a belief system centralized in Haiti, it's from the Hoodoo-infused variant of Vodou found in New Orleans, Louisiana, where the most positive pop-culture celebration of the faith revels in unabashed glory: the jazz funeral. (If you're not familiar, Hoodoo is a folk spirituality developed by enslaved Africans in the US, especially in the Deep South.) The ritual of celebrating after the burial of a vodouisant with music, chanting, and dancing is a Vodou tradition carried over from Sub-Saharan Africa where, while unarguably a sad affair, the death of a loved one brought the joy of knowing that they had now reunited with the ancestors.

These jazz funerals (originally called "brass band funerals" since "jazz" wasn't a thing 'til the twentieth century) were seen as disrespectful by the white New Orleanian aristocracy. Nowadays, though, city officials of all colors and income brackets have come to embrace the macabre musical parades as a living cultural landmark of the city (as officials have also done with Vodou, in general, to help generate those tourist dollars).

Because it was a valuable port city that controlled trade on the Mississippi River and acted as a gateway to international trade, the city of New Orleans (the actual city, not the folk song or the Amtrak train) had a long tradition as a military base for the French, Spanish, and Americans (depending on who controlled the city at the time) wherein the military brass bands were always available and on the lookout for gigs to supplement their income. The roving epidemics of yellow fever, malaria, smallpox, and cholera that came with being a swampland port metropolis provided plenty of funeral gigs at which these military brass bands could play.

Solemn dirges to the final resting place fell in line with colonial Catholic protocol, but once the body was properly laid to rest, the Vodou-inspired celebration of good times to come for the departing soul allowed the band to play upbeat music, which was made extra danceable, loud, and triumphantly joyous by the use of bold brass instruments. The soul's release from the body was an especially joyful occasion during slave days when death was a slave's only release from toil and abuse. As time went on, official slavery ended and New Orleans eventually became more integrated and proud of its hometown jazz due to its profitability. Consequently, the funeral processions became bigger, grander, and more openly celebrated affairs even though their origins in Vodou spiritual and magical beliefs remain relatively unknown.[124]

African Diaspora Takeaway:
NOT KEEPING QUIET

Oftentimes when someone we know experiences a loss, we become profoundly awkward. We want so much to say just the right thing so as to avoid making them even more sad…which often leads us to do the worst thing: not say anything at all.

Many African diasporic cultures don't have this problem. Death, whether it be in the form of ancestor worship, necro-magic, or even the fatal hardships/effects of slavery, was (and still is) an ever-present reality in the daily life of Africans in the New World. And when someone died, there was much noise, celebration, and dancing to be made. The awkwardness of "how do I talk to someone who just experienced a loss?" didn't largely factor into things when communication through music, dance, and rituals mandated that one's shyness take a back seat to the ceremonies at hand.

So, your African diaspora takeaway challenge is to not awkwardly hide away and avoid conversation the next time you're in the presence of someone who you know is going through a loss. Really, the best thing you can do is just swallow your awkwardness and ask the person how they're doing and if they need anything. Trust me, you're not going to suddenly remind them of the death (they know, it's most likely on their minds 24/7). Rather, this allows them to control the conversation for what they need.

---

124   Rosy Edwards, "New Orleans jazz funerals: Where life is celebrated through the joy of music," *Metro*, Oct. 8, 2017, https://metro.co.uk/2017/10/08/ new-orleans-jazz-funerals-where-life-is-celebrated-through-the-joy-of -music-6965499/ (accessed Jun. 4, 2018).
"New Orleans Jazz Funeral Service Rituals," *Funeralwise*, https://www .funeralwise.com/customs/neworleans/ (accessed Jun. 4, 2018).

Maybe they just need to vent and talk. Maybe there is a specific thing you could do to help them out. Or maybe they've just been talking about it with someone else and really don't want to keep on talking about it right now. Don't push anything, just ask them how they're doing and if they need anything, and let them control the conversation.

No matter how much you want to help someone get over grief and be happy again, grief isn't something that needs to be or even *can* be expedited. It has to be experienced fully and profoundly, from beginning to end. There are no shortcuts. We can still be there for them, but trying to rush someone back into happiness through avoiding acknowledgment of their grief just isn't helpful. Grief is a part of us, a part of life. It's sad, yes, but it's what the soul needs to do. Grieving *is* healing, however painful.

Deities & Legends

BARON SAMEDI

In Vodou, the *Lwa* (pronounced "lwah," sometimes "LOW-ah") are the spiritual intermediaries between the Supreme Creator and humans. Each Lwa has a distinct personality and style, and out of all of them, Baron Samedi is probably one of the best-known in pop culture, thanks to his eccentric personality and caricaturized depiction in popular movies such as Dr. Facilier in Disney's *The Princess and the Frog* and as the aptly named Baron Samedi in the James Bond classic *Live and Let Die*. As the patron Lwa of death, graves, cemeteries, smoking, drinking, and obscenities, he's one of the most transgressive deities of any religion.

Appearance-wise, Baron Samedi is often depicted with a skeletal-thin frame, with a glass of rum or a cigar in his gloved hand and wearing a dapper purple frock coat and top hat. Particularly, he is known for his disregard for tact and decorum as well as for his lascivious debauchery, but he does it all with an urbane air of suaveness all his own.

His fluid disregard for gender norms and his willingness to go beyond the binary of man/woman, straight/gay, masculine/feminine, earth/underworld, living/dead makes him a popular figure. To the queer community and those who feel the need to transgress boundaries without shame or who feel they don't fit into a singular category of labels, Baron Samedi is a Lwa they can relate to.

According to tradition, it is said that you can only die if Baron Samedi digs your grave. Because he is a capricious, spur-of-the-moment kind of personality, he may choose not to dig your grave, thus letting you live through whatever is going on with you, if petitioned to do so or if he just doesn't feel like digging your grave for no reason in particular.[125]

MAMAN BRIGITTE

Maman (French for "Mama") Brigitte is a Vodou Lwa of death and the wife of Baron Samedi. A perfect match: she's just as obscene, capricious, vice-indulgent, and down for a good time as her husband. She's particularly iconic for infusing her rum with chili peppers and smoking long cigars.

What makes her one of the most unique of all Vodou Lwa is her appearance: she's a white woman. And not just any kind of white, mind you. She's a redhead with green eyes, one of the whitest shades of whiteness a person can be (trust me, I know). It might seem odd at first glance, but it all makes sense when you remember Vodou is a syncretic religion of African beliefs and European Catholicism.

Because the slaves in the Americas had to hide their traditional practices under the guise of Christianity, vodouisants masked the Lwa with the outward appearance of Catholic saints. In the case of Louisiana Vodou's feminine death deity, Ireland's own St. Brigid was used as the visual "cover" (St. Brigid, in turn, being a Catholic rerendering of the Irish Celtic goddess Brigit).

Considering that New Orleans was a penal destination of sorts for Irish prostitutes who were forced to drain the Louisiana swamps alongside black slave women back in the day, these constant cross-cultural interactions the female slaves had with the redheaded Celtic working girls and

---

125 Penczak, *Gay Witchcraft: Empowering the Tribe*, 2003.

their tales of the popular St. Brigid all contributed to giving Maman Brigitte her physical appearance, her bawdy behavior, and her name.

Like her husband, Maman Brigitte is a psychopomp who protects cemeteries and gravestones, but she was especially involved in healing spells, particularly for fatal illnesses (a patronage of St. Brigid as well as the charge of Irish nuns in Louisiana during epidemics). Her dominion of healing also included spiritual healings for a fresh start in life, and she's often seen as a patron and protectress of interracial marriages.[126]

IKÚ & OYÁ

In Santería, Ikú and Oyá are Orishas of death. As the legends go, humans were once able to live forever, but since no one could die, the pangs of starvation became a serious problem since there came a time when there wasn't enough food to feed the overpopulated world. Mankind petitioned the supreme god to help them, and so the supreme god tasked Ikú to go and kill a few people every so often to keep the population under control, but Ikú refused because he didn't want to be hated and feared by humans for having the *Sophie's Choice* task of choosing which innocent people would have to die. The supreme god agreed that he was placing Ikú in a no-win situation, and thus he unleashed disease unto the world so that Ikú wouldn't have to select his victims.[127]

Oyá (whose name means "darkness") was the wife of the war deity Oggun, whom she used to accompany to the battlefield (before leaving him for Shango, Orisha of justice). She holds command over the spirits of death, mostly because she is the mother of many of these death spirits. A number of legends tell of her leadership and encouragement of women to stand up for themselves, take action, and reject the false idea of men being superior to women. Herself a powerful sorceress, she is a patroness

---

126 Caroline Wise, "Maman Brigitte She Comes from Angletere: Thoughts of a Brighid Devotee on the Earthquake in Haiti," *Mirror of Isis*, https://mirrorofisis.freeyellow.com/id523.html (accessed Jun. 4, 2018).

127 "Iku," *Divine Moon*, http://divinemoonblog.org/post/47648362389/iku (accessed Jun. 4, 2018).

of magic workers and the wind (both the physical movement of air and the metaphorical winds of change).[128]

OMOLÙ

Omolú is the Orixa (Candomblé's Portuguese spelling of "Orisha") of life and death. According to legend, he contracted smallpox as a young child, which left him permanently hobbled and scarred (physically and emotionally). Due to his contagious disease, he was kept away from others and became something of a loner, but by being outside of society, he gained a profound knowledge of it because he could observe and understand it without the trappings of being subjected to its influence. Because of this upbringing, he is sympathetic to outsiders, the lame, and those ostracized by society.

His control over life and death comes primarily from his giving and curing of diseases, appropriate for both his disgust toward human society and his empathy toward those who are suffering. Due to this empathy and patronage of healing, he's one of the most popular Orixas in Candomblé.

His appearance, however, remains a mystery because he always wears a headdress with floor-length dried raffia fronds that hide his body (effectively making him look like Cousin Itt from *The Addams Family*). Rumor has it that this headdress was given to him by his mother to hide his smallpox-scarred body from others (though it's still contested as to whether she meant to protect the public from his grotesque appearance or to protect him from the cruel ridicule of the public).[129]

128 "Oya," *CubaYoruba*, https://cubayoruba.blogspot.com/2007/01/oya.html (accessed Jun. 4, 2018).

129 "The Orixa Omolu," *Church of Candomble*, Jun. 27, 2016, http://churchofcandomble.com/the-orixa-omolu/ (accessed Jun. 4, 2018). M. Stan, "Omolu," *UCR Panda Blog*, May 7, 2009, http://ucrpandas.blogspot.com/2009/05/omolu.html (accessed Jun. 4, 2018).

11

SUB-SAHARAN & AFRICAN DIASPORIC MAGICAL COMMUNITY

CAMPFIRE STORIES

The only guarantee in life is death. We can have the best-laid plans all set, have backup plans, backup plans to the backup plans, and every other little detail meticulously prearranged, and still, there's no guarantee on anything. I expect to wake up tomorrow. I expect that the joke I texted my friend an hour ago won't be the last thing I said to him. I expect to not be at the wrong place at the wrong time. Yet still ... these are just expectations, not guarantees.

Something like this happened when I was reaching out to ask people who practice traditional sub-Saharan death practices of Africa to come here and share a story or a facet of their magic with us. A number of people expressed interest but then just disappeared and ghosted on us. And just like that, my expectations and plans came to an unforeseen and grinding halt. Truly nothing is guaranteed in life.

Regardless, the world keeps on turning, time stops for no one, and deadlines and commitments don't just disappear because we've experienced unforeseen misfortune whether professionally or personally. So, in true Sub-Saharan and African diasporic fashion, when in times of crisis, let's seek the help of the ancestors. There's no rule that our community contributors can't come from beyond the grave, and so let's gather 'round the campfire to listen to some morbid African folktales as passed down through the ages from those who have already passed on.

The Cost of Immortality

The Ashanti people have a story about death that tells of how their earliest ancestors didn't like having to die and lose loved ones, which inspired them to petition the gods to allow them to live forever. The gods complied, and all death disappeared from existence. However (because there's always a "however" in folktales), the people soon realized that not only could animals not be slaughtered for food, but also new crops couldn't grow and humans could no longer conceive. The people complained, and so the gods explained to them that death and new life (destruction and creation) go hand in hand; without one, the other couldn't exist. Weighing their options, the people decided it was worth it to forego immortality and have death in the world if it meant new life could continue coming into the world.[130]

How a Dog Doomed Us All

The natives of Nigeria have a story explaining how humankind lost out on the chance of immortality all because of one dog. They say that the chief creator god was very kind and loving, and he was especially fond and proud of his creation of humans. When the very first human died, he saw how sad that made everyone, and that, in turn, made him sad. So, he tasked his messenger dog with telling the humans the secrets to an

---

130   Bryant, and Peck, *Encyclopedia of Death and the Human Experience.*

above-ground funerary ritual that could resurrect the unburied dead, thus making death impermanent. The dog went on his mission, but he became distracted by all manner of things and took many long rests.

Meanwhile, more humans kept dying, so the chief creator god, in his frustration, asked a sheep to relay the funerary rights in the hope that it would be able to follow through on the assignment, unlike that dog. He was right, and the sheep expeditiously relayed everything to humankind. However, sheep were notoriously stupid, and so the message that ended up getting relayed was that the chief creator god wanted humans to bury their dead. Sometime later, the dog finally got around to telling everyone the real message, but no one believed him because they had already received the supreme god's command from the sheep. From then on, people buried their dead and lost out on the secret rituals of living forever.[131]

Killing Death

Our closing story for the night is a West African tale about youngsters who set out to kill Death. As the story goes, a plague swept through their land leaving three youthful brothers orphaned and alone. Every single person they knew and loved had been killed by the invisible disease, and so in their rage-filled grief, they planned to enact revenge on Death and give him a taste of his own medicine.

With nothing left for them in their ghost town of a village, they determinedly journeyed out into the world to find and kill Death. All they found, however, was ridicule from the people they met who told them they were on a fool's errand and that no one can ever find Death because Death is the one who finds you. Stubbornly resolute (like only headstrong youths can be), they ignored everyone's advice and continued their vendetta quest.

Eventually, they came across an old man who, instead of laughing at them, gave them a dire warning that no good could come from their mission. The brothers snapped back at the old man, and in response to their

131 Elphinstone Dayrell, *Folk Stories from Southern Nigeria, West Africa* (London: Longmans, Green, and Company, 1910).

rudeness, the old man told them where they could find Death. Excitedly, the boys ran off and prepared themselves for the grand encounter they'd been eagerly anticipating.

As directed, they found the auspicious looking tree the old man described to them, where he said Death would be waiting underground. As they began to dig, they came across a buried box containing seven gold coins. Visions of wealth and everything they could do with that money filled their heads. Killing Death no longer seemed that important anymore.

More than anything, though, they were hungry, but they couldn't go to town carrying all this money; they'd be attacked and robbed. So, they agreed that two of them would stay there with the box and one of them would go to the nearest village to buy some food. While out in the nearest market, this one brother began to get *The Treasure of the Sierra Madre*-esque ideas that it'd be even better if he didn't have to split all those found riches with anyone. Acting upon impulse, he bought some poison, laced the food with it, and happily headed back to feed his brothers.

When he got back to the auspicious tree, there was no one in sight, but the treasure box was still there. Before he could wonder what happened, his brothers jumped out from hiding and killed him. Relieved that the treasure now only had to be split two ways (or, in their minds, maybe less in the near future), they hungrily gobbled up the food and succumbed to the poison soon after.

The next day, the old man arrived on the scene, unsurprised by the boys' three corpses. He warned them that no good would come from trying to find Death, but they wouldn't listen. Now that they had found Death, the old man hoped they were happy.[132]

132 Amy Friedman, and Meredith Johnson, "Tell Me a Story: Searching for Death (A West African Tale)," *UExpress*, Apr. 1, 1999, https://www.uexpress.com/tell-me-a-story/1999/4/1/searching-for-death-a-west-african (accessed Oct. 5, 2018).

ENJOY THE PARTY WHILE IT LASTS

To get a particularly macabre insight into working with the spirits of the African diasporic community, I've invited back our friend Danielle Dionne. We last saw her in the Egyptian leg of our global trek when she recounted to us her morbid tale of meeting Anubis. However, this fellow traveler of ours also had quite a morbid experience in meeting another dark deity of death, the Vodou Lwa Baron Samedi.

It makes sense, though, that Danielle would have a number of macabre encounters with such shadowy spirits considering that she's not only a psychic medium, but also a hospice volunteer and vocal advocate for the death-positive movement, particularly in the Death Cafés that she hosts. Yes, she literally works with people who are slowly dying, and brings together those of us fascinated by morbidity to talk all things death. So, here she is again to share with us an important piece of advice from Baron Samedi, during a fateful trip down in old New Orleans.

New Orleans had been calling me for a long time. The city of sex and death. It was on a magical retreat during ritual when I would first encounter Baron Samedi. In vision, I found myself in a cemetery. Shadows were cast in purple fluorescent and dark shades like a black light. There stood a tall, well-dressed man in a top hat. He wasn't alone; other figures were off in the distance. He had a skeletal-like face and smiled a big grin as he leaned against a vault. Intrigued and slightly uncomfortable, I passed him by. He nodded to me and laughed aloud. He said nothing, and neither did I.

After my initial New Orleans trip, I would visit twice more within the year. The Crescent City was like a lodestone, magnetically pulling me to return. Each journey proved to be its own initiation of sorts. I returned in January during one of the coldest spells New Orleans had seen in recent memory. It was a challenging time, and I was stressed. My family was facing difficulties regarding unemployment, the recent death of my grand-father, and looming decisions for my grandmother. While I was grateful to be pursuing a full-time spiritual business, I had fallen into a bit of burnout. I was questioning big life decisions. Everything from quitting my well-paid hospital job to decisions around marriage, family, friendships, magical traditions, and my fertility haunted my mind. Indecisive, I found myself at the crossroads and back in New Orleans.

I was compelled to purchase a Baron Samedi doll at a local voodoo shop. I placed it on a makeshift altar, my bedside table at the hotel. I poured out a shot of rum and left it as an offering in honor of the Baron. I couldn't shake the image of him from my memory. I was moved to ask for his guidance. I quickly learned Baron Samedi is direct and loud!

After a boozy New Orleans Saturday night, I dreamt of a dimly lit party with black and purple fluorescent lights. The alcohol flowed and the party was heated. It smelled of rum, cigars, and hot peppers as I watched figures dance closely together around me. I began to dance as well. The party turned to a sexual frenzy as I watched others fornicate. I turned to face my partner behind me and was instead met by the laughing, skeleton-like face of a man in a top hat. I then realized what kind of party this was!

He was laughing at me with a loud and outrageous roar. He mocked me openly in front of the partygoers, what I assume were the ancestors and Guede spirits. He chided me as someone spending too much time focused on death and the dead. That I was too afraid to live a real life! He challenged me to make decisions, right then and there at the crossroads of the living and dead. Yes or no? I made my decisions and loudly pronounced them, strangely empowered and also mortified.

Baron Samedi was right: I was taking life too seriously. He was certainly the most lively death ally I had ever encountered. He was outrageous, lewd yet paradoxically charming, debonair, and wise. This smug skeletal spirit had called me out. With that simple clarity, and humiliation, I had reaped my necessary answers. As well as a severe headache the next morning.

Baron Samedi loves a good party and encourages us to enjoy it while it lasts. Live your authentic life. Death comes for us all. What will you do with your time to make it count?

—DANIELLE DIONNE

PART 4

INDIA & SOUTHEAST ASIA

Now I am become Death,
the destroyer of worlds.
J. ROBERT OPPENHEIMER
(quoting the *Bhagavad Gita*
upon successfully detonating
the world's first atomic bomb)

As we head eastward and ride the rail lines back across the Sahara and Arabian Deserts, we find a passage to India. Here is the birthplace of Hinduism and Buddhism, which are two of the world's most ancient religions that are not only still actively practiced to this day but also command a sizeable portion of all religious adherents on earth (around 1.6 billion of us, or about 22 percent and growing).[133] Though as you've probably noticed by looking around, India is predominantly Hindu. While it's true that the Buddha was an Indian-born Hindu who kind of flipped the script on things and started his own philosophical worldview (similar to Jesus and

133 "The Changing Global Religious Landscape," *Pew Research Center*, Apr. 5, 2017, http://www.pewforum.org/2017/04/05/the-changing -global-religious-landscape/ (accessed Nov. 15, 2018).

his native Jewish background), Hinduism was already quite ancient before his birth and provided the foundational worldview on which Buddhism is based.

In a very overly simplified manner, Indian culture is essentially Hindu culture and vice versa. Buddhism, however, really found its roots further east, especially in Southeast Asia where it's still maintained in its strictest forms, albeit infused with local lore and ghostly belief in the hereafter. Nevertheless, both of these religions have a radically different approach to death and the afterlife than any place we've yet traveled, so let's get exploring!

12

HINDUISM

Cultural

To be fair, Hinduism technically has no definitive date of origin, founder, or regulated internal structure. It just evolved along with the peoples who inhabited what is now modern India and Pakistan. A big thing to remember about ancient eras is that death was much more present in the lives of our earliest ancestors. High infant mortality rates, low life expectancy ages, a lack of medical advancements, and living at the whim of weather and warlords made death much more of a frequent reality back then in the ancient past. Nowadays, with all the medical and scientific miracles that have been developed, which we take for granted, as well as how much less war there is around the globe compared to the past, we are blessed to not have to think about death on a daily basis like our ancient ancestors once had to.

In such hard times, tomorrow was certainly not guaranteed, and therefore all actions you took on any given day were that much more important. Everything you did had a real consequence in the ancient era either for better or for worse; philosophically, this became "karma," the cosmic reciprocity wherein everything you do eventually comes back to you.

The Grand Illusion

Time, however, is seen as cyclical in Hinduism, not a straight line from birth to death. The spirit lives on and gets reincarnated many times over, and so good/bad behavior in a past life could result in being better/worse off in the next life. Nonetheless, life is seen as a grand illusion; none of this is really real since everything in life is temporary. The only *real* thing, the only everlasting thing, is the universal spirit, and a human spirit's goal is to attain awareness of this and reunite with the universal ALL.

Doing this is harder than it seems. Because we're living in the material world, all this stuff around us and experiences we have seem so real and permanent. The spiritual goal of a Hindu, however, is to be able to look beyond the human misperception of reality (*maya*) and see the universe for the united impermanence that it truly is. Once you can do this, your spirit can transcend the grand illusion of earthly life and reunite with the infinity.

With each lifetime, you are given a chance to do this, and if you fail, then no worries. You'll be reborn into different circumstances to try again, and you will continue to try again over and over until you succeed (it's kind of like a difficult video game with infinite lives where if you do exceptionally well during a run, you get a continue code so you can restart from a more advanced level, but a big failure can lead to a restart further back).

Suicide Solutions

Due to the illusory nature of life, detachment from worldly things is seen as a sign of great spiritual advancement. So, what do you think is the ultimate detachment from life that anyone could make to show their rejection of the material world? That's right, suicide. Suicide in traditional Hindu culture isn't so much a controversial topic as it is an ambivalent one. It is at the same time abhorred and greatly respected … it just depends on one's perception of the motivation behind this supreme act of detachment.

You see, in the beginnings of Hinduism, ascetics used to ritualistically set themselves on fire once they attained full awareness of the illusion that is life. They wanted to enter immediately into the universal ALL rather than risk having future life experiences diminish this awareness and muddle their current clarity, which would doom them to another rebirth. That doesn't really happen much anymore, but the modern version of this is that some elderly Hindus just decide that they've had enough with life and willfully disengage from anything that would keep them going. Rather than inflict self-harm, they simply stop eating, drinking, and taking their medication (if they have any). Though this isn't common by any means, it's seen with great admiration and respect to some hard-core traditionalists in India as a continuation of the ancient ascetics' ultimate act of detachment from this world.

Suicide out of depression, however, is greatly frowned upon and shunned. Rather than a rejection of the illusory nature of the world, it's seen as the exact opposite: succumbing to the temporary pains and sorrow of maya when it becomes too real. The only exception is for people who have just lost a spouse. Killing yourself because you cannot live without the love of your life (via years of actual marriage, not some preliminary infatuation *Romeo and Juliet* nonsense) is given a pass and seen as tragically romantic and worthy of respect and understanding. Other than that, though, sorrowful/hopelessness-induced suicide karmically ensures an even worse life in your next reincarnation.[134]

134 Jayaram V., "Death and Afterlife in Hinduism," *Hinduwebsite*, http://www .hinduwebsite.com/hinduism/h_death.asp (accessed Jun. 5, 2018).
"Hinduism: beliefs about life after death," *British Broadcasting Corporation*, 2014, http://www.bbc.co.uk/schools/gcsebitesize/rs/death/hindubeliefrev2 .shtml (accessed Jun. 5, 2018).
Kenneth P. Kramer, "Hinduism," *Encyclopedia of Death and Dying*, http://www .deathreference.com/Gi-Ho/Hinduism.html (accessed Jun. 5, 2018).

All Fired Up

As for the dead body, which certainly isn't permanent, Hinduism prescribes a loose ritual to follow for its final disposition. Breath is profoundly sacred in the Hindu tradition, and during a person's last breaths, the spirit is gathered into the major organs of the body from where they then make their way to the heart chakra. With the final breath, the spirit shoots up from the heart chakra to the crown chakra on the top of the head and erupts into the universe. However, there are still residual bits of spirit in the organs left in the body, and to free them, the body needs to be cremated (burial would result in spirit residue becoming trapped underground).[135]

Antyesti is the name for these ancient funeral rites, though they are perceived as more of a rite of passage into the soul's next reincarnation. In this ritual, an outdoor pyre is assembled (preferably on the banks of a river) for cremation. There are three exceptions, though: (1) children can be buried in the ground, (2) ascended masters can be enshrined in a mausoleum, (3) a watery grave in the Ganges is permitted (the Ganges is the holiest river in India whose sanctity is believed to be able to wash away all karmic impurities from one's lifetime).[136]

Assuming the antyesti is for an adult cremation, the eldest son places water (preferably from the Ganges) into the parent's mouth while the family recites sacred mantras. Then the body is dressed in a white shroud (for men and widows) or a red shroud (for married women whose husbands are still alive). The big toes are tied together, and a tilak is painted on their brow (the iconic red dot and/or white stripes in the center of the forehead). The body is then carried to the funeral pyre and placed in the center.

If it's the death of a father, then the eldest male child is tasked to light the fire. If it's the death of a mother, then the task falls to the youngest male child. Once the body disintegrates and the residual bits of soul are

---

135   Jayaram V., "Concept of Death, Hell and Afterlife in Hinduism," *Hinduwebsite*, http://www.hinduwebsite.com/hinduism/death.asp (accessed Jun. 5, 2018).

136   Wendy Doniger, *The Rig Veda* (New York: Penguin Classics, 2005).

released, the cremated remains are gathered together and thrown in the nearby river to be purified. Afterward, those who handled the body and/or who were touched by the smoke from the pyre need to bathe in the river to purify themselves.[137]

Don't Drink the Water

Though traditional and beautiful, those who continue to practice these ancient funerary rituals are creating major environmental and public health issues all over India. With about 1.3 billion people[138] (and growing) living in a congested manner on one relatively small swath of land on earth, that's a lot of dead bodies to be burning into the air and dumping into the same river ecosystems on a regular basis. Heavy deforestation of the subcontinent is also rapidly increasing to provide the funeral pyre wood for the growing number of deaths in a growing population. To combat this, the Indian government has begun funding non-wood-burning crematories around the country, but this has met bitter resistance from the many preferring a traditional *antyesi* over an eco-friendly one.

Moreover, the rivers of India are essential resources for laundry, bathing, and drinking, especially in the most impoverished areas, but the growing amount of corpses and cremated remains being placed in them are making these rivers even more unhealthy for human use (because of all the blood, fluids, and residual fecal matter that escape a putrefying body and travel downstream as well as all the inorganic cremated remains).[139] Though the ecological damage is very real, old habits here die hard, especially when the compensation for environmental degradation is social advancement in your next reincarnation.

---

137 Kramer, *Encyclopedia of Death and Dying*
     "Hindu beliefs on Dying and Death," *Funeralwise*, https://www.funeralwise
     .com/customs/hindu/beliefs/ (accessed Jun. 5, 2018).
138 "Population, total," *World Bank Group*, 2017, https://data.worldbank.org/
     indicator/SP.POP.TOTL (accessed Jun. 5, 2018).
139 Kramer, *Encyclopedia of Death and Dying*.

Hindu Takeaway:
FOR THE LAST TIME

When was the last time you enjoyed something for the very last time? Think back to someone you know who has died; what was your last interaction with them like? Would it have been different if you knew it was going to be the last time you ever saw them? Would you kiss your lover differently if you knew it was your last night together? Would you choose different topics of conversation if you knew it was the last time you and your best friend would ever meet? Would your words be more kind if you knew it was the last time you'd talk to your parents or children?

The concept of impermanence underlies Hinduism. Nothing lasts forever. Good times, bad times, joys, and sorrows. All things must pass. However, things do become a little more magical when you know it'll be the last time you ever do it. Time moves a little more slowly, details become a little more vivid, and you take stock of every precious second, memorizing the place and scene so you can revisit it in your mind's eye again and again regardless of changes in the physical world.

Imagine how magical (literally and figuratively) your life would be if you perceived every experience, every encounter, every taste, scent, and touch as if it were for the last time. For your Hindu takeaway challenge, try it for at least a whole day. It'll be one of the most magical days you've ever lived, even if nothing special at all happens. Just simply be more present in the moment and treat every moment during the next twenty-four hours as if it were your last. Who knows, it just might be.

Deities & Legends

CHITRAGUPTA

Chitragupta is a Hindu deity and the top bureaucrat when it comes to the afterlife. He keeps meticulous notes on every single little thing you do in life and then, when you die, factors in all these things to determine what will become of you in your next reincarnation. In a way, he's the de facto distributor of your lifetime of karma.

His origin legend tells of how the great god, Lord Brahma, placed the deity Yama in charge of the lands of the dead. Excellent with the bigger picture, Yama was terrible with the little details and with staying organized. In his overworked confusion, he sometimes distributed the wrong karma to the wrong people by sending the good to hellish realms and lower caste rebirths while also sending the wicked to peaceful realms and higher caste rebirths. Brahma meditated for thousands of years on what to do about this, and as a result of this meditation, Chitragupta was born from his body.

From then on, Chitragupta kept meticulous notes on everything every living thing did, and souls always went to their correct afterlife destination and rebirth. Altogether, his volumes of notes make up the Akashic Records (a compendium of the events, thoughts, words, emotions, and intentions of all beings ever to have occurred in the past, present, and future). To do this, Chitragupta invented writing, which he then taught to mankind to use. Though Yama's assistant, it's quietly understood that Chitragupta is the one who really has all the actionable power after death.[140]

KALA

In the Hindu pantheon, Kala is the deific personification of time, and therefore technically the deity of death. Befitting the embodiment of time, Kala is very impersonal and detached from all people, gods, and occurrences. He's also regarded as the god of inevitability since statistically everything is eventual if given enough time. In India, he doesn't have as strong of a following as other deities, mostly because it's believed that time cannot be swayed or petitioned; it marches on regardless of our human wants or needs.[141]

140 Aayush, "Lord Chitragupta—Who helps Lord Yamaraj to maintain karmic accounts," *Detechter*, https://detechter.com/lord-chitragupta-who-helps-lord -yamaraj-to-maintain-karmic-accounts/ (accessed Jun. 6, 2018).

141 Janmajit Roy, *Theory of Avatāra and Divinity of Chaitanya* (New Dehli: Atlantic Publishers & Distributors, 2002).

YAMA (HINDUISM)

Yama is a death deity in both Hinduism and Buddhism. In Hinduism, he's the lord of death and the underworld. Unlike many other cultures' deities of death, Yama is considered to be very fond of humans and attempts to help them whenever he is not too swamped with ruling the underworld. However, he draws the line at injustice, and those who commit injustices incur his wrath.

He gained the position of lord of the dead quite by accident, though. According to legend, Yama was once human, one of the very first humans, to be precise. He was also the very first human to die, and so when he arrived in the empty underworld, the gods decided to make him the ruler of it and elevate him to godliness so as to be able to do so. It's said that his human origins are a big reason why he is so fond of us.[142]

The Hindu underworld, however, is not a permanent place, but rather a temporary location where souls go after death while they await rebirth. Depending upon their karma, it can be a good or bad time. If the person was good, their soul gets to relax and chill out for a while to accumulate its strength back (kind of like a spa). If the person was wicked, then they'd be purified through horrific punishment (the likes of which *Hellraiser*'s Cenobites would be proud).

Once purified, they could be reborn and try again at being a good person and transcending *maya*. And while technically Yama oversaw all of this, due to his penchant for justice (or just downlow sadism), he primarily spent his time purifying the wicked.[143]

---

142   A. A. MacDonnell, *Vedic Mythology* (Strasburg: Von Karl J. Trübner, 1897).

143   Anna L. Dallapiccola, *Dictionary of Hindu Lore and Legend* (New York: Thomas & Hudson, 2004).

13

BUDDHISM

Cultural

Buddhism is a religion inspired by the inevitability of suffering and death. The Buddha himself was a Hindu royal in ancient India whose new philosophies and cosmic worldviews were all based upon the even more ancient foundations of Hinduism. However, the ultimate turning point that instigated his search for answers that Hinduism just couldn't satisfy was the existential nihilism that came from witnessing a corpse.

The Buddha & the Corpse

Though scriptural accounts embellish his early life with supernatural and suspiciously auspicious phenomena, the straightforward story about the Buddha's fateful corpse encounter in adulthood is that Siddhartha

Gautama (later to be titled *Buddha*, meaning "awakened/enlightened one") lived sometime between the sixth and fifth centuries BCE and was born into the lap of luxury as the son of a royal chief near the foothills of the Himalayas (in what is modern-day Nepal). Naturally, he was spoiled beyond belief, given everything he ever wanted, and lived in an aristocratic bubble away from the stark realities of the masses.

Around the age of twenty-nine, his father consented to him leaving the extensive palace grounds and touring the kingdom (the only prohibition previously placed on him). Unbeknownst to Siddhartha, however, the tour was all staged, since his father made sure that only the young and beautiful were allowed to be seen on the processional tour route so as to keep his son insulated from all unpleasantness of real life.

Nevertheless, an old man managed to be overlooked and was spotted in the crowd by Siddhartha, who recognized him as an oddity. Never having seen a person crippled and twisted from advanced age, Siddhartha asked his charioteer what was wrong with that man, to which he was given the answer that that was old age, a fate for everyone. Morosely intrigued, Siddhartha asked his charioteer to show him more about the real lives of his subjects.

Consenting, the charioteer took Siddhartha off the preplanned route and into the side streets of the capital city. Disturbed by reality, Siddhartha was especially uneasy to see a person riddled with sickness and disease. Again, he asked what that was all about and was told that that is what illness looked like and that it would happen to everyone sooner or later, often many times over.

The unofficial tour continued until Siddhartha commanded the charioteer to stop and explain why so many people were crying and wailing around a motionless man on the ground. At this moment, he was told about death, witnessed its sorrow firsthand, and learned that it was an inevitability for us all. Everyone we love, including ourselves, is doomed to die.

With his worldview and preconceived notions on life thoroughly rocked, Siddhartha couldn't get the corpse or inevitability of all this suffering and death out of his mind. Eventually, he abandoned his family, home, and affluence to wander and ponder on what seemed to be life's endless cycle of suffering (being involuntarily born into a world where you will labor, toil, get sick, age, and suffer until death, only to be reborn and do it all over again and again and again). From this, Buddhism was established, Siddhartha's suggestions on how to best deal with the inevitable downsides of life and expedite enlightenment so that you can escape the wheel of being endlessly reborn into a world of inevitable suffering.[144]

At the end of his own life, the Buddha is said to have died from food poisoning around age eighty, from either spoiled or poorly prepared mushrooms or pork. Allegedly, he was given this meal in good faith while traveling, and the death wasn't intentional. Still, it's common belief that the Buddha knew the food was bad but accepted it anyway because he was already quite old, had health problems, was in constant pain, and was just ready to go.

Upon his death, his followers had him cremated as per their Hindu tradition. From this precedent, most Buddhists tend to greatly prefer cremation, though there are no precepts against alternatives. Organ donation, in particular, is also greatly supported and seen as a way to get some good karma after death.[145]

The Body-Breakers

Aside for the preference of cremation, Buddhist texts and teaching don't really outline or mandate specific funerary practice, and so Buddhist corpse handling varies greatly from denomination to denomination. Additionally, there is great variance within each denomination due to regional folk beliefs influencing Buddhist practices in various corners of the world.

---

144 Andre Ferdinand Herold, "The Life of Buddha," trans. by Paul C. Blum, *Sacred-Texts*, 1927, http://www.sacred-texts.com/bud/lob/index.htm (accessed Jun. 7, 2018).
"Buddha Biography," *Biography.com*, Mar. 19, 2018, https://www.biography .com/people/buddha-9230587 (accessed Nov. 15, 2018).
145 Pallavi Thakur, "How did Lord Buddha die?" *SpeakingTree*, May 26, 2017, https://www.speakingtree.in/allslides/how-did-lord-buddha-die (accessed Jun. 7, 2018).
"Buddhist Funeral Service Ritual," *Funeralwise*, https://www.funeralwise.com/ customs/buddhist/ (accessed Jun. 7, 2018).

So, in a sense, a Buddhist funeral is really a native folk funeral dressed in the philosophy of Buddhism.

Going north to the Himalayas (where the Vajrayana school of Buddhism is most prevalent), the high altitude, hard soil, and lack of wood provide few options for corpse disposal, and so they've developed an infamous and eco-friendly solution: sky burial. A sky burial begins by burning juniper incense and chanting sutras around the body. Then, a *rogyapa* (which translates to the intense name "body-breaker") begins to disassemble the cadaver by hacking it into small pieces. With help from the juniper smoke and sections of flesh that the body-breakers have sliced off the corpse, vultures are attracted. These vultures begin to consume the corpse, ripping it into pieces and scattering its remains into the sky and throughout the lands. Whatever remains is pulverized into a paste that can be fed to smaller scavenger birds.

In addition to being extremely practical, the Vajrayana Buddhists see sky burials as a final act of generosity to the natural world before leaving it, giving your last earthly possession (your body) to the animals for their nourishment. Mystically, this practice also acts as an omen for the living as to whether the deceased was karmically good or wicked. If all goes according to plan as outlined above, then the person supposedly had good karma and would be reborn into a better position during their next incarnation. If the vultures refuse to eat the corpse or only pick at it a little, the person is deemed to have been too filled with bad karma for the vultures to want and they would suffer in the afterlife for a while before rebirth. In this case, the body would be fed to nonflying scavenger animals as a last way to eke out a bit of good karma and ease some of the afterlife suffering.[146]

T.B.D.

This infamous practice of sky burial is outlined in the even more infamous piece of eighth-century-CE literature known as the *Tibetan Book of the Dead* (though its real name is the *Bardo Thodol*). Like the Egyptian *Book of the Dead*, this Tibetan version acts as a handbook for the soul of the

---

146 Meg Van Huygen, "Give My Body to the Birds: The Practice of Sky Burial," *Atlas Obscura*, March 11, 2014, https://www.atlasobscura.com/articles/sky -burial (accessed Jun. 7, 2018).

recently deceased, filled with dos and don'ts, secrets, cast of characters, and what to expect in the afterlife. While it is read aloud to a person on his/her deathbed, it's also encouraged to be read and studied by the living in preparation for death so as to help make things easier and facilitate their time in the afterlife before the next reincarnation.[147]

Flowers for the Dead

Over in the jungles of Southeast Asia, Theravada Buddhism is the denomination most heavily practiced, and in Thailand, a Theravada funeral is an expensive affair. There's even a Thai saying that goes "the dead sell the living," meant in reference to how the death of a loved one would often drive the surviving family into debt to pay for their funeral.[148]

After about a week of bathing and chanting rituals on the part of the family, the corpse is escorted in procession to the crematory, and it's carried in a counterclockwise circle around the building three times. Once inside, the presiding monk is given a white robe from the surviving family as a gift on behalf of the deceased for the monk's services and everyone pays their final respects. Only close family stays to be present during the actual cremation, but all attendees who show up offer a flower to be burned with the body as a symbolic gesture. The reason these are such expensive affairs is because the family is expected to provide food, drink, and entertainment for *everyone* on every night of the weeklong funerary rituals as well as the day of cremation. Understandably, expenses can add up really quickly.[149]

147 Chogyam Trungpa, and Francesca Fremantle, *The Tibetan Book of the Dead: The Great Liberation Through Hearing In The Bardo* (Boulder, Shambhala Publications, 2000).

148 Larry S. Persons, *The Way Thais Lead: Face as Social Capital* (Chiang Mai: Silkworm Books, 2016).

149 Richard Barrow, "What to expect if you are invited to a Thai Funeral," *Buddhism in Thailand*, Aug. 5, 2011, http://www.thaibuddhist.com/what -to-expect-if-you-are-invited-to-a-thai-funeral/ (accessed Jun. 7, 2018). Nattha Thepbamrung, "Soaring Cost of Dying," *Bangkok Post*, Dec. 15, 2013, https://www.bangkokpost.com/news/special-reports/384890/soaring-cost -of-dying (accessed Jun. 7, 2018).

Crocodile Flags

The actual funeral rites in Cambodian culture are very similar to those in Thai culture thanks to the majority's strong adherence to Theravada Buddhism. However, Cambodians are special in their use of white crocodile flags (long, vertical-hanging flags that have the geometric silhouette of a crocodile). These flags are hung outside a house to publicly show the community that a death has occurred in this home.

It's a 500-year-old tradition stemming from an incident whereby a daughter of King Chan Reachea was killed by a crocodile while swimming. As vengeance, the crocodile was killed and left to rot in public, hanging on a pole outside the palace like a human execution. As often happens, the common folk wanted to imitate and be like the wealthy upper class and show solidarity with their leader, so they also began hanging murdered crocodiles outside their own homes when one of their loved ones died.

Once selling crocodile skins became big business, however, people began stealing the hanging crocodile corpses from outside mourning families' homes. In response, people resorted to simply drawing a crocodile on a white flag, which then turned into the modern, more elaborate crocodile silhouette flags we see today flown in mourning here in Cambodia.[150]

Blood Bridges

King Chan Reachea also helped instill in Cambodia the supernatural fear of bridges and a horrific legacy of child death. During his sixteenth-century reign, there emerged a superstition that if bodies were buried underneath a bridge during construction their souls would provide extra magical strength and stability to the finished structure. The purer and more innocent the blood, the stronger the magic. The king wanted to have the best bridges of all his predecessors, and so he ordered the executions and burials of countless people (especially children since they were

---

150   Roth Meas, "Crocodile flags, a rite of death," *The Phnom Penh Post*, Aug. 17, 2012, https://www.phnompenhpost.com/7days/crocodile-flags-rite-death (accessed Jun. 8, 2018).

the most innocent) underneath each new bridge, causing his subjects to believe that, although sturdy, these new bridges were haunted.

During the dictatorship of the Khmer Rouge in the 1970s, this superstition was revived when children began to go missing en masse. Being the height of the Cambodian genocide, the superstitious masses believed the children were being spirited away by resistance fighters and sacrificed to supernaturally reinforce strategic bridges that the ruling regime wanted destroyed. The reality, though, was equally depressing. So many kids went missing during this time because they were being kidnapped by the Khmer Rouge and forced into children's armies. The dark legacy of haunted bridges and child soldiers still haunts the Cambodian people, albeit not necessarily in a supernatural way.[151]

Buddhist Takeaway:
POPPING YOUR COMFORT ZONE BUBBLE

Death is much more than just physical. There can be all kinds of deaths. The death of a relationship, of a marriage, of an era, of old ideas, and so on. In fact, we go through many deaths throughout our lives, most noticeably the death of childhood innocence the moment we realize that the world is an unfair place where reward isn't based upon merit, the wicked receive no comeuppance, and we live under the whim of the corrupt powers that be. Try as we might, the childhood protective bubble of cartoons, familial love, and primary school ethics cannot last forever.

This bubble-popping realization is what inspired the Buddha to seek out something more. The moment he saw old age, sickness, and especially death, his life of blind optimism and pampered naïveté died. He had been reborn into a more cynical, determined, and philosophic adult. Without the internal death of his preconceived notions on life, the world would've never known Buddhism.

So, for your Buddhist takeaway example, you are now challenged to get out of your own bubble and do something out of your comfort zone. It doesn't have to be an elaborate to-do; it can be as simple as going on stage

151   Meas, "Crocodile flags, a rite of death."

and singing karaoke, trying out a new restaurant from a culture whose cuisine you've never tasted, or even letting your friend set you up on a blind date with that person she's always telling you about. Bring about the death of your discomfort and be reborn into a more confident you.

Deities & Legends

CHUYỆN MA

Chuyện Ma is the Vietnamese equivalent to "ghost stories." Throughout all of Southeast Asia, ghosts are understood by many to be very real, and they play an active part in the fears and daily precautions of everyday people. They take a variety of shapes and forms, sometimes human, sometimes animal, sometimes other. The most common type of ghosts, however, are ancestral spirits.

Usually, ancestors in Vietnam are venerated as helpful protectors residing in the afterlife, but this is only on the condition that they had a good death, a proper burial, and are continuously given regular offerings of food, money, libations, and luxury goods to enjoy as provisions in the next life. However, if an ancestor experienced a bad death (murder, suicide, freak accident, sudden illness, etc.), was not given a proper burial, or is ignored after death, then they return as an angry ghost bent on haunting their living family members (and sometimes others if their grief is profound enough). They wander the earth searching for and stealing the offerings that their family has not given them, and they cause fatal accidents so others can share in their spectral suffering.

The ghosts of MIA soldiers from the Vietnam War with the United States have been spirits of particular concern. In the mayhem of defending their homeland, many Vietnamese went off to war, never to return. To this day, many families still don't know what happened to their relatives and are haunted (psychologically, at least) by the fact that their loved ones (and now ancestors) most likely experienced a bad death and never received a proper burial. In an act of desperation, numerous families have erected and maintain empty graves in absentia near their homes, in the countryside, along roadways, and anywhere else they can in the hopes that whatever little they can do will be enough to satisfy these tragic familial spirits.

But it's not all doom and gloom in the spirit world. It's believed that spirit mediums can establish a special relationship with the ghosts of the damned. With enough money, you can hire a medium to outsource their work to these ghosts-for-hire who can wander the world unseen and collect information that living people could never get. Just like modern private eyes, spying on allegedly unfaithful lovers is one of the most popular tasks for them.[152]

KRASUE

Krasue is the Thai name for a specific undead specter that appears in folklore all across Southeast Asia. Each culture has a different name and a slightly different variation of the Krasue, but the commonalities they share are that the Krasue is a nocturnal spirit who can fly through the air and has the head of a beautiful young woman and a body of exposed internal organs hanging from her neck. So, if you saw her, she would literally appear as a jumble of floating viscera attached to a seductively beautiful female head. She's also said to have an eerie glow around her and to roam the countryside (especially around farms and swampy areas) on the hunt for human blood.

She has a number of origin stories, but there's a running theme though many of them that women who engage in magic become Krasue. Sometimes the woman is the innocent victim of demonic possession; other times, becoming a Krasue is the consequence of the woman engaging in magic and working with demons. Because of this "magic woman" association with Krasue, literal witch hunts still occur in rural Southeast Asia. Women who are perceived to be odd, outsiders, or easy scapegoats are accused of transforming into Krasue at night and causing harm to the community (most

---

152   Jesse W. Nash, and Elizabeth Trinh Nguyen, *Romance, Gender, and Religion in a Vietnamese-American Community: Tales of God and Beautiful Women* (New York: Edwin Mellen Press, 1995).
Heonik Kwon, *Ghosts of War in Vietnam* (Cambridge: Cambridge University Press, 2008).

often through miscarriages). The blame can be burdened on the accused's family, too, since being a Krasue can also be a symptom of being related to a female worker of magic.

Despite officials trying to play down these perceived superstitions, sightings of Krasue are quite frequent, and now with modern technology, people are uploading videos and photos of "Krasue sightings" all over the internet. Nevertheless, scientists insist on ruining the fantasy by offering an explanation. According to them, the culprit is methane gas balls emitted from rotting organic material (popularly known as will-o'-the-wisps in the West). Rotting organic material is common on farms and swamplands (thus explaining why Krasue are commonly sighted there), and the sphere shape with fire trailing can appear, at quick glance, as a head with entrails in tow.[153]

YAMA (BUDDHISM)

Yama is a death deity in both Hinduism and Buddhism. In Buddhism, his exact duties and level of sadism vary from culture to culture. In general, though, he rules the temporary underworld and makes sure that the cycle of life, death, and rebirth runs smoothly and according to one's appropriate karma.

In cultures associated with Theravada Buddhism, Yama goes beyond the role of administrator of the dead to also be the instigator of death. In particular, he punishes the living with catastrophes, sickness, old age, and tragedies so as to remind them of their own mortality and the impermanence of everything (the hope being that this will prevent humans from becoming too attached to anything in the material world and let them focus on their karma instead).[154]

---

153 Julia Luangrath, "Krasue," *Pseudoparanormal*, Mar. 20, 2012, http://www
.pseudoparanormal.com/2012/03/krasue.html (accessed Jun. 8, 2018).
Benjamin Baumann, "The Khmer Witch Project," *Ghost Movies in Southeast
Asia and Beyond: Narratives, Cultural Contexts, Audiences*, ed. by Peter J. Bräunlein
and Andrea Lauser (Boston: Brill Academic Publishers, 2016).
154 Nanamoli Bhikkhu, and Bodhi Bhikkhu, *The Middle Length Discourses
of the Buddha: A Translation of the Majjhima Nikaya* (Boston: Wisdom
Publications, 2001).

14

INDIAN &
SOUTHEAST ASIAN
MAGICAL COMMUNITY

FORCE MAJEURE

Since the most ancient of times, peoples around the world have believed in a force majeure, a universal power beyond themselves and what seems possible that crashes into our life in unforeseen (and often unwanted) ways. Call it nature, God, the Tao, the Universe, etcetera... the force of the cosmos often comes into conflict with our own wants and preferences. In the case of my London-born celebrity friend, Radhika Vekaria, this involved the untimely death of a loved one.

Despite her many life accomplishments and dedication to bettering humanity (she's a recent recipient of the Global Peace Song Award, a US ambassador for Round Table Global, and a champion of various international causes) she's still human, and isn't immune to grief.

Why this person? Why now? These and other such unanswerable questions can corrode our faith and our happiness no matter who we are, where we're from, or what we've done. For Radhika, the Vedic philosophies behind her faith and upbringing lend solace to her times of grief. So, visiting us here from her home in L.A., let her share some ancient insight into how Vedism helped her when a particularly painful force majeure changed her life forever.

My name is Radhika. I am a creative artist in Los Angeles, where I have launched my latest music project called "Her Departure." Throughout the experimentation of this work I found my deep realisation of the elements of nature—Air, Earth, Fire, Water. Lyrically and sonically, it is a culmination of how I have witnessed the world since childhood and moved through it as human, and more so a woman.

My ancestral lineage from the last two centuries comes from India via East Africa. My name translated from Sanskrit means "one with unending love." I never resonated with my name growing up. I do now. As my spiritual practise has allowed me to dive into philosophy that I took for granted, I know now that love never dies. Neither does anything else. There is only natural law, cause and effect. That is the root of what I understand to be the faith I have known. Vedism.

One of the predominant discussions from Vedism—the root of modern Hinduism—is nature and our place within it. We cannot be immune from the universal forces, the cycles of nature: birth, life, and death. The idea of reincarnation is deeply ingrained in us. Perhaps this practise is a preemptive coping mechanism for life's losses that the heart will find too much to bear. However, it is my belief that a philosophy over 4,000 years old has some deeper truth to it. We can never fully decide upon this until having our own experience through what is the heaviest test for the human and its soul.

I lost my father fourteen years ago. Too young for any child to lose theirs. However, I believe that my spiritual practises like meditation, exposure to sutras, rituals, and Vedic-rooted celebrations and stories allowed me to feel the grace and universal power through the loss and thereafter. The main three forms of energy in the universe, depicted by the three lords, Brahma, Vishnu, and Shiva, are, respectively, the Creator, the Sustainer, and the Destroyer. Every single part of life, on this planet and beyond exists because of Nature's continual sequence in these three aspects.

As a child I used to look at awesome forces such as hurricanes and feel that there is a greater power than us that ultimately decides. We are powerless to stand in the way of what Nature and her laws decide to carry out. I revered her then, and I do more now. I didn't realise before that Vedism is not a religion but a way of life. A way of moving through this world with an acute and intimate respect and understanding of how the larger picture of our lives is formed.

One of the fundamental ways to remain or return to this state with immediacy is through breath. Our breath is the first thing we have after we are born and the last thing we do before we die. It is our greatest ally, our longest standing and most powerful of friends. Deep Ujjayi breathing is an instantaneous, electric path to the present. It develops Prana (life-force energy). Ujjayi breath is a closed mouth breath, taken over the back of the throat deeply with an inhale and exhale. At first one can feel a little light-headed; however, this fundamental yogic practise is the root of all actions taken by the body to move toward the soul. The breath returns us to the present and to practise this comes more easily if committed to regularly, even for a few minutes a day. Memories from the past or anticipation of the future keep us from being in the present and instead rouse our emotions in turbulent waves. This is suffering. The idea is not to eliminate pain, but how long it stays in each wave is up to us.

We are told that the Soul never dies. Only the body is dropped once the last breath is exhaled. There are no boundaries when it comes to being a child of Hindu communities. You go to funerals, see the body of a loved one, brought into the home they once resided in, to be adorned and ritualised by rice, water, flowers, and multiple essences of Nature that all bless and release the Soul that once was hosted by the flesh. There is a reason for these rituals that allows for the Soul to be at peace and depart. And cremation, though a truly painful event to witness always, exercises intense

grief, forcibly making us accept that the person is indeed gone. There is
nothing to hold on to but the memory, and denial is not an option.

However, the more beautiful part that is underlying it all is the driving
difference between the seen and unseen. The body is matter, returning to the
earth. And the ashes fly into the wind, or are poured into the river—some-
times returned to the all-powerful Ganges in India. But always back to
nature. The Soul, however, lives on. And it may even be reborn the instant
we say goodbye. Who knows, somewhere on this planet may be the Soul
of my father in a body of a different skin tone or religion, or speaking a
language I may never hear. Whether or not that's the case, there is a connec-
tion. I feel it. And in that, there is never the need to miss him for too long
because I will feel the vibration of the same earth beneath our feet and same
heavens that we look upon.

—RADHIKA VEKARIA

THE CHANT OF REBIRTH

Our next community member is Dannie Phan, who comes to us all the
way from the heart of Little Saigon in Orange County, California. Despite her
living in the OC, I first met Dannie in Santa Barbara while in college there at
the University of California. Though life after college has made it a bit more
difficult to hang out like we used to, we've managed to stay in touch through
the years, and she has gone on to establish herself as a very adept photographer, documenting life, love, and death through her camera (check out her
work at www.donegeemedia.com).

Part of her work sometimes involves photographing Buddhist funerals, giving her an insider's trained eye to witness these rituals in a way
most people wouldn't easily see. For our journey here, Dannie has come
to share a Vietnamese funerary chant and what it means to the many Vietnamese diaspora communities all over the world who are grieving.

The funerary chant that we Vietnamese Buddhists use the most would be
"Nam Mô A Di Đà Phật," which is basically a call to Amitabha Buddha
in hopes to be reborn into the Pure Land, a place where there's no pain
or suffering, so that one can attain enlightenment. It's thought that this

chant can help in purifying bad karma, and so it's often also used for meditation purposes, but I've also heard family use it as a greeting or salutation to monks.

It's a short phrase that can be repeated dozens of times; often, prayer beads are used for counting one's progress for large gatherings like a funeral. Monks use bells and drums to count down and signal the number of remaining chants. After a death it can be heard repeatedly at all hours during the mourning process. If it's not being chanted by an individual, there are recordings that can be played at home throughout the night. Depending on the speaker's cadence it can sound very robotic or hauntingly beautiful.

After the body gets blessed by monks, the coffin is packed with the deceased's prized possessions to take to the afterlife. The sealing of the coffin before burial represents the separation of the deceased from the living, and all family present are expected to turn away. We look away so they can go. Seeing the mourning faces of loved ones could keep a lingering spirit from moving on. This process is repeated when a coffin is placed into the grave. While looking away, individuals will focus on chanting "Nam Mô A Di Đà Phật" in meditation but these two moments are typically the hardest part for people and for my family. It's perfectly normal for people to cry and wail as they chant this call over and over again.

—*DANNIE PHAN*

PART 5

EAST ASIA

Empty-handed I entered the world
Barefoot I leave it.
My coming, my going—
Two simple happenings
That got entangled.
DEATH POEM OF FOUR-
TEENTH-CENTURY ZEN MASTER
KOZAN ICHIKYO

Heading northbound from the jungles of Southeast Asia to the mountains and fertile farmlands of East Asia, it soon becomes apparent that death isn't the driving force behind religion and spirituality anymore. With the notable exception of ghosts, the mysteries of the afterlife aren't really as much of a religious focus here. Due in part to Taoism and Mahayana Buddhism's focus on the ephemeral, the afterlife is de-emphasized as a distraction from living here in the present moment.

Nevertheless, death is a big part of life, and so each culture and faith here in East Asia touches on it in some way. Our travels here will begin in China where the fluid, laissez-faire attitude of Taoism and the ultra-rigid, hierarchical classism of Confucianism developed two very interesting views on death and dying. After this, we'll continue north through the steppes of Mongolia to the Korean Peninsula, where land-space issues have forced quick modernization of funerary rites and rituals. Finally, we'll ferry over to Japan where the animistic and magical native tradition of Shinto still lives on side by side (and sometimes intertwined) with the austere and stoic mentality of Zen Buddhism.

15
CHINA

Cultural

TAOISM

Taoism is a religious and philosophical tradition based on observances of the natural world. As an ultra-simplified explanation, one could say that Taoism witnesses how nature seems to live in perfect balance with itself and flowingly achieves its goals with ease, and so Taoists try to mimic the balanced flow of nature so as to obtain the same benefits of harmony and ease.

The catch is, however, that the flow of nature and the universe at large doesn't necessarily lead to the fulfillment of your personal desires and wants. It always tends to lead to fulfillment of your needs and for the greater good, but if your wants don't align with your needs or the greater good, then the flow of nature won't take you to them. Going against the flow for personal gain causes unnatural pressure, stress, and difficulties for yourself that should be avoided. Finding the path of least resistance, like nature does, will lead you to a happier life overall, albeit sometimes without the things you think you want.

Taoist philosophy has existed in China as long as there have been humans interacting with nature and trying to survive in it. Taoist teachings, though, weren't really organized or written down until around the sixth or fourth century BCE when the legendary figure of Lao Tzu (from the Chinese "Lǎozǐ," which is an honorific title literally translating to "old man") compiled his musings on the observable universal truths of the natural world into what is now the *Tao Te Ching*. A slim handbook, it makes no mention of gods, deities, the afterlife, karmic punishments, or any other supernatural magic. It simply outlines how nature achieves its goals, how you can achieve your goals by following nature's example, and how not following nature's example will result in a tough life of self-imposed hardships.

Full-Taoist Alchemists

Being China's first and oldest unified philosophy, Taoist teachings have greatly influenced Chinese (and consequently East Asian) society, but their omission of answers on death and the great beyond have often caused people to fill in the blanks. Religious Taoism (established some 200 to 400 years after organized Taoist philosophy itself) is essentially Chinese folk beliefs and superstitions loosely held together by Taoist philosophy, and when it comes to death, Chinese folklore is filled with demons, ghosts, and realms of afterlife magic.

Taoist observance of the natural world dictates that death is inevitable, but ancient superstitions argue that there's a way around this. The search for an elixir of immortality is historically an important aspect of religious Taoism, and for at least the past two millennia, this obsession to defy death by Taoist alchemists has led to revolutionary discoveries such as gunpowder, rocketry, acupuncture, and a host of varying medicines.[155]

---

155   Peter Wang, "Top 20 Ancient Chinese Inventions," *China Whisper*, Nov. 21, 2012, http://www.chinawhisper.com/top-20-ancient-chinese-inventions/ (accessed Jun. 12, 2018).

Aside from alchemic experimentation, there were other everyday things that every Taoist could do that were believed to keep death at bay and prolong life, including sexual techniques (like "edging"), breathing techniques, exercise, tai chi, vegetarian diets, and living a moral life.[156]

Funerary Spiritual Defense

Once death inevitably *does* happen, though, the Taoist funeral is full of symbolism that has varied from community to community and throughout China's long history. In general, the family comes together to wash the body and dress it in its finest clothes (but never red since that could cause the soul to become a wandering ghost). Mirrors and reflective surfaces are covered due to the worry that seeing the reflection of the dead will cause you to die too. With the corpse in the casket (traditional ones have three humps on the lid), an altar is set up with a memorial photo, tea (symbolic of yin energy), rice (symbolic of yang energy), water (symbolic of yin-yang unity), a lamp (symbolic of wisdom), and five pieces of fruit that are red, white, yellow, green, and black (symbolic of the five elements: fire, metal, earth, wood, and water).[157]

Admittedly, religious Taoists don't know what happens to the soul after death, but they do firmly believe in a soul and in otherworldly spiritual beings. In the funeral itself, most of the rituals are done to help ward off evil spirits from harming the newly exposed, defenseless soul. Such protection measures include heavy incense, chanting, traditional instruments playing discordant music, imitating iconic postures of deities, and the burning of paper items and "ghost money" that can be used by the dead in the afterlife.

Afterlife affluence is very important for two very distinct reasons. First, it provides the soul with bribe money and leverage should the next world be a bad place. The logic is that if the next place is bad, then there

---

156 Henri Maspero, *Le Taoïsme et les religions chinoises* (Paris: Éditions Gallimard, 1971).

157 Jenny Goldade, "Cultural Spotlight: Chinese Taoist," *Frazer Consultants*, Aug. 11, 2017, https://www.frazerconsultants.com/2017/08/cultural-spotlight -chinese-taoist-funeral-traditions/ (accessed Jun. 12, 2018).

will be just as much (if not more) corruption, so these offerings allow the deceased some judicial flexibility to help them get by, learn the ropes, and possibly escape. However, if the next life is a good place, then those with a lot of wealth and affluence will naturally want to hang out with other wealthy, affluent people and bypass the poor and working classes (just like in real life). These offerings allow the deceased to make the right social connections in the next world so that they can have the best afterlife possible.[158]

Funerals are also dangerous places for the living. All of the attention attracted by the colorful, loud, perfumed ceremony may ward off demons, but it also attracts jealous spirits who weren't ever given their own proper funeral and thus became wandering ghosts. These envious spirits come to cause harm to the funeral attendees, and so to prevent this, the mourners are encouraged to pray for the souls of these ghostly funeral-crashers, thereby creating a purifying barrier that will free the specters from their earthly prison should they get too close.[159]

Taoists understand that nothing happens in a vacuum. There is a reason why ghosts become evil, and by remedying that reason, evil leaves the ghost. Getting into a magical battle with ghosts to exorcise them from existence might also work, but the natural path of least resistance is to soothe the underlying problem. Working smarter, not harder, is always preferred in Taoism.

Taoist Takeaway:
THE FUTILITY OF FOREVER

Nature is the great teacher in Taoism. She teaches by example, and one of the most unsettling examples is how nothing lasts forever. Weather

---

158 Heidi Ng, "Hong Kong's Taoist funerals: the superstition, symbolism and how to stop your soul being dragged into the coffin," *South China Morning Post*, Jul. 19, 2017, http://www.scmp.com/lifestyle/article/2102955/hong-kongs -taoist-funerals-superstition-symbolism-and-how-stop-your-soul (accessed Jun. 12, 2018).

159 "Daoist Funeral Traditions," *The Daoist Encyclopedia*, Nov. 7, 2009, http:// en.daoinfo.org/wiki/Daoist_Funeral_Rites (accessed Jun. 13, 2018).

passes, landscapes change, and living things die. Nevertheless, that doesn't stop humankind from attempting to live past our species' natural expiration date. Like religious Taoists in their pursuit for an elixir of eternal life, modern science is constantly trying to unlock the secrets to near-forever longevity.

Think about it, though: What would the world be like if human life could be prolonged seemingly forever? Look how decrepit we become at age one hundred. As we age, we become more reliant on others for assistance with everyday tasks. Our senses diminish. Our pains become more pronounced and linger into the chronic. Adding more years to life has never shown an increase in the quality of life, only a steady decline in comfort and well-being.

But let's imagine there's a magical remedy that keeps us eternally youthful along with a life span of 500 years as the new norm. Accidents will still happen, and living 'til near forever will only exacerbate the tragedy, pain, and grief over people who die "young." Rather than carrying the painful stone of grief inside you for eighty-some years, it'll be hundreds, and that many more years is now stolen from each child and "youngster" who is killed within their first hundred years of life.

Environmentally, it would also become more of a strain on the earth and more difficult to feed, clothe, and shelter everyone (especially if we want to do so in an equitable way). And unless progressive measures like a universal basic income are implemented, we'd be at an uncomfortable impasse wherein technology will automate most jobs, yet we'll need more jobs to be able to give exponentially more people a way to earn income. Add to that inflation rates, all the farms/pasturage needed to grow that much more food, and still leaving room and rights for wildlife… things become quite tricky.

But let's scale things back and look at the immediacy of forever. Should scientists discover some magical elixir that'll make you everlasting, you *know* that patented product will be expensive. How much would *you* pay to prevent death for an extra hundred-some years? Exactly. So, then the megawealthy will be the only people to afford the elixir, and we'll be faced with a dystopian situation wherein the megawealthy will live for centuries while the masses pray to make it through their seventies. The current oligarchy of the wealthy will just become worse.

So, your Taoist takeaway challenge is to de-romanticize living forever. Yin and yang exist in balance, but we tend to only see death and eternal life as always bad or always good. Take an active approach to looking at the opposite of these preconceived notions. How does death play a beneficial role in the universal design? How would living forever be detrimental to ourselves and the world at large? And if you feel so inclined, get in touch with those who have passed on and ask them for insight into how their mortality wasn't such a bad thing (and may have been a great thing) now that they've transcended the material world and have a broader perspective on life and death.

CONFUCIANISM

Confucianism is the other half of the same coin that is traditional Chinese belief systems. While Taoism is the more free-flowing, nature-based, and magical side, Confucianism is the strict, logic-based, and bureaucratic side. Essentially, both aim to help people live a better life. It's just that Taoists say humans are naturally good and taking it easy via nature's example is the best way to live a good life, while Confucians say humans are naturally corrupt and by keeping everyone (including yourself) in line via rigid protocols and hierarchy, everyone can benefit from a better life.

This thinking spawned from the philosophy's eponymous founder, Confucius (which is the Latinized version of the original Chinese "Kǒng Fūzǐ," meaning "Master Kong"), who lived from 551 to 479 BCE. Surrounded by the horrors of civil war that resulted from the decaying decadence of a falling imperial dynasty and by the ensuing warlord power struggles, Confucius believed the remedy to all this suffering was a stronger centralized government that could control and protect the population from themselves. If wise people (meaning "men," because this is ancient China) ruled through nonpartisan law and each person knew their place in society and never overstepped their bounds, harmony would be the natural result.

The Model Family

Because of its emphatic focus on dictating the proper behaviors and interactions of each stratum of society, Confucianism (like Taoism) wasn't too concerned about the afterlife. According to legend, when a disciple of Confucius asked him about life after death, Confucius humorously chastised him by asking why he was trying to understand the afterlife if he didn't even fully understand this life he was living in now.[160] Still, people's natural curiosities about what happens to them after death couldn't be brushed aside, and so (again, like in Taoism), religious Confucianism developed, which was basically Chinese folk beliefs structured within the philosophical framework of Confucianism.

The only concrete things Confucius said about the afterlife were in regard to the spirits of our familial ancestors, which makes sense since Confucius used the hierarchy of the family as the prime exemplary model of a harmonious society: male/father ruler, obedient female/wife, children (sons over daughters) striving to support their parents, parents striving to provide for their children. In Confucianism, just because a family member died did not mean there was an excuse to stop honoring them. If you venerated your ancestors, they'd provide a supernatural link to anything and everything beyond your present reality as well as cosmic assistance in earthly endeavors. Families often keep tablets at home with the names of their deceased ancestors chiseled onto them to help keep their memory alive and provide easier contact.[161]

Chinese folk tradition added to Confucianism by saying that these ancestors lived in a dark, murky realm where offerings of money and goods had to be given to them regularly to help support them there. Unsupported ancestors could come back to haunt the family. Well-supported ancestors might be more inclined to help their generous family. Conveniently, an entire business of selling flammable miniatures of luxury items from

---

160 Kǒng Fūzǐ, *The Analects of Confucius: A Philosophical Translation*, trans. by Roger T. Ames, and Henry Rosemont, Jr. (New York: Ballantine Books, 1999).

161 Myron Cohen, "Confucian Teaching: Filial Piety and Ancestor Worship," *Asian Topics: Columbia University*, http://afe.easia.columbia.edu/at/conf_teaching/ct03.html (accessed Jun. 13, 2018).

watches and iPhones to cars and currency of ridiculously large denomina-tions (which calls into question the crazy inflation rate the hereafter must have) has developed to provide you the opportunity to make your ances-tor's afterlife their best life.[162]

Confucian Familial Piety

As for the funeral itself, much of the same rituals and rites of those found in Taoism are followed due to both religions arising from Chinese folk tradi-tions. The main differences are the lack of magical symbology in Confucian funerals as compared to Taoist ones, as well as the heavier emphasis on a division of genders and the prominence of men over women.[163]

After death, the most popular way to show continued filial piety to one's ancestors is to maintain their graves, and so in early April of every year, the Qingming ("Pure Brightness") Festival is celebrated. This is a national holi-day in China dedicated to families traveling to their ancestors' graves, spruc-ing them up, doing some groundskeeping, offering them annual supplies of effigy goods and money to use in the afterlife, and spending time in remem-brance of them (somewhat similar to the *Día de Muertos* tradition in Mexico).

Particularly in the rural areas of modern China, the growing urbaniza-tion and state-sponsored embrace of capitalism (or as the Chinese powers-that-be and nouveaux riches like to call it, "socialism with Chinese char-acteristics"[164]) has made traveling to ancestral lands and static graves inconvenient, but this is easily remedied by paying professional mourners to travel to your family's graves during the Qingming Festival and do all the rituals for you while you watch via a smartphone livestream.

Of course, with the extreme (and growing) population of China, over-crowding in cities is a big problem for the living, let alone finding space

162   Vittoria Traverso, "In China, Ghosts Demand the Finer Things in Life," *Atlas Obscura*, Oct. 19, 2017, https://www.atlasobscura.com/articles/china-ghost -festival-burning-money (accessed Jun. 14, 2018).

163   Christian Jochim, "Chinese Beliefs," *Encyclopedia of Death and Dying*, http://www .deathreference.com/Ce-Da/Chinese-Beliefs.html (accessed Jun. 13, 2018).

164   Ben Westcott, "Socialism with Chinese characteristics? Beijing's propaganda explained," *CNN*, Mar. 10, 2018, https://www.cnn.com/2018/03/10/asia/ china-npc-communist-party-phrases-intl/index.html (accessed Nov. 16, 2018).

to permanently bury every single dead person individually, and a growing number of cities are prohibiting any new land for cemeteries, thus forcing cremation as the only legal and practical option. But this also means leaving no more tombs to maintain and show devotion to one's ancestors. In response, the Chinese funeral industry has adapted by providing QR codes along with a decedent's cremated remains so that a family can scan it with their phone and be taken to a digital tomb for them to be able to take care of and show their filial piety (in much the same way you'd care for a Tamagotchi pet or a FarmVille homestead).[165]

Hanshi History

Originally, this Qingming Festival started as the Hanshi ("Cold Food") Festival from a legendary incident of accidental manslaughter back in the seventh century BCE. According to the stories, Jie Zhitui voluntarily followed his lord, Prince Ji Chong'er, into exile and proved to be a loyal companion who entertained the prince, kept up morale, and even carved off a hunk of his own thigh for his lord to eat when starvation appeared imminent. When Chong'er was returned to power, however, he overlooked Zhitui when bestowing aristocratic job positions to all who had helped him during his exile.

Disheartened by his lord's lack of loyalty and appreciation, Zhitui became a hermit in the forest, refusing all contact with the outside world. Chong'er eventually felt bad and set the forest on fire to force Zhitui out to apologize to him, but the fire killed him instead. In honor of Zhitui (and personal guilt), Chong'er decreed that no fires can be lit on this day every year, and thus the people must eat only cold food.[166]

---

165 "Ancient Chinese tomb-sweeping festival goes hi-tech," *British Broadcasting Corporation*, Apr. 4, 2017, https://www.bbc.com/news/world-asia-39487437 (accessed Jun. 14, 2018).

166 Caitlin Doughty, "TOMB SWEEPING DAY!!!" *Ask A Mortician*, Apr. 4, 2017, https://www.youtube.com/watch?v=WVFr7ynB8s8 (accessed Jun. 14, 2018). Wes Radez, "How to Celebrate the Qingming Festival," *Chinese American Family*, Oct. 2, 2018, http://www.chineseamericanfamily.com/qingming -festival/ (accessed Nov. 24, 2018).

How did this Cold Food Festival become the macabre Qingming Festival of today? The Tang dynasty, that's how. You see, this Cold Food Festival grew to a multiday festival when fire was forbidden, but it originally took place in winter, which made it a dangerous time for children, the sick, and the elderly, who were more susceptible to wintertime cold. Additionally, the wealthy were having multiple ancestor-veneration ceremonies throughout the year that were so self-servingly and ostentatiously lavish that they became a living parody of insincere bad taste and took away from the real sacred focus of ancestor veneration. So in the eighth century CE, the Tang dynasty moved the Cold Food Festival to early spring to prevent so many people from dying and combined it with a one-time, empire-wide annual ancestor veneration festival for all subjects, thus solving two problems at once.[167]

Erotic Funerals

And before we venture on, there is one more thing we need explore. You know the marketing maxim "sex sells," right? You're aware of how advertisers often utilize human sexual allure to catch people's attention and sell a product? Well, imagine you had to put on an event wherein the amount of attendees was equal to the amount of honor your family would get. This is the issue facing many Chinese upon the death of a family member; the larger the crowd of mourners the more prestige and greater honor their deceased loved ones receive. So how do you draw a big crowd to garner more honor for your dead relative? By hiring funeral strippers, of course!

Don't think one solitary "day shift" stripper gyrating off to the side. Think multiple "A-Team" strippers dancing to loud music with lasers, fog machines, stages, and poles right up next to the casket. Mostly happening in the countryside, many rural Chinese (in an effort to achieve their Confucian-inspired obligations of postmortem filial piety of acquiring more honor for their newly deceased relatives) are drowning in debt from paying several times their annual income on funeral strippers. Still, these families

167   Donald Holzman, "The Cold Food Festival in Early Medieval China," *Harvard Journal of Asiatic Studies* 46:1, Jun. 1986.

voluntarily go into severe debt over funeral strippers because at the end of the day, they do, indeed, draw big crowds to funerals.

Needless to say, the Chinese government is *not* happy about this growing popularity for what they see as superstitious, debt-inducing, misappropriated sexual decadence for the dead, going so far as to set up a national hotline for people to leave anonymous tips on any funeral stripper activity goings-on (yes, it's a real hotline). Meanwhile, over on the island of Taiwan, the lack of a crackdown on funeral strippers and the use of them by high-profile politicians (one of whom had fifty in a single cortège) has made it much more commonplace, albeit just as disapprovingly ridiculed (in public anyway).[168]

In all seriousness, though, author Caitlin Doughty (of the YouTube series *Ask A Mortician* fame) brings up the important point about cultural relativity when looking at practices like these. To us in the West, erotic funerals might seem tragically ludicrous (or even ludicrously tragic), but to the people who are going into severe debt to pay for funeral strippers, it's a logical means to a highly desired end.

They are truly sincere in trying to fulfill their Confucian duties of filial piety by giving their deceased family member the most honor possible via attracting the biggest crowd at a funeral possible, and it just so happens that sex reliably draws a crowd. It's a growing phenomenon because it works, and it's done out of genuine love for one's dearly departed. Conversely, the "close family and friends only" Western funeral would seem unbelievably disrespectful to many rural Chinese. Everything's relative.

168   Caitlin Doughty, "Let's Talk FUNERAL STRIPPERS," *Ask A Mortician*, Mar. 23, 2018, https://www.youtube.com/watch?v=bFM_w_tN2B4 (accessed Jun. 14, 2018).
Samuel Osborne, "China vows to crack down on funeral strippers," *Independent*, Feb. 21, 2018, https://www.independent.co.uk/news/ world/asia/china-funeral-strippers-crack-down-rural-attract-mourners -death-a8220866.html (accessed Jun. 14, 2018).
Yvette Tan, "Why do some Chinese funerals involve strippers?" *British Broadcasting Corporation*, Feb. 24, 2018, https://www.bbc.com/news/world -asia-china-43137005 (accessed Jun. 14, 2018).

Confucian Takeaway:
UNEARTHING THE FAMILY TREE

In Confucianism, venerating your ancestors is a pillar of the faith. In a certain light, one could say that necromancy is an integral part of this cultural tradition. So, let's get back to the basics for a second and do a little bit of Necromancy 101.

At its most basic level, necromantic acts usually involve reaching out to dead relatives, but do you even know who your ancestors are? I'm not talking about people who have died in your lifetime; I'm talking about great-grandparents and beyond. And no, just knowing their names isn't enough.

Who were they? What did they do? What were their goals and aspirations? A lot of us in this modern world know our geographic roots, but we know little to nothing about the entire tree between those roots and us as the leaves on the very top (and yes, if you were adopted into a family, you are grafted onto that family tree and receive the same nutrients the other leaves receive).

Your Confucian takeaway challenge now is to do some research into your dead ancestors. At a minimum, this means finding out a factoid about them. At best, this means taking a trip to their graves, handling their cremated remains, or visiting the sites of their great achievements and terrible accidents. A tree whose leaves are close to its roots is called a shrub, and no living person on earth is that closely descended from their prehistoric roots to have a family shrub instead of a family tree. So, if you want to tend to your family tree, give a little humanity and familiarity to everyone making up the essential trunk.

Deities & Legends

EIGHTEEN COURTS OF HELL

Since the three major religions in China (Taoism, Confucianism, and Buddhism) all generally refrain from talking too much about the afterlife, Chinese folk traditions have filled in the gaps and created an elaborate underworld called Diyu that is separated into eighteen levels. This afterlife realm is a perfect amalgamation of all three big religions in China; it has the ephemeral suffering of Buddhism, the magic and demons of Taoism, and the rigid hierarchy and bureaucracy of Confucianism.

Being based on folk traditions, the descriptions and stories about Diyu vary greatly throughout China's cultural regions (being more prominent in poorer, rural regions) and often conflict with one another, but the universal theme is that it's a place where the soul suffers a bit to purge it of its impurities so that it can be reincarnated pure. Everyone is destined to come here, but depending on your impurity after a lifetime on earth, you could spend anywhere from a few minutes to near eternity in this realm. Regardless, though, everyone got their karma comeuppance here after death.

Originally, there were some 84,000 different divisions of hell, but the Tang dynasty simplified things so that there only needed to be eighteen divisions (called "courts"), each with their own subruler who reported to the overseer Yánluó. In its own way, Diyu is similar to the ironic punishments featured in Dante's *Inferno* and *Purgatorio*, and we'll do a lightning-round rundown right now of all these eighteen courts of horrors.

Court 1: Chamber of Tongue Ripping—Those who were gossips or spread lies would have their tongues ripped out.

Court 2: Chamber of Scissors—Those who were homewreckers or broke apart families would have their fingers cut off.

Court 3: Chamber of Iron Cycads—Those who caused discord within the family are hung from iron cycads (think palm trees but more squat and stout).

Court 4: Chamber of Mirrors—Those who never suffered on earth for their wrongdoings are shown their true wickedness and the consequences of their actions via magic mirrors.

Court 5: Chamber of Steam—Those who were hypocrites or caused trouble for personal amusement would have scalding hot steam blown on them nonstop.

Court 6: Forest of Copper Columns—Those who were arsonists or used fire to harm others would be bound to columns of glowing red-hot copper.

Court 7: Mountain of Knives—Those who killed living beings (including animals) with knives are forced to climb a mountain of upward pointing knives.

Court 8: Hill of Ice—Those who were adulterers, schemers, or preyed on the elderly would be left naked and exposed in the freezing cold on a hill of ice.

Court 9: Cauldron of Oil—Those who were thieves, rapists, made false accusations, or were physically abusive would be boiled together in a large cauldron of oil.

Court 10: Chamber of Oxen—Those who were abusive toward animals would be gored, trampled, and broken by vengeful oxen.

Court 11: Chamber of Rocks—Those who were abusive toward babies or abandoned their children would have to stand in a putrid lake while holding a giant rock above their heads until they ran out of strength and were crushed while asphyxiating on the fetid water.

Court 12: Chamber of Pounding—Those who voluntarily wasted food would be forcibly fed hellfire by demons. (I know, the name is a bit of a misnomer.)

Court 13: Chamber of Blood—Those who were just all-around disrespectful toward others would be forced to wade through a pool of blood.

Court 14: Town of Suicide—Those who committed suicide would be forced to wander an abandoned town where the wind of sorrow and the rain of pain never cease.

Court 15: Chamber of Dismemberment—Those who stole from the dead and raided tombs would have their bodies hacked to pieces.

Court 16: Mountain of Flames—Those who were corrupt would be thrown into a volcano.

Court 17: Chamber of the Stone Mill—Those who were abusive of their power or preyed on those weaker than themselves would be ground in a stone mill by demons and fed to dogs.

Court 18: Chamber of Saws—Those who took advantage of legal loopholes, committed financial crimes, or were dishonest in business matters would be sawed in half (vertically).

(Note: After the punishment, you'd be regenerated to suffer it all over again and again until you spent your due time in that court.)[169]

MENG PO

In Buddhist-inspired Chinese folk beliefs, Meng Po is the morose, elderly tea server of the underworld, who is the last person the soul meets in the afterlife before its next reincarnation. Her duty is to ensure that you get a fresh start on your next earthly go 'round, and she does this by offering you a magical tea called *mi-hun-tang* ("waters of oblivion") that gives you permanent amnesia of your past lives and time in the underworld. However, the amount everyone drinks can vary, thus explaining why some people have stronger past-life memories than others.

According to legend, Meng Po's background is that she is an immortal who had a very rough time while residing on earth and wanted to forget her memories of trauma, sorrow, and horrific experiences (all of which would never go away since she can live forever). So, she developed the mi-hun-tang tea, but in her compassion, she decided not to drink it, rather preferring to serve it to the souls of others before their next reincarnation.

The irony is that though she created it for herself and her own suffering, if she drank it, she wouldn't remember how to make it and thus would be unable to give it to anyone else. Compassionately, she chose to forego

169 Prof. David K. Jordan, "The Jade Guidebook: A Visitor's Guide to Hell," *UC San Diego Department of Anthropology*, Jan. 30, 2009, http://pages.ucsd .edu/~dkjordan/chin/yuhlih/yuhlih-intro.html (accessed Jun 15, 2018). "The Eighteen Layers of Chinese Hell," *China Underground*, Apr. 27, 2011, https://china-underground.com/2011/04/27/the-eighteen-layers-of-chinese -hell/ (accessed Jun. 15, 2018).

her own miracle so that we may all receive it; her sacrifice is our blessing. Though it may seem sad to lose emotional memories, Meng Po serves the tea for the greater good of the soul because the amnesia prevents karmic cheating, giving people an authentic chance to ultimately escape from the wheel of rebirth.[170]

YÁNLUÓ

Yánluó is the Chinese version of Yama (the ruler of the underworld in Hindu and Buddhist traditions), but this time he's the actual deity of death rather than just the administrator of deathly affairs. Appropriately serving as overseer of the courts of hell, he wears the robes of the official judges of medieval China, but he also has bulging eyes, deep red skin, and a permanent scowl expressed on his face.

As a judge, it's up to him as to which court (or courts) of hell you will be sent to and how long your stay there will be. Despite this power, though, he's regarded as a very fair judge, and in the traditions of the Mahayana school of Buddhism, he usually just follows what your karma dictates. His strongmen "bailiffs" were two demons with human bodies, but one had the head of an ox and one had the face of a horse (just the face, not the entire head). They served as psychopomps who would guide the souls of the recently deceased to Yánluó's courtroom for sentencing. In some stories, he was demoted to overseer of the Chamber of Oil due to his habitual leniency in adjudicating cases.[171]

170   Xueting Christine Ni, *From Kuan Yin to Chairman Mao: The Essential Guide to Chinese Deities* (Newburyport: Weiser Books, 2018).
      "Meng Po," *Deities Daily*, Dec. 18, 2012, http://deitiesdaily.tumblr.com/post/38227184791/december-18th-2012-meng-po (accessed Jun. 14, 2018).
171   Harry Leong, "King Yama," *The Jade Turtle Records*, Feb. 10, 2011, http://jadeturtlerecords.blogspot.com/2011/02/king-yama_10.html (accessed Jun. 15, 2018).
      Sheng Yen, *Orthodox Chinese Buddhism: A Contemporary Chan Master's Answers to Common Questions*, trans. by Douglas Gildow and Otto Chang (Berkeley: North Atlantic Books, 2007).

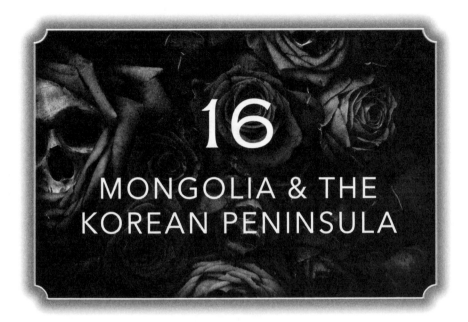

16

MONGOLIA & THE KOREAN PENINSULA

Cultural

MONGOLIA

Despite having had the largest contiguous empire in human history, Mongolia often gets overlooked when it comes to culture. It makes a brief appearance in the medieval sections of world history books and then seems to vanish as if were an extinct civilization. Mongolians do live on, though, and often in much the same way as their ancestors did in the time of the Great Khans.

From Sky to Coffin

The main reason Mongolians get overlooked is because they're a land-locked country that's not convenient to visit, they are right next to the cultural powerhouse of China, and their centuries of nomadic ways prevented the establishment of attractive glittering cities and permanent historical sites during their apogee for us nowadays to flock to as tourists. Religiously, they've been (and are) a mix of native shamanism and Vajrayana Buddhism. However, as shamanic Buddhist nomads for most of their history, they've developed some pretty interesting views and rituals on death and dying.

Arguably, their most famous funerary tradition is sky burial. Yes, the same limb-hacking, vulture-eating final disposition that we saw when we were back in Tibet. Beyond both cultures being heavily influenced by Vajrayana Buddhism, they both have similar terrains and environments that not only make this possible but also extremely practical: high elevations, lack of available wood, non-arable ground, etc.

Nevertheless, burial is not unheard of, and it's becoming increasingly practiced as Mongolia modernizes and begins to regard its own traditional sky burials as backward or in poor taste to twenty-first-century respectability. For these new funeral rites, the first thing done upon death is collection of any iconic items of the deceased (signature pair of glasses, a lucky pocket watch, that one piece of jewelry they always wore, etc.) and getting rid of them since it's believed that the strong attachment the soul has to those items will prevent it from wanting to leave for the next world. After this, the body is removed through a window or cut hole in the wall of the home as a protection measure because evil spirits will be waiting at the doorway for the fresh corpse.

Meanwhile, close family members (always males) are tasked with making a coffin and upholstering its exterior in red fabric (a remnant of Mongolia's communist era). Inside the coffin, the bottom is upholstered in green fabric (representing the earth) and the lid in blue fabric (representing the sky/heavens). Finally, the body is wrapped in a white shroud (unless it was an untimely death, in which case it's a red shroud). While this is going on, another male relative constructs a miniature, rudimentary yurt made of iron that will be placed on top of the grave after the burial and will serve as a home for the soul in the next life. By having such a hands-on participation in the final disposition of the dead, the family expedites the grieving process and comes to terms with the loss of their loved one.[172]

The Tomb of Genghis Khan

When you think of Mongolia, the first thing that comes to mind is probably the infamous Genghis Khan, the supreme and brutal ruler who utilized his charisma and military strategy to unite nomadic clans of wandering horsemen into a united empire that devastated the medieval world. However, despite being the iconic leader and founding father of modern Mongolia, his gravesite remains one of the greatest archeological mysteries to this day. No one knows where it is, and scholars speculate that it very well might be the greatest tomb find in history, with an unprecedented hoard of preserved treasures from conquered cultures throughout his vast empire, including historical relics from civilizations he completely wiped off the face of the earth.

What we *do* know is that on August 18, 1227 CE, Genghis Khan died around the age of sixty-five. Most accounts from foreigners say he died as a result of battling the Xia of China. A lot of internal accounts say that he died from falling off his horse in a hunting accident. And still many others claim he was stabbed to death in the bedroom by a Chinese princess whom he had taken hostage. While all those have different levels of veracity and dubious sources with obvious agendas, a commonality in the details of all of them is how Genghis himself had requested that when his time came, he be buried without fanfare in an undisclosed location to remain anonymous. Whether this was out of fear of tomb raiders, not

---

172   Jenny Goldade, "Cultural Spotlight: Mongolia," *Frazer Consultants*, Nov. 10, 2017, http://www.frazerconsultants.com/2017/11/cultural-spotlight -mongolian-funeral-traditions/ (accessed Jun. 15, 2018).
Sandrine Ruhlmann, "Objects and Substances of Funeral Mediation in Mongolia: Coffin, Miniature Yurt and Food Offerings," *Material Religions*, Apr. 8, 2015, http://materialreligions.blogspot.com/2015/04/objects-and -substances-of-funeral.html (accessed Jun. 15, 2018).

wanting his death to stop the expansionary momentum of his troops, or some personal reasons, we don't know.

Being a well-oiled machine drilled to take orders without question, an elite squadron of his soldiers carried his corpse and any/all items with which he was to be buried out to the middle of nowhere. They killed everyone who saw them on their long march and rode thousands of horses over the burial site to destroy any evidence of its existence. Then they killed everyone who saw them on the ride back. Their draconian discipline helped them keep Genghis's secret, and to this day, no one knows where his grave is, only that it's somewhere in Asia.

Since his death, foreign empires the world over have searched for Genghis Khan's burial site with all kinds of technology, including satellite imagery, yet success remains elusive. And here's the morbidly interesting thing about all of this… only foreigners are interested in finding the Great Khan's tomb. The Mongolians themselves believe the tomb shouldn't be found, as per Genghis's wishes. As protection measures, Mongolia had a number of potential locations internationally certified as UNESCO World Heritage Sites, making invasive scientific expeditions and research off-limits to everyone.[173]

This speaks on a very profound level to the respect of a decedent's last wishes. Yes, the discovery of Genghis Khan's tomb would spark international attention and establish an international tourist location that would pump so much foreign money into the struggling Mongolian economy (let alone the pricelessness of whatever treasures might be entombed in there). Collectively, however, Mongolian sentiment seems to be fairly unanimous

---

173 Domagoj Valjak, "To keep Genghis Khan's grave a secret: The funeral escort killed anyone who crossed their path," *The Vintage News*, Mar. 3, 2017, https://www.thevintagenews.com/2017/03/03/to-keep-genghis-khans-grave-a-secret-the-funeral-escort-killed-anyone-who-crossed-their-path/ (accessed Jun. 19, 2018).
Erin Craig, "Why Genghis Khan's Tomb can't be found," *British Broadcasting Corporation*, Jul. 19, 2017, http://www.bbc.com/travel/story/20170717-why-genghis-khans-tomb-cant-be-found (accessed Jun. 19, 2018).
"Where is Genghis Kahn buried?" *History.com*, Feb 27, 2013, https://www.history.com/news/where-is-genghis-khan-buried (accessed Jun. 19, 2018).

that if their most iconic leader wanted to be found, he would've been and certainly had the means to do so. Respect for the dead remains strong here in the steppes of Asia—a respect not often seen in the modern West, where the next of kin's personal preferences often do (and legally can at times) override a decedent's last wishes.

Mongolian Takeaway:
HONORING LAST WISHES

Last wishes are a tricky thing in the funeral industry. In the best of circumstances, the decedent has left clear instructions on what they'd like done with their body, and the next of kin is in agreement. In the worst of circumstances, there's either no death plan made or the surviving family foregoes the decedent's last wishes on everything. You see, most people don't draft and notarize last wishes in a legally binding way. Usually, an elderly (or wisely proactive) person will just tell someone what they want once death is immediately imminent... but that doesn't ensure anything.

Don't think it's all malicious, though. One of the more common deviations from following last wishes revolves around wanting to do "the right thing." Maybe dad has arranged to donate his body to science (fun fact, if you donate your body to science, they'll usually pay for a cremation when they're done and have the cremated remains delivered to you free of charge), but when the moment comes for you, the legal next of kin, to sign his body over to the research institute, you might suddenly have an emotional urge to give him a "proper" burial. No research team is going to pry your father's corpse out of your arms simply because your father authorized his body for donation. Usually, whatever the next of kin wants is what the medical and funerary professionals will abide by.

The Mongolian people's devotion to Genghis Khan's last wishes for over almost 800 years, even when they have so much to personally gain from going against his wishes, is awe-inspiring. Yet, as exemplified above, it's a very difficult thing to do. Could *you* do it?

If you've done the previous takeaway challenges, you've already gotten your last wishes in order, but do you even know what your loved one's last wishes are? Your Mongolian takeaway challenge now is to talk with your loved ones (especially parents, spouses, adult children who are unmarried, and those whose bodies will become your legal responsibility as next of kin) and find out what they want done. The important thing here is to have them explain their rationale and impetus behind why they want what they want. In this way, when the time comes, you can always refer back to and have comfort in understanding why they want you to take them off life support or want an economical no-frills cremation, thus making the decision and following their directive much easier (though still difficult).

KOREA

Once a united peninsula stretching out into the Pacific Ocean, dividing the Yellow Sea from the Sea of Japan, Korea has had it pretty rough as far as national sovereignty is concerned. For most of its early history, it was three separate kingdoms vying for total control and was eventually overtaken by the Mongol Empire and the Yuan dynasty of China. Then the peninsula was conquered by the Japanese during World War II, and after that the nation was split in two with the Soviet Union and China effectively running the northern half and the United States effectively running the southern half.

To this day, this north-south divide with the totalitarian Kim dynasty of North Korea and the US-backed democracy of South Korea remains as a political reality. This history has led to very unique funerary practices north and south of the thirty-eighth parallel that divides modern Korea.

Korean Kingdoms

First, though, we'll look at historic Korea during the era of its dynastic kingdoms, whose death rites are far different than those of today. Heavily influenced by Confucian China, death rites followed strict hierarchical protocol and separation of genders. Most uniquely, men and women were not allowed to be there during someone's last moments if they were of the opposite sex, no matter if the dying person was a close friend or immediate family member. Following this, a wail of sorrowful guilt (known as a *kok*) would be sounded by those in attendance as a way to ask for atonement if any lack of filial piety had somehow attributed to the death.

Also like Chinese tradition, most subsequent funerary rites in Korea during its various dynastic kingdoms revolved around appeasing the soul so as to not have it become a restless ghost wandering the earth. Primarily, three bowls of food, three pairs of shoes, and three payments of money would be left in the entrance of the house so as to be hospitable to and accommodate the three arriving psychopomp spirits. Failing to do this or any signs of disrespect would turn away the spirits and leave no one to escort the deceased's soul to the next life.

At the burial site, an exorcist would perform a ceremony over the grave to remove any malicious spirits that may be inhabiting it. After burial, the family would return to the site three days later with offerings of food. All throughout these funerary rites from the moment of death, men were expected to be stoic and unemotional (other than the initial *kok*) as befitting a gentlemanly scholar (the ideal of Confucian manhood). Women were expected to be over-the-top, exaggeratedly emotional (because, y'know, Confucian patriarchal expectations of women) in the belief that the more hysterically and irrationally sad women became in their mourning, the more prestigious the deceased must've been in life.[174]

North Korea

Nowadays in totalitarian North Korea, subsistence survival dictates funerary customs. Being a deeply poverty-stricken nation, North Koreans cannot afford the luxuries of time, money, or resources to give deceased loved ones a decent funeral. While one's best clothes are preferred, people are buried in whatever their surviving family can spare. This has led to guilt-ridden fears that such an improper send-off has doomed the decedent to become a restless ghost. The financial inability to show filial piety also haunts the hearts of those left behind. Moreover, poverty also places extra burdens on the three-day mourning period since expenses and the

---

174 Mimsie Ladner, "On Death, Dying, and Funerals in Korea," *Seoul Searching*, http://www.myseoulsearching.com/2013/02/korean-funeral.html (accessed Jun. 19, 2018).
Korean Embassy, "Funeral Rites," *AsianInfo.org*, 2000, http://www.asianinfo .org/asianinfo/korea/cel/funeral_rites.htm (accessed Jun. 19, 2018).

disrepair of both transportation and communication infrastructure prevent sfriends and families from being able to come see the deceased within the historically mandated three days.[175]

The funeral industry is also pretty nonexistent, and where it does exist, only the aristocratic elite can afford their services. For the masses of the common people, either the family handles everything or, if you look hard enough, elderly people in the community can be contracted (not because they're professionals, but because they've just been around a lot of death and have more experience with what to do). Certain mountains are set aside as general cemeteries, but it's up to you and your family to find a spot, dig the grave, and transport the body (all difficult to do on rocky, mountainous terrain without proper equipment).

The only exception to this familial burden is for military leaders. Basing their power on the dual cults of personality and militarism, all high-ranking military officials are mandatorily given a grand, elaborate send-off in public halls, but who is responsible for putting all this on and paying for it? That's right, the common people.

Most famously, the deaths of the two recent leaders of North Korea (Kim Il-sung and Kim Jong-il) caused mass grieving hysteria brought on by severe cult worship of these "Great Leaders," though critics have argued that the true extent of the nation's grief is impossible to quantify since it's unknown who were truly sad and who were just playing the part because it was expected of them given the repercussions of being labeled treasonous if they weren't seen as being sad enough.[176]

175 Justin Nobel, "Christmas and Death in North Korea," *Funeralwise*, Dec. 24, 2015, https://www.funeralwise.com/digital-dying/christmas-and-death-in -north-korea/ (accessed Jun. 19, 2018).

176 Mina Yoon, "What happens when you die in North Korea? A funeral system explained," *NK News*, Apr. 4, 2014, https://www.nknews.org/2014/04/what -happens-when-you-die-in-north-korea-a-funeral-system-explained/ (accessed Jun. 19, 2018).
Je Son Lee, "In North Korea, sometimes the dead come back," *NK News*, Sept. 22, 2015, https://www.nknews.org/2015/09/in-north-korea-sometimes-the -dead-come-back/ (accessed Jun. 19, 2018).

South Korea

Nowadays, down past the demilitarized zone into South Korea, much of the superstitions around traditional funerary customs have been abandoned in favor of a more Westernized, funeral industry approach. The most striking change is that cremation has overtaken burial as the most common final disposition choice, but it only did so in the recent past (the 1990s) because cemeteries were running out of space for new burials. Compared to many other nations around the world, South Korea is a small, mountainous country with a large population, thus available good land is at a premium. With land values so high and the need to save good land for the living and agriculture, the government makes it very difficult for new cemeteries to be established, so cremation became the only real other option for the populace.

One of the most philosophical death trends going on in South Korea right now is the mock funeral. This is exactly what it sounds like: a staged funeral taking place while you're still alive so that you can see what it's like to be dead before you actually die. The biggest reason for this (aside from morbid curiosity) is that it's a chance to both accept death as an inevitability and to avoid suicide should you be entertaining such visions.

More than just sitting in a box and hearing people say good things about you, this is an intensive experience attended mostly by the terminally ill and those who are seriously considering suicide (though it's also becoming popular for business/company motivational retreats). Funded by groups of funeral providers, designated centers lead people through an all-encompassing free program including dressing in traditional funeral attire, writing their last will and testament, being hammered shut in a pitch black wooden casket, and being left there for a time. Participants have shown to have a greater appreciation for life and a more centered calmness toward their own mortality upon completion of the mock funeral.[177]

177   Choe Sang-Hun, "South Koreans, Seeking New Zest for Life, Experience Their Own Funerals," *New York Times*, Oct. 26, 2016, https://www.nytimes .com/2016/10/27/world/what-in-the-world/korea-mock-funeral-coffin.html (accessed Jun. 19, 2018).

Korean Takeaway:
ALTERNATIVES

There's always more than one way to do something. Granted some ways are better than others, but "better" is oftentimes relative. Both North and South Koreans have had to find alternatives to their historical funerary traditions as forces outside their control forced them to change. In North Korea, poverty and poor infrastructure have forced them to be creative when it comes to traditional burial customs and timelines. In South Korea, the lack of burial space has made the alternative final disposition of cremation more popular. But what about you? Have you ever thought about death alternatives for yourself?

Usually, people only think their options are burial or cremation, open casket or closed casket, and maybe donating their body to science. There's so much more out there, though. Would you like an eco-friendly burial where you can decompose back into the earth? How about water cremation (aka alkaline hydrolysis) wherein, as an alternative to fire (and guzzling up all those fossil fuels), your body is placed in a mixture of water and lye and dissolved into a material similar to cremation "ashes"?

And if you are cremated, why don't you have your remains help save a coral reef? There are so many things you can do, but because we don't *need* to find alternatives, most people don't look into them (and since people don't request them, few funeral homes invest into offering or advertising them). So, your Korean takeaway challenge is to do a deep dive into all the final disposition alternatives available and see which one seems like the best way to go for you. With the internet and libraries, there really isn't anything you cannot learn about. Saying "I can't because I don't know" is the same as saying "I don't want to learn."

Deities & Legends

ERLIK

In Mongolian mythology, Erlik is the deity of death and the ruler of Tam (a hell-like underworld). His origins and subsequent rulership of Tam are oddly similar to Milton's seventeenth century epic poem *Paradise Lost* (which depicts the fall of Lucifer from Heaven and his subsequent rulership of Hell).

According to legend, Erlik was the first and most beloved living creation of the creator god Ulgan. However, Erlik was supremely prideful, which led to his questioning of and refusal to blindly follow Ulgan's cosmic laws just because Ulgan said so. The two clashed, Erlik lost, and Ulgan banished him to a place of terrors beneath the earth.

Erlik never got over this, and since he cannot stand up to Ulgan directly, he takes his frustration out on Ulgan's most accomplished creations, human beings. He does this by sending disease, death, and general misfortune to people. Because of his pride, though, he can be appeased by being worshiped as a high god, particularly through offerings of animal sacrifice.

His fiery domain of Tam is where the wicked are sent to be punished. In his sadism for more victims, Erlik is believed to tempt people to do wicked things so as to ensure that their souls will be his upon death. And if his name sounds kind of familiar, both the Marvel supervillain (Erlik Khan) and the dinosaur genus *Erlikosaurus* are named after him.[178]

GHOST WOMEN OF KOREA

The heavy Confucian influence in East Asian culture had historically divided men and women into their own places in society with men wielding all power and women being subservient, and Korea was no exception. Due to this division and lack of interaction between the sexes, men (the

---

[178] "Erlikosaurus," *Prehistoric Wildlife*, http://www.prehistoric-wildlife.com/species/e/erlikosaurus.html (accessed Jun. 19, 2018).
"Erlik," *Encyclopedia.com*, https://www.encyclopedia.com/environment/encyclopedias-almanacs-transcripts-and-maps/erlik (accessed Jun. 19, 2018).
V. A. Burnakov, "Erlik khan in the traditional worldview of the khakas," *Archaeology, Ethnology and Anthropology of Eurasia* 39:1, Mar. 2011.

writers, storytellers, and leaders in society…because Confucian patriarchy) developed a mystification of women. The unknowns about women and the unknowns of death merged together and caused men to make the major ghouls in Korean folklore be women. Three in particular stand out.

Mul gwishin are the best known in the West. They have deathly pale skin, long black hair covering their faces, and are soaking wet (inspirations for the ghost girls in the Japanese films *The Ring* and *The Grudge*). Officially, they are the wandering souls of those who died a watery death. They lurk in any body of water (including bathtubs), and attempt to grab and drown living people for company due to their perpetual loneliness. In Korean slang, *mul gwishin jeokjeon* ("water ghost tactics") is a phrase referring to metaphorically pulling people down out of jealousy for their success.[179]

Cheonyeo gwishin are the ghosts of females who died as unmarried virgins. You see, in Confucian thought, daughters are put on this earth to serve their parents and brothers, marry well, and produce more sons to continue to nurture the ancestral line. Women who die as virgins are seen as having failed these main points of filial piety around which their whole existence revolves (I know, I know…but again, Confucian patriarchy). In being "failures," they are thought to have unfinished business and wander the earth restlessly. In particular, they're believed to haunt their family until the family sets up a ghost marriage (a legally recognized marriage between two unmarried dead people/corpses), which has created an underground black market of matchmakers and corpse trafficking that still lingers on in East Asia (especially rural China, where the practice

179   Benjamin Welton, "10 Monstrosities From Korean Folklore," *The Trebuchet*, Jun. 27, 2016, http://literarytrebuchet.blogspot.com/2016/06/10 -monstrosities-from-korean-folklore.html (accessed Jun. 20, 2018).

originated). In appearance, they are similar to the mul gwishin in having a deathly pallor and long, unkempt hair that can obscure their body.[180]

Gumiho (also called *kumiho*) is a shape-shifting ghost whose main appearance is as a beautiful woman with nine fox tails (sometimes also with fox ears and a muzzle-like nose). It is said that when a fox lives to be 1,000 years old, it becomes a gumiho who hungers to devour human organs. They prefer the shape of a beautiful woman because they've found it to be the easiest and most proven way to attract men to a secluded place where they can prey on them. Very similar to the nine-tailed *kitsune* of Japan, the biggest difference is that these Korean ghost foxes are malicious predators while kitsune are just mischievous tricksters. In addition to hanging around graveyards scavenging for the organs of freshly buried cadavers, gumiho have the opportunity to turn into full humans if they can abstain from eating human meat for 1,000 days (a feat rarely done).[181]

JEOSEUNG SAJA

Jeoseung Saja (also spelled *Jeoseung Sacha*) is the Korean equivalent to the Grim Reaper. He's the personification of death whose duty it is to take the souls of the recently deceased and guide them into the afterlife. He's always a male, always has a human physique (albeit with pale skin and sunken eyes), and always wears a Joseon dynasty–style traditional Korean *gat* (tall, wide-brimmed hat) and all-black formal wear (*hanbok* in South Korea, *Joseon-ot* in North Korea). Known to hang around places of recent death (hospitals, accident scenes, mortuaries, cemeteries, etc.), he

---

180   Kyle Hovanec, "Korea Haunt: The Most Famous Korean Ghosts," *SeoulSync*, http://seoulsync.com/culture/traditional/famous-korean-ghosts (accessed Jun. 20, 2018).
Vicky Xiuzhong Xu and Bang Xiao, "Ghost marriages: A 3,000-year-old tradition of wedding the dead is still thriving in rural China," *Australian Broadcasting Corporation*, May 2, 2018, https://www.abc.net.au/news/2018 -04-07/ghost-marriages-in-rural-china-continue-to-thrive/9608624 (accessed Oct. 30, 2018).

181   Mimsie Ladner, ""Who's Who: Korean Ghosts, Goblins, and Gumiho," *Seoul Searching*, http://www.myseoulsearching.com/2013/10/korean -ghosts-goblins-gumiho.html (accessed Jun. 20, 2018).

can only be seen by people who are about to die. He can also be seen in dreams (though dreaming of him means you're going to die soon too). Officially, though, even if you see him, he would only come for your soul if he said your name aloud.[182] Nowadays, he's a popular character featured in Korean television dramas and popular art across all media.

182 "Jeoseung Saja," *Le Grenier de Clio,* https://mythologica.fr/coree/jeoseung.htm (accessed Jun. 20, 2018).

17
JAPAN

Cultural

SHINTO

Shinto is very interesting because it's a unique rarity in the modern world. It's an animistic religion (believing all things animate and inanimate are sacred and have a spirit called *kami*) that has survived wholly intact to modern times as a major belief system in one of the most technologically advanced and economically powerful countries on earth. Having never been colonized by a European power and after centuries of strictly enforced immigration and emigration prohibitions, outside influences in Japan were kept to a minimum for most of its history, thus allowing its native religion of Shinto to flourish and thrive without much competition.

The only real outside influence the Japanese had before the early modern era was from China and Chinese-influenced Korea, but more on that later.

The Religion That Isn't a Religion

Truth be told, Shinto isn't even regarded as a religion in Japan. It's been so ingrained in the culture and national consciousness since early human history on the islands that the beliefs of Shinto are seen as just how the world is and not a theological philosophy for the world. "Religion" is seen as mostly associated with Buddhism and Christianity (the other two current big faiths in Japan), and modern Japanese culture is a mix of Shinto and Buddhism (with Christian traditions here and there for "funsies"). In fact, there's a popular self-effacing joke in Japan saying how they're "born Shinto, marry Christian, and die Buddhist," referring to the different religious rituals that are popularly practiced at each of these major stages of life for pretty much everyone, regardless of personal adherence.[183]

The Impurity of Death

In purely Shinto views of death, the afterlife is a dark, gloomy place with a river that separates it from the world of the living. It's believed that during large festivals and through specialized rituals, the living can interact with the dead for communication and magical favors. There's also a special, enhanced connection to spirits of your ancestors, all of whom are easier to contact and more inclined to assist you (especially with protection magic) through rituals.[184]

Death itself, however, is seen as impure. The cessation of life, departure of your *kami*, and putrefaction of the cadaver are regarded as the antithesis to the life-giving, vibrant, clean purity that Shinto adherents seek to embody. Because of that, cemeteries are forbidden on holy grounds such as temples and shrines, and priests (who are considered too pure to han-

---

183   R. Kisala, "Japanese Religions," *Nanzan Guide to Japanese Religions*, ed. by P Swanson, and C. Chilson (Honolulu: University of Hawaii Press, 2005).

184   "Understanding Shinto: Japanese tradition and ritual provide comfort for mourners," *eCondolence.com*, http://www.econdolence.com/learn/articles/shinto-understanding-shinto/ (accessed Jun. 20, 2018).

dle a corpse) are absent at funeral services but can aid in leading mourning rituals. The family (and in older times, the village community) undertakes the responsibilities of funerary and burial arrangements.

This impurity associated with death partly explains why Japan has *the* highest cremation rate in the world (close to 100 percent).[185] Fire is seen as a purer, cleaner final disposition compared to burial, and because (like in Korea) land space is extremely limited in modern Japan, having cemeteries to accommodate everyone would cause major issues. But a Japanese cremation is different from a Western cremation in that it's a more communal, family affair with macabre duties and morbid symbolism designed to help overcome grief and attain closure.

The burning of the body is the same. Fire from an industrial Japanese crematory does the same biological degradation as fire from an industrial Western crematory. You see, a little-known fact about cremations is that it doesn't reduce your body to "ashes" (which are technically called "cremated remains," or "cremains" to be cute, and expedient amongst funeral industry personnel). All of your organic matter is burned away, but a lot of your bigger inorganic bones remain intact (albeit highly charred and fragmented). In the Western funeral industry, crematory operators rake these bones fragments into a big industrial blender (awesomely called a "cremulator") that grinds the bones into the sandy powder that you receive back as "ashes."

Why do we do this? It's because it's actually illegal in a number of US states to return cremated remains that are "recognizable" as skeleton bits, but mostly it's because the funeral industry believes it's too distressing for the family to see these bones (another example of death being hidden from the modern world).[186]

---

185 "Ashes to ashes: How common is cremation?" *The Economist*, https://www
.economist.com/graphic-detail/2012/10/31/ashes-to-ashes (accessed Jun.
20, 2018).

186 Michael Brown, "What really happens when you die?" *The Guardian*, Feb.
15, 2008, https://www.theguardian.com/lifeandstyle/2008/feb/16/
healthandwellbeing.weekend2 (accessed Jun. 22, 2018).

Bone Collecting Ceremony

The Japanese funeral industry believes the exact opposite about hiding the reality of death from grieving family members, and the traditional cultural ritual of *kotsuage* emphasizes witnessing and interacting with the identifiable bone fragments left over from the cremation process. This is done by pulling the charred and fragmented bones out of the cremation machine on their tray and letting them cool. Then the family comes with special elongated chopsticks with which they pick up each fragment of bone and place in an urn.

One must always start from the feet up (so the person can be "upright" in the urn), and people can help each other by lifting the bones together or passing them to one another (outside of a kotsuage, it's a major social faux pas in Japanese culture to mutually lift things or pass things with chopsticks since that's symbolic of this funerary ritual). At the very end, non-immediate family can gather the remaining cremation dust (a ritual called *bunkotsu*) to keep for their own funerary shrines at home.[187]

Shinto vs. Buddhism

In regard to that national Japanese self-effacing joke I mentioned earlier, the one about being born Shinto, marrying Christian, and dying Buddhist, it's like that because no one wants to die Shinto when there are better options available. Via a Shinto death, you have a nonoptimal afterlife destination, a limited ability to grieve (Shinto emphasizes a stoic approach to loss and regulates outward grief to only during designated rituals), and no guarantee to reunite with your loved ones in an afterlife. So, it's easy to see why most Japanese opt for a Buddhist funeral because Buddhism has a more positive, hopeful spin on what happens after death and gives more leeway with emotions.

187   Richard Martin, "Japanese cremation ashes rituals: Kotsuage and Bunkotsu," *Scattering Ashes*, Jun. 21, 2013, https://scattering-ashes.co.uk/different -cultures/japanese-cremation-ashes-rituals-kotsuage-bunkotsu/ (accessed Jun. 22, 2018).

Buddhists get reincarnated over and over until they reach a state of blissful nirvana, so all the focus of a Buddhist funeral is on the decedent's rebirth, rather than the eternal unknown and uncertainty of the Shinto afterlife at a Shinto funeral. Faced with those options, the Japanese overwhelmingly prefer Buddhist funerary ceremonies over Shinto ones, even if they weren't really Buddhists in life.[188]

Shinto Takeaway:
KEEP MOVING

In the legendary film *Gone with the Wind*, the character of Scarlett O'Hara is constantly at odds with the overwhelming difficulties of life that fate (and often she herself) deals to her. Though visually and emotionally battered by each dealt tragedy, she knows that she has no other option but to keep moving forward and persevere. Even when things are undeniably overwhelming, she does what little she can in the moment and trusts that, little by little, moment by moment, she'll overcome whatever difficulty presents itself to her.

Shinto has the same stoic resolve as that Southern belle when it comes to confronting the difficulties of death and dying. The death of a loved one is a supremely sad and emotionally crippling experience that everyone will experience sooner or later, and often more than once. Though our personal world has just been shattered, the world at large keeps moving without us. A time to grieve is important, but tragic is the tale of those who can no longer move forward, being left behind as the world continues. The stoic attitude of self-control through adversity is exemplified in Shinto's approach to the death of others (much akin to the "Keep Calm, Carry On" motto in Britain during the blitzkrieg of World War II).

And when stoicism is too hard for the present moment, Shinto adherents switch to Buddhist funerary protocol. They keep going even if they have to progress in way that is different from their usual because their

---

188   Elizabeth Kenny, "Shintō Mortuary Rites in Contemporary Japan," *Cahiers d'Extrême-Asie* vol. 9, 1996, https://www.persee.fr/doc/asie_0766-1177 _1996_num_9_1_1124 (accessed Jun. 22, 2018).

usual way is too difficult for this particular moment. There's no shame in that. And so, your Shinto takeaway challenge is to build up your ability to keep moving. Don't shy away from life experiences because they're difficult or require a lot of effort.

While there's no way to fully prepare for losing a loved one, the more you build up this internal discipline in other areas (such as sticking to a diet or exercise regime, putting business before pleasure, or foregoing immediate gratification in order to save for something greater later on), the more you will trust yourself to keep moving forward when a grand tragedy does come to pass. Yes, it's uncomfortable and involves work that isn't all fun, but that's what training is. Developing strength takes action, and you *will* be sore from each "workout," but you'll be stronger from it for the next burden you'll have to carry. And there will *always* be more burdens placed upon you in the future.

Who knows, maybe with your newly developed strength and discipline, you can even help shoulder the burden of others lost in grief over that same loved one. Just keep moving. The world will not stop for you no matter how bad you feel, so learn how to just keep moving.

ZEN BUDDHISM

When it comes to Buddhism in Japan, the Mahayana branch of the faith reigns supreme. However, when it comes to Buddhist death in Japan, one Mahayana school's morbid rituals and funerary rites are the favorite: Zen Buddhism. This school of Mahayana Buddhism emphasizes minimalism away from the dependence on scripture, iconography, and outside distractions. The focus is on the mind, from which all things arise, are interpreted, and acted upon. To control your mind is to control your world.

In particular, it's the Sōto sect of Zen Buddhism that's most popular in Japan. In death rituals, almost all Japanese Buddhists follow Sōto protocol regardless if they, in life, adhered to another sect of Zen Buddhism, to another school of Mahayana Buddhism, or even to Buddhism at all for that matter.

Historically, Zen Buddhism originated in China during the Tang dynasty in the eighth century CE. There, it was called Chan Buddhism, and was the product of mixing Mahayana Buddhism with Taoism, wherein Buddhist self-discipline of the mind and Taoist reverence for not fighting against the natural flow of life merged together into a unique practice. When Chan Buddhism arrived in Japan from Korea and became renamed "Zen," it was funerals and death that ultimately allowed it to gain traction and flourish throughout the archipelago.

Posthumous Prominence

By virtue of its minimalism, Zen ceremonies weren't very flashy and couldn't attract much attention to gain new followers like the grand ceremonies of other Buddhist traditions of thirteenth-century Japan could. What Zen *did* have going for itself, though, was the uniqueness of not having funerary rites for laypeople, only for ordained monks. Thus, if a Zen layperson was in need of funerary rites, they'd be posthumously ordained as a monk so that the proper rituals could then be performed. This after-death ascension in social importance appealed to the common folk of medieval Japan.

Meanwhile, among the upper echelons of Japanese aristocracy, Zen and its minimalist chic were becoming very en vogue as a refined alternative to other, more garish schools of Buddhism, and the Zen funerals of the aristocracy followed the same austere protocols and postmortem ordination as those of the lower classes. This great equalizer of the economic classes in their death ceremonies further fueled interest in Zen among the large masses of the poor and helped make the Sōto Zen funeral the popular standard for most Japanese to this day as well as the most popular school of Mahayana Buddhism in the country.[189]

Theater of the Macabre

In the early days of Buddhism in Japan, no other aristocrat in Japanese history took more advantage of their death to create a theater of the

---

189 William M. Bodiford, "Zen in the Art of Funerals: Ritual Salvation in Japanese Buddhism," *History of Religions* 32:2, 1992.
Bernard Faure, *The Rhetoric of Immediacy: A Cultural Critique of Chan/Zen Buddhism* (Princeton: Princeton University Press, 1991).

macabre and teach the Buddhist lesson of fleeting impermanence to the masses than Tachibana no Kachiko (also known as Empress Danrin). She lived and ruled during the very beginning of the now-legendary Heian period of Japan in the ninth century CE. Though extremely educated and an ultradevout Buddhist, she was best known in her own time for her exceptional beauty, which overshadowed everything she did.

All anyone could ever compliment her on was her beautiful looks, which she regarded as superficial and frivolous. Frustrated by this (even on her deathbed at age sixty-five), she mandated in her will that the elaborate funeral ceremonies and rituals reserved for Empress of Japan be prohibited. Instead, she willed that her corpse be dressed in a simple, unadorned kimono and be thrown out into the streets of Kyoto like trash to be eaten by dogs and decompose in public view.

By doing this, she hoped to show the public that beauty (even her legendary beauty) was impermanent. The masses would witness how her beautiful body would bloat, become infested by maggots, and rot in all its ugly putridness. Naturally, the entire court and royal family were stunned, but since she was the empress, no one dared defy her last wishes. The spot of her open-air decomposition can still be seen today in Kyoto at what is now dubbed "the Crossroad of Corpses."[190]

Sakura Sakura

Much like the exemplary cadaver of Tachibana no Kachiko, a more internationally well-known icon of Japan gained its fame due to its poetic symbolism of death and impermanence: the cherry blossom. One of the national flowers of Japan, cherry blossoms bloom for only a short window of time every year, and their petals' fragility leaves them susceptible to even the slightest winds that will inevitably destroy them. Zen Buddhism

---

190   Zack Davisson, "Katabira no Tsuji—The Crossroad of Corpses," *Hayakumonogatari Kaidankai*, Oct. 31, 2013, https://hyakumonogatari .com/2013/10/31/katabira-no-tsuji-the-crossroad-of-corpses/ (accessed Nov. 19, 2018).

utilized cherry blossoms as a metaphor for the fragility of life and the brief, passing nature of existence on the earth.

The samurai further popularized the death imagery of the cherry blossom since they resonated strongly with how the flowers never get old, wither, and die. Rather, much like many samurai themselves, cherry blossoms are cut down in their prime when they are still their most attractive and vibrant. Though physically fit and oftentimes well-educated, a healthy and attractive samurai could have his life extinguished at his bodily peak, albeit at the end of a katana blade rather than a moderate breeze. Years later, the Japanese kamikaze pilots of World War II similarly adopted the morbid metaphor of the cherry blossom for their own foreseeably short-lived lives.[191]

Death Poems

Paying artistic tribute to the Buddhist tenet of impermanence reached new levels of Zen mastery in the form of *jisei* (death poems). Often in the form of a haiku or a tanka (a five-line haiku), these literary farewells to life were often written by samurai on the eve of battle, by warriors and noblemen upon committing ritualized suicide (*seppuku*), or even by monks and regular folks reflecting on the ephemeral nature of life itself. Sometimes they could be comical, sometimes they could be poignant, but they were always personal Zen reflections on death as a natural part of life.[192]

The closely related dark cousin of the death poem, the suicide note, is also infamous in Japan. Though declining, Japan has consistently held high rates of suicide compared to similarly developed countries. Nowadays, the statistics average out to about fifty-nine lives lost every single day per

---

191 Wesley Baines, "The Symbolism of the Cherry Blossom," *Beliefnet*, http://www.beliefnet.com/inspiration/the-symbolism-of-the-cherry-blossom.aspx (accessed Jun. 25, 2018).

192 Eugene Thacker, "Black Illumination: Zen and the poetry of death," *The Japan Times*, Jul. 2, 2016, https://www.japantimes.co.jp/culture/2016/07/02/books/black-illumination-zen-poetry-death/#.WzFgfKdKhPY (accessed Jun. 25, 2018).

year in Japan due to suicide.[193] Particularly grim is the statistical evidence that since 2014, suicide has become the leading cause of death for children (aged ten to nineteen) in Japan, and this child rate is only increasing despite the overall suicide rate in the country declining.[194]

Suicide Forest

These high numbers are a result of a mix of Japan's expectations of social uniformity and its cultural tolerance of suicide as honorable. You see, in Japan, to stand out or be different is socially frowned upon. "The nail that sticks out gets hammered" is a good metaphor, and this severe disapproval of individuality over the communal whole has its consequences. At best, these expectations of social uniformity have made Japan one of the safest, least crime-ridden, most efficient, healthiest, and cleanest industrialized nations for its size and population. At worst, they've made many Japanese an internal pressure cooker of depression, isolation, unrealistic expectations, untreated mental health issues, and suicidal thoughts.

No place in Japan is more notorious for suicide than Aokigahara forest on the northwestern slopes of Mount Fuji. This forest has become a morbid mecca for the suicidal in Japan (much like the Golden Gate Bridge or Niagara Falls in the US). During a hike among all the beautiful flora and fauna in the forest, you'll encounter numerous suicide prevention signs and, quite possibly if you wander off-trail, bodies hanging from the trees at various stages of decomposition (especially in March, the end of Japan's fiscal year).

Most of this popularity as a suicide destination comes as a result of its past popularity building upon itself (infamous for being infamous), but a lot of it also comes from both its association with the mythical practice of *ubasute* (abandoning the elderly alone to die in nature because fam-

---

193 Annemarie Luck, "Suicide in Japan: the Reasons, the Statistics, and the TELL Support," *Tokyo Weekender*, Aug. 18, 2017, https://www.tokyoweekender.com/2017/08/suicide-in-japan-the-reasons-the-statistics-and-the-tell-support/ (accessed Oct. 31, 2018).

194 Olivier, "Child suicide in Japan: the leading cause of death in children," *Humanium*, Feb. 27, 2017, https://www.humanium.org/en/child-suicide-in-japan-the-leading-cause-of-death-in-children/ (accessed Oct. 31, 2018).

ily resources can no longer support unproductive members) and it being featured in two highly popular and influential Japanese books: the 1960s novel *Tower of Waves* by Seichō Matsumoto, wherein doomed lovers take their own lives in Aokigahara, and the 1990s nonfiction how-to book *The Complete Manual of Suicide* by Wataru Tsurumi, wherein specific tips on how to kill yourself in Aokigahara (among other places) are outlined. Much to the disapproval of the locals and the Japanese government, the forest has become something of an international hotspot for necro-tourism where foreigners and Japanese alike come due to their dark fascination and morbid curiosity and in the hopes of stumbling upon a real corpse out in nature.[195]

AIBO, Robot

In modern Japan, the tragedy of unexpectedly losing a loved one also applies to pets … even if those pets are electronic. End-of-life ceremonies for nonsentient objects and artificial intelligence is a new trend. Robot funerals (think funerals for robots, not funerals worked by robots) have become a recent phenomenon, but they're not for just any robots; they are held for Sony AIBO robotic dogs in particular. If you remember (or were alive back then), these were the toy robot dogs that were flying off the shelves in the late 90s and early 2000s that had very advanced AI that allowed them to act and react like actual pet dogs without any of the inconveniences of biological dogs (vet visits, food, water, potty training, poop walks, etc.).

These dogs, thanks to their advanced AI (which included the ability to become particularly familiar with various specific humans), became part of the family in many Japanese households, especially to the lonely and the elderly in need of companionship. The miracle of Sony AIBO dogs

195   Michael Nedelman, "Inside Japan's 'Suicide Forest'," *CNN*, Jan. 4, 2018, https://www.cnn.com/2018/01/03/health/japan-suicide-forest-intl/index .html (accessed Nov. 19, 2018).
Jordy Meow, "Japan's Suicide Forest: Aokigahara," *Offbeat Japan*, Jun. 6, 2018, https://offbeatjapan.org/aokigahara-the-suicide-forest/ (accessed Nov. 19, 2018).

(on which they were partly marketed) was that they could technically live forever, since, if there was ever an issue with their hardware or software, you could send your AIBO to Sony to fix it. That was true at least until 2014 when the company closed its AIBO repair department to cut costs. Since then, new generations of smarter AIBOs have been engineered (with their own repair departments established), but for the owners of the original AIBOs sold between 1999 and 2006, Sony never revived their repair operations.

This means that the remaining original AIBOs have been slowly "dying" due to their hardware or software inevitably malfunctioning, something their owners never thought could happen when they bought them twenty years ago. A cottage industry of first generation AIBO repair shops has since emerged, but without new parts in production by Sony, there's only so much these third-party repairs can do. Consequently, an AIBO "organ donation" system has come into being wherein the owners of a terminally failing AIBO donate their dog to a repository of dead AIBOs from which independent repair shops can salvage parts to help fix any other failing AIBOs that have a chance at being saved if only they have the right replacement part.

Before the donation, though, owners of first generation AIBOs are commonly holding Buddhist funerals for their dogs just as they would for any other loved one. Accompanied with prayer cards and personal messages tied to their necks like collars, Buddhist monks bless the AIBOs and perform the regular funerary rituals that they would for any other living being that had been loved. Then, instead of a burial or cremation, the Buddhist monks help donate the "dead" AIBOs to the donor repositories to help save the lives of "sick" AIBOs all over Japan. Still, these efforts are only delaying the inevitable, and there will come a time when the last AIBO becomes irreparable, reflecting the impermanence of all things, even AI.[196]

Zen Buddhist Takeaway:
THE POETRY OF DEATH

If everything is in the mind, then reality is subjective. A thing only exists in the way we perceive it, and everything we perceive is filtered through our physical senses, emotional distortions, and prior experiences/education. So, nothing is truly objective since no one can really see a singular thing in the exact same way as someone else, however similar. Thus, death is also subjective.

In Zen Buddhism, the death poetry of monks, samurai, and the literate middle class transformed the gloomy terrors of cessation into beautifully artistic interpretations of what dreams may come after the big sleep. Your Zen Buddhist takeaway challenge now is to write your own death poem. It can be a structured haiku, it can rhyme, it can be a simple couplet. However you want to poetically reflect and write about your own mortality is just fine. You may even surprise yourself with how life-affirming writing about death can be. Everything is subjective, so how do *you* see your own impermanence?

Deities & Legends

IZANAMI

Izanami (whose full name is *Izanami no mikoto*) is the Shinto goddess of creation and death who helped create the islands of Japan along with her husband Izanagi. According to the *Kojiki* (the oldest existing Japanese classic tale), Izanami was experiencing labor complications while pregnant

---

196 Justin McCurry, "Japan: robot dogs get solemn Buddhist send-off at funerals," *The Guardian*, May 3, 2018, https://www.theguardian.com/world/2018/may/03/japan-robot-dogs-get-solemn-buddhist-send-off-at-funerals (accessed Jun. 25, 2018).
Caitlin Doughty, *From Here to Eternity: Traveling the World to Find the Good Death* (New York: W. W. Norton & Company, 2017).}

with her son Kagutsuchi (deity of fire), which caused the child to inadvertently burn her birth canal, leading to further complications that eventually resulted in her death.

Inconsolable, Izanagi pleaded to the high gods that he be allowed to retrieve her from the underworld. The gods consented but told him to wait until they gave him permission to enter the underworld. The waiting stretched on for a long, long time, and Izanagi became so impatient and desperate that he went into the underworld to bring back his wife before being officially sanctioned by the high gods to do so. When he arrived, he found that she was still a rotting corpse, and by coming too soon, he halted her slow regeneration. Angered by this, Izanami chased her husband with fatal rage. He only narrowly managed to escape from the underworld and seal her in. This led to Izanami being the de facto deity of death and the underworld where she still rules, regenerating in darkness.[197]

SHINIGAMI

Shinigami are the Shinto equivalent to a proactive Grim Reaper. They are supernatural spirits that don't just escort you to the afterlife, they tempt and invite you toward your own death too. Most often, they do this by giving people suicidal thoughts, and lingering around stereotypical hot spots for suicides (cliffs, railroads, rooftops, etc.).

It's said that a human could become a Shinigami if they were murdered or killed while having ill-intent in their heart. These negative emotions would compel the soul to linger on earth attracting others to commit murders or kill themselves at the very same place that the Shinigami had died. Interestingly, though, Shinigami don't appear in Japanese literature or folktales until the Edo period (seventeenth–nineteenth century CE), leading scholars to believe that European stories of the Grim Reaper and

---

197 Mark Cartwright, "Izanami and Izanagi," *Ancient History Encyclopedia*, Dec. 6, 2012, https://www.ancient.eu/Izanami_and_Izanagi/ (accessed Jun. 28, 2018).

the Western emphasis on death as a negative led to the inception of the Shinigami rather than them being purely Shinto-inspired death spirits.[198]

TETSUMONKAI & THE SELF-MUMMIFIED MONKS

Tetsumonkai was an ascetic monk of the Shingon Buddhist order (a school of Vajrayana Buddhism) who wandered around Japan in the early 1800s. While drifting through the outlying Edo area (what is now Tokyo), he came upon a village plagued by an unknown disease that was making people go blind. He tried to help, but none of his medical knowledge was effective. A devout and deeply compassionate Buddhist, he was committed to increasing his spiritual power to help the village, and he did this via self-mutilation.

You see, Shingon Buddhist monks believed that one's spiritual and physical powers are inversely proportionate, meaning the weaker one is physically, the stronger his/her spiritual power is and vice versa. Additionally, they also believed that they could take on the suffering of other living beings, effectively healing the sick by taking on their sickness for them. So, Tetsumonkai gouged out his left eye to physically weaken himself and take on the village's plague of blindness. Miraculously, the plague soon ended, and Tetsumonkai became emboldened in his altruistic masochism to take on the Shingon challenge of *sokushinbutsu* (starving yourself in such a manner that your body mummifies) to become an "instant Buddha" and better help the villagers.

Tetsumonkai adopted a rigorous exercise routine to lose all fat (since the heat and moisture generated by fat in a dead body helps activate bacteria and accelerate decomposition), nourishing himself with only salt, tree bark, nuts, seeds, roots, and urushi tea (an infusion of the poison ivy relative *Toxicodendron verniciluum*, known as the base ingredient to create Japanese lacquer). This tea not only dehydrated him through fever-induced sweating, vomiting, and diarrhea, but it also built up a toxicity in his body

198 Geller, "Shinigami," *Mythology.net*, Oct. 28, 2016, https://mythology.net/japanese/japanese-gods/shinigami/ (accessed Jun. 28, 2018).

that would repel maggots from eating his corpse. All the while, he sat in perfect meditational stillness to waste away his muscles, thus further emaciating himself.

After about five years (yes, YEARS) of this, once Tetsumonkai knew he was close to death, the villagers helped bury him alive in a small crate just big enough for him to sit in the lotus position. With only a thin bamboo tube used for air, he would ring a bell every day until he died from slow suffocation. One thousand days after the bell stopped ringing, the villagers exhumed his body and placed his self-mummified corpse in the nearby temple.

Up until the twentieth century (when assisting with religious suicide was made illegal in Japan), hundreds of Shingon Buddhist monks attempted to become sokushinbutsu, but only about twenty-some succeeded. Nevertheless, they can still be seen on display in temples throughout the country (especially in the northern prefectures), including Tetsumonkai himself. Their shrines are honored as macabre mementos of monks who arduously prepared themselves to die for the magical benefit of the masses.[199]

199   Ichiro Hori, "Self-Mummified Buddhas in Japan. An Aspect of the Shugen-Dô ('Mountain Asceticism') Sect," *History of Religions*, 1:2, 1962.
Caitlin Doughty. "The Self Mummified Monks," *Ask A Mortician*, Mar. 24, 2017, https://www.youtube.com/watch?v=FlmMtZ4J3qQ (accessed Jun. 28, 2018).

18
EAST ASIAN MAGICAL COMMUNITY

ACCEPTANCE OF THE INEVITABLE

In my own personal spirituality, I guess you could call me eclectic. Though if that's too much of a cop-out fence-sitter answer (which it kind of is), I'd say I'm more Taoist than anything. Taoism has been my guiding principle for the latter half of my life now since I first began really studying it (in the curriculum of my Catholic high school's World Religions class of all places). So, I thought it'd be nice to get some personal time with you outside of being a global tour guide and share a bit of my own experience with loss that was softened by a parable from ancient China on the Tao and death.

There are many variations on this parabolic legend, but the general story tells of how the wife of Zhuangzi (an influential Taoist philosopher from the fourth century BCE) became ill and died. Hearing about her passing, one of Zhuangzi's oldest friends, named Huizi, decided to travel to pay him a visit to help out and be there for him during this difficult time.

However, when Huizi arrived and approached Zhuangzi's home, he heard his friend playing joyful music and singing. Worried that his friend had snapped under the weight of grief, he tried to bring Zhuangzi back to reality and remind him that this wasn't appropriate behavior. His wife was gone forever, and he should be sad.

Zhuangzi sagely countered by explaining that he already had his moments of sorrow over his loss and that to dwell upon it after getting the grief out of his system didn't make much sense. He knew she was dying for a while while she was ill, he was prepared for it, and he had accepted it. It just didn't make sense to him that he should be expected to mourn in a prescribed, formulaic way when he had already accepted she was going die. The best thing he could do now was be happy, as she would've wanted him to be. It would dishonor her and her period of illness to suffer as if her death was a surprise.

This Taoist lesson on acceptance of the inevitable and how that affects the grieving process was something I learned firsthand. This was back when I was in college, a couple weeks before I was set to study abroad in South America. At the time, maternal grandparents lived with my immediate family all in the same house together, and one night, my grandpa sat me down, out of the blue, to give me grandfatherly advice on living for an extended time in another country (from his own experience being stationed abroad during the Korean War).

But then he held an extended pause, locked eyes with me, and said that if he dies while I'm away, he doesn't want me coming to the funeral. I brushed it off with something like "Oh, Grandpa... I'll see you when I get back." His face remained serious, and he kept telling me again and again that he didn't want me wasting a whole bunch of money to fly all the way back to California just to see him dead and lying in a casket. He said all this with an assertive, matter-of-fact calmness without the hint of any of it being a joke. He made sure that I understood he was serious.

About three months into my South American adventure, I received a long-distance call from my sister. Grandpa had died. He just never woke up one morning. Although old, there were no signs that he was going to pass away that particular night, let alone anytime soon. At that moment, I knew that he knew all along. How he knew, I have no idea, but he *knew* he was going to die during my year abroad. Being the patriarch of a large, extended Mexican family, his "unexpected" death brought about a profound amount of heavy grief to everyone... except me.

Mind you, this was the first death of a close loved one that I had experienced, and I had always imagined that I'd be more depressed, more despondent in grief. I remember wondering why I didn't feel more broken with grief than a lot of my family back in California who were there with the body to get closure.

The only explanation I can give is the one Zhuangzi gave to his friend in that legendary Taoist tale. Thanks to my grandpa's own acceptance of his imminent death and his forcing me to accept his imminent death before the fact, I was better prepared for it. Of course I was sad, but he gave me the gift of a shorter, less painful grieving period, and to worriedly ruminate on "not being sad enough" would be to miss the point of that gift entirely. So, I was okay with being okay about it. I had accepted the way things came to be... before they came to be. Honoring his wishes, I didn't go to the funeral. He gave me the closure I needed before I knew I'd need it... all thanks to him being able to accept his own death and openly talk about it with me.

EASTERN MOURNING RITUALS

Back again to talk about death in Buddhism is our friend Dannie Phan. When we recently met her in Southeast Asia, she gave us a very behind-the-camera view (befitting a photographer like Dannie) on a Buddhist funerary chant. Now, though, I've invited her back again to give a more personal account of what it's like to be a young person living in the West who suddenly has to dive back into millennia-old Eastern mourning rituals upon the loss of a loved one. As she'll explain, sometimes it can be awkward, but in the end, holding strong to her cultural traditions passed down through the generations is well worth it in helping to ease a very difficult time.

> Over the course of ten months in 2017 we lost three people on my mother's side of the family—a person from each generation. My parents have our funeral traditions well-documented and often guide our extended family. Many of these traditions and superstitions that I'll list below are different than the Western approach to the mourning process but I feel that in many ways they're helpful to bring the community together to grieve for a substantial amount of time.

Vegetarianism:

> The very first thing that occurs is switching over to a vegetarian diet for forty-nine to one hundred days if you're an immediate relative or descendant of the person that has passed. This is probably the most challenging task for me since I have a habit of eating out with friends, finding pleasure in eating different foods, and trying new restaurants. After messing up the first week for my grandmother's passing I was pretty upset, but I decided that if I couldn't be vegetarian that I would at least be mindful and be thankful for what I was consuming. Every meal became a moment when I thought of her. For those that believe in the potential of reincarnation, one of the reasons for vegetarianism is that it recognizes that you and your loved one could be reborn into a different living being that you'd someday eat. I think this is very easy to forget since we live in a country where meat is processed and in packages.

Wearing White Instead of Black:

> When talking about the difference of Buddhist funerals with friends, the first thing that I bring up is the uniqueness of the clothes that we wear. White clothing is typically worn to symbolize the mourning of family members. Direct descendants are given white tunics and headbands blessed by monks to wear during every prayer for the next forty-nine days. Depending on your relationship with the deceased, your headgear will vary. Direct decedents will wear a plain white headband or hood. A

grandchild from a daughter would wear a white headband with a blue dot while a grandchild from a son would wear a white headband with a red dot. Great-grandchildren sport a golden headband. After many weeks of prayer, the tunics and headbands will get burned, concluding the ritual. For those that aren't familiar with this tradition, it could seem like we're associated with the KKK, and for the longest time I was embarrassed by this, but as an adult I've found that people are very open-minded and I became more comfortable about sharing these differences.

One Hundred Days of Mourning:

   Mourning traditionally lasts for one hundred days with prayer ceremonies every seven days for forty-nine days, where food and tea are offered. This extensive mourning process forces an entire family to mourn and heal together, adapting to the absence of the loved one. Every week I would have to see my entire family at the temple, and we would pray together, share a meal, and talk about how we were doing. I used to see it, as my younger cousins now do, as tedious and annoying to be obligated to go to temple every week. But as an adult, I see that some folks take longer to heal than others and they shouldn't have to go through it alone. We're pretty lucky to have a large family to create a tight-knit support network, but we'll see other, smaller families mourning at the temples, too, and my aunts and uncles will talk to them. Since we all have to wear our mourning outfits for prayer, other attendees at the temple would also know who was there suffering from a loss and strike up conversations to give condolences. Even strangers would talk to each other to give support.

Death Anniversaries:

   Every year on the death anniversary, the family will recognize the absence of the family member. Food and tea are offered similar to that during the funeral. Over time, this annual ceremony is less about mourning and serves as a way for families to reunite, share stories from the past, and continue to build a strong sense of community.

*When explaining them to friends or coworkers, these traditions often
seem unusual and sometimes excessive. I find that it helps with the healing
process and gives permission for those that need to grieve to have room to
do so, so I continue on with these traditions.*

—DANNIE PHAN

THE SILENCE OF THE TREES

In horror films, often the most frightening elements are the things left unseen and unheard. The silence that surrounds you while in an area known for violence, death, and hauntings is volumes more unsettling than a clichéd shout or yell. And if you cannot see the terrifying creature or madman that you *know* is around here somewhere, your adrenaline-filled mind begins to imagine them everywhere and in a form more frightening than they probably realistically are.

This is the situation Jordy Meow found himself in one fateful day when he wandered into Aokigahara, Japan's "Suicide Forest." Based in Tokyo, Jordy is a photographer specializing in capturing the hauntingly beautiful landscapes of abandoned and forgotten places that are scattered throughout the islands of Japan. You can check out his work on his websites, jordymeow.com and offbeatjapan.org, as well as in his book *Abandoned Japan*. Today, however, he's here to tell us the story of what exactly happened in that silent forest when he ventured off the main path and had nothing but clues from the unseen dead to find his way back.

*As an avid explorer of abandoned places throughout Japan, I am fascinated
by the arrangements of objects in spaces forgotten by time. One day, after
a trip to the many beautiful lakes surrounding Mount Fuji, my partner and
I still had some time left before having to head back to Tokyo. Aokigahara
was nearby and seemed like the perfect place to visit.*

*As we drove toward the forest, the mythical mountain disappeared and
left us alone under a thick canopy of heavy green leaves. While wondering
where we should stop, we found a parking area with a few cars in it as well
as a small, disused truck that was seemingly abandoned there. It looked
like the right place to start.*

This parking area happened to be the entrance for the trail to the famous "Wind Cave" within Aokigahara forest. However, we had arrived too late, and official access into the cave had closed just before we arrived. So, we found a different path around the cave and kept exploring. Immediately, the atmosphere changed. The air felt stale, as if we were the only ones moving it.

Fifteen minutes later, we saw a little path that was blocked by a sign forbidding visitors to go beyond it. Having already missed out on the cave, we ignored the sign and went down the path anyway. It was getting late by the time we reached the end of the thinning path, and this end point was marked with a bicycle that had been left to rust. And a bit further, we noticed something else. Colored tape.

My partner had read about this. Aokigahara was regarded as the foremost suicide spot in Japan. It was even highlighted in a popular Japanese "how-to" book for committing suicide. In the book, it recommends marking your path through this forest by tying tree trunks together with colored tape. The benefits of this were outlined as twofold: to make it possible to find your way out if you changed your mind, or to make it easier for forest rangers to find your remains.

With all the muddy soil, volcanic rocks, twisted roots, and detritus around, it was pretty hard to move quickly, and the density of the forest also made it difficult to walk in a single direction. We became totally dependent on the colored tape for orientation. That's when we found it.

A small clearing. A dark blue tie attached to a branch with a slipknot. A few steps away, a hanging rope fashioned into a noose. The surface of the ground underneath where two people had hung themselves and rotted away in the open air was swept clean, like a spiritual sanctuary. I couldn't stop thinking that this was left by a couple who shared a forbidden love, yet lived with intolerable pain. Their final moments spent in this immaculate space forgotten by time. A tragically well-known and all too common occurrence here in Aokigahara.

Shivering, and with our heads spinning, we hurried back to the parking area. The maze of tape shining in the dying light felt as if ghosts had set a trap to trick us into staying. Somehow, we made it back to the rusted bicycle. We were on the right track. Then we passed the "Wind Cave." All was dark by then, but as we turned a corner, a flashing vending machine welcomed us back to the world, to the land of the living.

We bought a warm drink from the vending machine and drove back to Tokyo, having survived thanks to the help of some colored tape intentionally left behind by a tragic couple who took their own lives amid the silent trees and stale air of Aokigahara.

—JORDY MEOW

PART 6

OCEANIA

*In language there is life. In
language there is death.*
HAWAIIAN PROVERB

Sailing south from the islands of Japan, we make our way to
Oceania, a far-flung region of the globe consisting of Australia and the numerous islands of Micronesia, Melanesia,
and Polynesia that are spread out all over the Pacific Ocean.
Here, we'll start our journey on the isle of New Guinea,
where Western influence is still at a minimum and ancient,
pre-Neolithic tribes, many of whom have yet to make contact
with the outside world, still practice their traditional death
rituals. After this, we'll head on down to Australia, where the
aboriginal tribes of the continent still try to maintain their
ancient rites and ceremonies despite the ceaseless onslaught
of missionaries, urbanization, and the modern world.

Finally, we'll embark into the heart of Polynesia. Getting
technical, the area of Polynesia is roughly in the shape of a
triangle, with Hawai'i as the northern apex and New Zealand and Rapa Nui (aka Easter Island) as the two base corners. Nowadays, these lands are a mix of independent nations,
self-governing dependencies, European overseas territories,

and member states of federated unions. Nevertheless, traditional culture remains strong, even in spite of the zealous spiritual and behavioral indoctrination of colonizers and missionaries. It would seem that these sunny shores of paradise on earth would be far removed from macabre rituals and morbid magic, but you cannot separate death from the human experience, not even here in paradise.

Cultural

NEW GUINEA

New Guinea is one of the most highly diverse human biomes on earth. A large island (second in size only to Greenland) north of Australia, its eastern half alone has more indigenous languages concentrated in a single country than any other place anywhere (839 that we know thus far).[200] It's

200 G. Seetharaman, "Seven decades after Independence, many small languages in India face extinction threat," *The Economic Times*, Aug. 13, 2017, https:// economictimes.indiatimes.com/news/politics-and-nation/seven-decades -after-independence-many-small-languages-in-india-facing-extinction-threat/ articleshow/60038323.cms (accessed Jun. 29, 2018).

also an anthropologist's dream due to having at least 1,000 different tribes in such a compacted area (with new ones still being discovered). Deep in the jungles and high in the mountains, tribes live a hunter-gatherer life with rudimentary tools and, sometimes, without ever having made contact with the outside world. It's here during the rare moments when the ultramodern comes into contact with the ultra-ancient on this island that humankind's ideas of death and the afterlife get strange.

Dialing the Dead

One example of this is how the island's remote Ambonwari tribe use cell phones to call their dead relatives. Isolated for about 60,000 years, they have long believed in necromantic communication with their ancestors, and the modern introduction of cell phones into their tribe simply facilitates that communication.

To call the dead with a cellphone in Ambonwari culture, you must first ask a shaman to find out the deceased's specific phone number, which he does through a trance ritual. Once you have that number, you can actually dial it and see if you've made connection, and that's where things get more fascinating. Apparently, if you successfully make contact (by sheer accidental luck) with an actual person who has that number, the voice on the other end is unquestioningly believed to be the ancestor's voice. If no one picks up, then it's assumed that the spirits are too busy with spiritual affairs to answer at this time, but they can still hear everything you say as a voicemail of sorts if you leave a message.[201]

Even on a mobile phone, however, the actual name of the deceased is taboo to say among the Kiwai tribe. To call or even say the name of the deceased (whether directly to the spirit or indirectly in conversation) is to catch the attention of their ghost and become targeted for disease-inducing curses from beyond the grave. Aside from self-protection, avoid-

---

201 Borut Telban, and Daniela Vávrová, "Ringing the living and the dead: Mobile phones in a Sepik society," *The Australian Journal of Anthropology* 25:2, 2014.

ing saying the names of the dead is also done so as to not renew the sorrow of those who were close to the deceased.[202]

Mortuary Cannibalism

Up in the highlands on the eastern side of the island, the natives here are known for a less celebrated macabre funerary ritual, mortuary cannibalism. If you're wondering what that means, your imagination is probably right; it's ceremoniously eating the corpses of the dead (voluntarily, not because you're facing starvation). While a number of world tribes do practice mortuary cannibalism, the Fore people are the most infamous, due to the plague of a horrific biological mutation that was spread through the eating of their own tribespeople.

This mutation is known today as "kuru disease," a neurodegenerative disorder similar to "mad cow" disease (also spread amongst cows being fed their own infected species) that leads to uncontrollable shaking, uncontrollable laughter, loss of coordination, and the death of neurons in the brain resulting in insanity. The name "kuru" comes from the Fore word meaning "to shake," due to the iconic tremors of the disease, caused by slowly losing control of your motor functions. While there is no known cure for kuru disease, very recently some tribespeople are unknowingly developing their own immunity via modern-day evolutionary bioresistance. As an additional preventative, modern awareness campaigns about the biological cause of kuru have effectively put an end to mortuary cannibalism in the region since the 1960s.[203]

Why did the Fore eat their dead, though? It seems like an unspeakable act to many cultures around the world, but the Fore had their reasons. They did it out of compassion and concern for their deceased loved ones. You see, they knew that if left to its own devices, a corpse would rot, putrefy, and be consumed by maggots and scavenger animals. If you've ever

---

202 Gunner Landtman, *The Kiwai Papuans of British New Guinea* (London: Macmillan, 1927).

203 Simon Mead, Jerome Whitfield, et al, "A Novel Protective Prion Protein Variant that Colocalizes with Kuru Exposure," *New England Journal of Medicine* 361:21. Nov. 19, 2009.

seen late-stage human putrefaction in person, it's quite the uncomfortable site. The Fore believe that it's much more respectful to the deceased if their family, friends, and community consume the body rather than letting maggots feast upon it or ever letting it go through the grisly process of putrefaction.

For the funerary feast itself, women were given the lion's share of the "food." Since women's bodies were believed capable of housing a spirit via pregnancy, the Fore felt women could also house and tame any spirits inhabiting the eaten corpse. Everything except the gallbladder was eaten, but the pièce de résistance was the brain, which, ironically, was where the kuru-causing abnormally folded prions resided.[204]

Granted, you could only get kuru if you ate the nervous system of someone with kuru, but because a person with kuru could show no symptoms of their disease for years and years on end, it would be impossible for a society lacking modern medical technology to know who had it. It's believed that someone in the tribe spontaneously mutated the abnormal prions around 1900 CE, died, and then those who ate that person got it, and as they died, more people got it from eating them and so on. Due to women doing more of the eating, they were disproportionately affected.[205]

Mortuary Cannibalism 2: The Revenge

The Korowai are another tribe on the island of New Guinea who also eat the dead. Unlike the Fore, though, this tribe continues to practice mortuary cannibalism, and since there was never a prion mutation within the tribe, contracting kuru disease is not a danger. They profess to only eat the corpses of witches called *khakhua*. These khakhua are believed to disguise themselves with magic to look like a friend or relative, thus giving them personal

---

204 Rae Ellen Bichell, "When People Ate People, A Strange Disease Emerged," *NPR*, Sept. 6, 2016, https://www.npr.org/sections/thesalt/2016/09/06/482952588/when-people-ate-people-a-strange-disease-emerged (accessed Jul. 2, 2018).

205 *Kuru: The Science and the Sorcery*, directed by Robert Bygott (2010; Mt. Lawley, Western Australia: Siamese Films).

and trusted intimate contact to drain the life force from their victims while they're sleeping.

Without access to modern medico-scientific knowledge, it's easy to see how a Korowai tribesperson's slow health decline and nightly wasting away from tropical diseases can come across as the result of some sort of supernatural vampirism. And since a person generally sleeps within the proximity of people he/she trusts (friends and family), the evil force must be disguised as one of those trusted people. To the Korowai, a khakhua is this disguised evil force causing unexplained illnesses in people.

However, it's when the sick person is on their deathbed that things get more dangerous and paranoia ensues. Believing their imminent demise is from khakhua witchcraft, they accuse one of their friends or family members of being the vampiric khakhua in disguise who has been slowly killing them. This effectively serves as a death sentence to whoever is accused because anything the accused says in denial of being a khakhua is believed to be a lie (because *of course* a khakhua would lie to save itself). Enraged by the victim's slow death and fearful of the khakhua claiming a new victim, members of the tribe form a hunting mob to kill the accused, and as poetic justice, they eat the corpse of the khakhua just as it had energetically "eaten" the life force of the victim.

Thus, here in the jungles of western New Guinea, many scenes reminiscent of the infamous Salem witch trials and the Arthur Miller masterpiece *The Crucible* are still taking place every year. No one in the Korowai tribe is safe from being accused of being a khakhua in disguise. Since the khakhua looks and acts just like the person they're pretending to be, anyone accused has no way to prove themselves otherwise. Moreover, it's believed that the accuser is always right, and documented stories abound of people screaming that they're innocent as their fellow tribespeople form a mob and murder them. Again, these screams are routinely ignored, believed to be the lies of the khakhua trying to trick everyone into mercy.

When asked if they feel bad for murdering their fellow tribespeople (who could even be their immediate family or friends since anyone can be accused), the Korowai explain that they aren't killing anyone innocent.

They are simply taking just revenge upon a khakhua. In fact, the final vengeance of eating their corpse isn't even seen as cannibalism among the tribe since they aren't eating people, they're eating khakhua.[206]

New Guinean Takeaway:
TRADITION FOR TRADITION'S SAKE

"Tradition" is often lauded as time-honored, representative of a certain people, and a stabilizing undercurrent that keeps people together amidst the changes of time. While this is all well and good, just because something is time-honored, representative, and stabilizing doesn't mean it's always good for you or the community. The problem comes when "tradition" is held on a pedestal that remains untouchable by criticism or critique. By not allowing "tradition" to be contested or modified, it can often be erroneously romanticized as a surviving vestige of "better," "simpler" times before the world got too fast and too complicated.

Here on the island of New Guinea, we've seen two examples of the dangers of tradition for tradition's sake, the continued practice of a custom just because it's the way things have always been done. The Fore tribe ended their tradition of mortuary cannibalism when they found out it was the cause for the kuru epidemic among their people. Yes, their tradition was always done with the best of intentions, but when new information came to light, they ended it for the betterment of their health and the future of their people. Imagine if they stubbornly refused to give up their tradition just because it was "tradition"; there'd be a whole lot more suffering going on. Similarly, imagine if the Korowai tribe questioned their tradition of killing anyone accused of being a khakhua; there'd be a whole lot more innocent people still alive.

Modern death in the West is shrouded in such "traditions" that the funeral industry relies on you not to question so as to increase their bottom line profits. Personal preferences aside, at the very least, a "traditional"

---

206   Paul Raffaele, "Sleeping with Cannibals," *Smithsonian Magazine,*
      Sept. 2006, https://www.smithsonianmag.com/travel/sleeping
      -with-cannibals-128958913/ (accessed Jul. 2, 2018).

burial of a casketed embalmed body is phenomenally detrimental to the environment…but hey, it's "tradition."

Your New Guinean takeaway challenge now is to question traditions in the death industry, in your own religion, and in everything else you do on autopilot just because it's the way things have always been done. After all, if you're following a tradition without insight into its history, your actions are done without meaning, and if you realize it's harmful to others, to animals, or to the environment, you're now an accomplice. Question everything. Accept only what is demonstrably true. Be willing to change if logic, experience, and reason prove your traditional beliefs wrong.

ABORIGINAL AUSTRALIA

Australia today is not the Australia that existed throughout most of human history. Nowadays, it's a white-majority, English-speaking, largely Christian nation still technically under the rule of the Queen of England. In line with these demographics, Australia's modern funerary rituals are largely those of Christianity with the final disposition option of casketed burial or cremation.

Losing the Past

Previous to the late eighteenth century CE, though, Australia was predominantly inhabited by dark-skinned tribes with rich traditions, cosmologies, and worldviews centered around shamanism and animism. Today, however, most aboriginal Australians are conservative Christians due to this Western faith being brutally instilled in them through forced conversions, having their children taken away to be given a "proper" (aka Eurocentric) education, and the decimation of their people and sovereignty at the barrel of a gun. In this day and age, only about 3 percent of Australia's population are aboriginal natives, and most of them have been absorbed into the Western European culture of urban Australia.[207]

207 Nicholas Biddle, and Francis Markham, "Census 2016: what's changed for Indigenous Australians?" *The Conversation*, Jun. 27, 2017, https:// theconversation.com/census-2016-whats-changed-for-indigenous -australians-79836 (accessed Jul. 10, 2018).

Because of all this, many of aboriginal Australians' traditional practices aren't practiced anymore outside of staged and touristy productions, selling their culture as an exoticism just to survive. Their funerary traditions are somewhat of a different story, though. Bits and pieces are still vehemently adhered to while others have been abandoned. Despite not having a universal culture across the continent, the majority of aboriginal Australian tribes' death rituals focus on assisting the deceased's spirit to the afterlife and keeping them appeased there so they don't come back to haunt the living.

World Firsts

The oldest archeological evidence of funerary rituals by Australian natives involved both cremation and burial. Not only the oldest cremation and burial on the continent, these finds are also the oldest evidence of cremation and burial in the history of humanity, dating around 40,000 years old. These weren't just arbitrary victims of fire or the coverings of a corpse; everything was done in a precise and meticulous way that suggests a ritualized ceremony. Additional evidence around the continent shows that some of the surviving bone fragments from cremations were kept and worn as jewelry by the family, evidence of possibly the earliest memento mori on the planet. The exception, however, would be the peoples of Northern Australia; they were more the burying kind.[208]

Those Who Shall Not Be Named

When talking in generalities about the many native tribes across Australia, there are a few similarities in the way they interact with the dead. One of them is that before the actual final disposition, the family of the

---

208 Danny Kingsley, "World's oldest burial redated to 40,000 years," *Australian Broadcasting Corporation*, Feb. 20, 2003, http://www.abc.net.au/science/ articles/2003/02/20/788032.htm (accessed Dec. 11, 218).
"Aboriginal vs. Non-Indigenous Funeral Traditions Among Australians," *In the Light Urns*, Apr. 2, 2015, https://www.inthelighturns.com/funeral -information/aboriginal-vs-non-indigenous-funeral-traditions-among -australians/ (accessed Jul 10, 2018).

deceased was expected to facilitate the spirit's task of exiting the corpse. Two rituals in particular among aboriginal Australians were performed to do this. First, there was the Smoking Ceremony, in which native plants (particularly *Eremophila longifolia*) were ritually burned in the deceased's home to both purify the space and help the spirit rise to the heavens.[209]

The second ritual is still actively honored today and involves a prohibition against the name of the deceased. In practice, this involves not being allowed to say or write the name of a deceased person. Either mutually understandable references about the person have to be said or a brand new postmortem name is given to the deceased as a safe way to speak and write about them. If another person in the family/community had the same name as the deceased, then they would have to change their name since that name now belonged to the dead.

Many tribes also still enforce a prohibition against looking at photos of the dead (photos of when they were alive and of their corpse). The belief behind this seeming erasure of their existence is to prevent their spirit from returning from the afterlife. Saying their name or seeing images of their bodies encourages the spirit of the deceased to remain in this world, and in many aboriginal cultures, lingering spirits are often believed to cause mischief and all manner of haunting problems for the living.

This prohibition against names and images goes into effect at the moment of death and is expected to be obeyed by everyone, including non-natives, though the level of strict adherence to this varies from culture to culture, family to family, and region to region. Particularly in postmortem medicolegal bureaucracy (such as preparing a death certificate or compiling medical reports on a decedent), this has led to difficulties in providing after-death funerary/hospital services that are heavily reliant on a person's name. After all, how can you document, make funerary plans

209 Sadgrove, Jones, and Greatrex, "Isolation and characterisation of (-)-genifuranal: the principal antimicrobial component in traditional smoking applications of Eremophila longifolia (Scrophulariaceae) by Australian aboriginal peoples," *Journal of Ethnopharmacology* 154:3, Jul. 3, 2014.

for, or even write about a dead person if you are prohibited from using their name and image? Moreover, tradition mandates that a family member *must* be the first person to announce a death, making informing the next of kin on the death of a family member quite complicated should that person die without family present.[210]

Aboriginal Australian Takeaway:
TABOOS

From not saying the names of the deceased to not keeping any photos of the deceased, Australia's aboriginal peoples have established a number of taboos concerning their dead. Their belief in spirits and hauntings shows an understood concept of some sort of existence after death that can interact with the living world, but even so, the dead are left to their own affairs. Whether based on the foundation of a healthy separation between the planes or on the fear that mostly harm can come between the planes intersecting, aboriginal Australians let the dead be dead.

What are some taboos around death (and in general) that are still practiced in your religion or culture? Why are those taboos there? Are they to protect you from something? Is this protection necessary or a vestige of a superstitious and scientifically debunked belief from the past? Why do you always have to do a certain thing this way and not that way?

Your aboriginal Australian takeaway challenge is to do some digging and find out the origins and reasonings behind the taboos that you adhere to in your own life. Taboos are often placed upon a people for a reason: sometimes for protection, sometimes as a tactic for someone else's personal gain. But you'll never know which is which until you dig deep and learn why something is not allowed.

210   Jens Korff, "Mourning an Aboriginal Death," *Creative Spirits*, https://www
      .creativespirits.info/aboriginalculture/people/mourning-an-aboriginal-death
      (accessed Jul. 10, 2018).
      Cameron Stewart, "Naming taboo often ignored in breaking news," *The
      Australian*, Jul. 13, 2013, https://www.theaustralian.com.au/business/media/
      naming-taboo-often-ignored-in-breaking-news/news-story/5ea91f685d3a866f
      87c48a26061ce7e1 (accessed Dec. 11, 2018).

Deities & Legends

ETERNAL DREAMING

"Eternal Dreaming" is the title given to the aboriginal Australian concept of life and death within the larger context of the "Dreamtime" (the cosmology of all existence). In its essence, it's the belief that everything (all worlds, people, living beings, etc.) is connected in an endless cycle of rebirth throughout the various planes of existence. Each plane is so distinctly jarring in its dissimilarities from the others that it seems as if we're constantly waking up from another dream with each rebirth.

Consequently, all deaths are regarded as rebirths into whichever plane of existence is next in the cycle. Because of this endless continuity, the separation between what is "real" and what is a "dream" becomes blurred, and thus all experiences are believed to take place in a fuzzy, dreamlike state of reality called "Eternal Dreaming."[211]

MOKOI

Mokoi are evil spirits who play a pervasively terrifying role in the everyday life of the Yolngu people indigenous to what is now Australia's Northern Territory. They are the tribe's de facto deities of death. To the Yolngu, death is considered something unnatural. Humans are believed to be able to live forever. Thus, every single death is believed to be unnatural and caused by the Mokoi in their eternal pursuit of causing human misery. The decay of old age, freak accidents, murders, sickness, and every other possible event that results in death is seen as a supernatural curse caused by the Mokoi.

The Mokoi's whole existence centers around causing tragic chaos and sorrowful misfortune at every possible moment to anyone at all, and their favorite way to do this is by kidnapping children in the night and eating

---

211 M. H. Monroe, "The Afterlife in Aboriginal Australia," *Australia: The Land Where Time Began*, Apr. 15, 2013, http://austhrutime.com/afterlife.htm (accessed Jul. 11, 2018).

them. This extreme willingness to cause harm makes them popularly invoked beings by malicious magic workers among the Yolngu. However, it is well known that whoever invokes the Mokoi would eventually fatally succumb to their own invocation's wanton, wicked ways.[212]

212 Douglas L. Oliver, *Oceania: The Native Cultures of Australia and the Pacific Islands*, vol 1 (Honolulu: University of Hawaii Press, 1989).

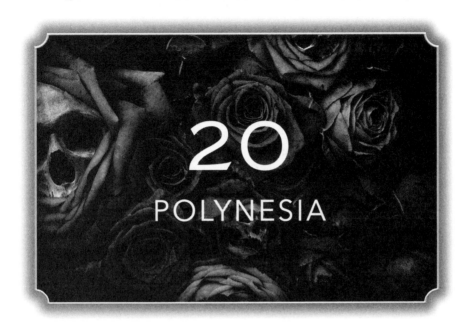

20
POLYNESIA

Cultural

Accompanying a Corpse in New Zealand

Heading out from Australia, we'll start this leg of our trek on the nearby islands of New Zealand. Here, the Māori people have traditionally held large, grand funeral celebrations known as *tangihanga*. Each individual tribe has its own embellishments to this death ritual, but in general, the structure and intention are similar.

The corpse (*tūpāpaku*) is never allowed to be alone from the moment of death, and as soon as possible, it's transported to an open clearing (*marae*) that is reserved for all-purpose religious ceremonies. Upon arrival, a welcoming ceremony of dancers, chanters, and singers greet the body as the family takes their place along the flanks of the corpse, which will remain

235

in state for viewing for two days. During this time, the extended family (dressed in dark colors with *kawakawa* leaves worn as a garland around the head) will stay by the body at every moment, only taking quick breaks for food, naps, and nature's periodic calls.

While the body lies in state, all those who are present are invited to come before the deceased's corpse and get everything off their chest. Whether it be expressing words felt yet never said, airing grievances, criticizing and chastising, or just having a heartfelt goodbye talk, everyone is encouraged to let everything out in this safe space where no conversation with the deceased is considered inappropriate.

After the two days of visitation, the body is then buried (nowadays with Christian rites) and then exhumed about a year later so that the bones can be painted with ochre and hidden away in a private place by the immediate family. The conclusion of the mourning period is the *hākari*, a communal feast in celebration of the deceased's soul successfully making it to the ancestral world of *Hawaiki*.[213]

This afterlife realm with the ancestors was believed to have a real-world entry point in what is now considered the most haunted place in all of New Zealand. At the very northwestern tip of the North Island's Aupouri Peninsula is Cape Regina (called *Te Rerenga Wairua* in Māori, which means "leaping-off place of spirits").[214] It's a desolate area surrounded by a frenzy of erratic waves at what was believed to be the edge of the known

---

213 Rawinia Higgins, "Tangihanga—death customs," in *Te Ara - the Encyclopedia of New Zealand* (Wellington: Manatū Taonga Ministry for Culture and Heritage, 2011). https://teara.govt.nz/en/tangihanga-death-customs (accessed Jul. 25, 2018).
Kristen Capano, "Tangihanga: A Look Into a Traditional Maori Funeral," *Seven Pounds*, May 25, 2017, http://blog.sevenponds.com/cultural-perspectives/tangihanga-look-traditional-maori-funeral (accessed Jul 25. 2018).
Moana Maniapoto, "Tangihanga—A dying tradition," *E-Tangata*, Aug. 15, 2015, https://e-tangata.co.nz/reflections/tangihanga-a-dying-tradition/ (accessed Jul 25, 2018).

214 Barry Mitcalfe, "Te Rerenga Wairua: Leaping Place of the Spirits," *Te Ao Hou* Vol. 35, Jun, 1961, http://teaohou.natlib.govt.nz/journals/teaohou/issue/Mao35TeA/c20.html (accessed Jul. 25, 2018).

world. This foreboding landscape is the location of Piwhane/Spirits Bay, wherein a large 800-year-old pōhutukawa tree marks the entrance to the land of the dead.[215]

Breathless in Fiji

North of New Zealand (in what is technically Melanesia) lies the Republic of Fiji. Well known in the West for their eponymous artesian bottled water, what is lesser known is their ritual of funerary strangulation. Granted, today's Fijian funerals are essentially Christian affairs due to the lasting impact of South Seas missionaries, but back in the old days, funerary strangulation was a regular occurrence.

It's pretty much just what it sounds like. Upon the death of someone (and by "someone" I mean a man, because patriarchy of the times), the widow would be ritually sacrificed via strangulation. This Fijian strangulation ritual started with the intention of helping the departed in the afterlife. Specifically, the dead man's widow was killed so as to solve the issue of the profound loneliness each one would have while apart. Since the deceased one couldn't return to life, the living one had to die for the couple to be reunited. However, the ritual slowly devolved into a sociopolitical affair with much ado. Where once only self-selecting widows asked to be killed out of severe grief, now all widows were socially expected to ask to be killed lest they be dishonored and ostracized by society for not loving their husband enough.

The widow's brother would be in charge of the actual strangulation, and being similarly honor-bound and avoiding ostracization compelled him to be his sister's executioner (plus unprecedented levels of prestige would be granted to him after the act). Of course, if the widow was beautiful or had much status, a suitor would often challenge the brother to what was essentially a tug-of-war with each of the widow's arms. If the brother won, the widow would be strangled. If the suitor won, the widow's life would be spared, and no one would be dishonored since (supposedly) both the

---

215 "Spirits Bay (Kapowairua)," *iTravel NZ*, http://www.itravelnz.com/listing/ spirits-bay-kapowairua.html (accessed Jul. 25, 2018).

widow and the brother were committed to go all the way (thus gaining true honor and fulfilling the societal expectations of everyone).

Eventually, the rituals turned into whole big choreographed productions wherein everyone knew that the suitor would be rigged to win yet everyone had to play the part and go through the motions. Nevertheless, there was still always the chance that a power-hungry brother would have an upset win and sacrifice his sister out of disapproval of his would-be brother-in-law or in order to gain status and prestige among the people.[216]

Dying Expensively in Tonga

Just to the southeast of Fiji is the Christian Kingdom of Tonga, where the firm matrilineal hierarchy, the societal class structure, and general expectations of the community often force families to hold lavish funerals and supply everyone with food, drink, lodging, and entertainment until after the burial. Since the entire extended family is societally mandated to be present, this makes funerals in Tonga expensive affairs, usually with an average low cost of US $10,000.

In addition to being financially taxing, Tongan funerals are emotionally taxing. Profound displays of wailing (whether sincere or not) are expected during the entire mourning period until burial. After burial, however, families often joke about how ludicrously tragic (or even tragically ludicrous) their wailing antics were, showing they're very self-aware and are ever mindful of how they are being perceived by the community during these death rituals.[217]

216 Samantha Russell, "Two Funerals and a Baby," *From Mushrooms to Mangoes*, Apr. 24, 2012, https://bulasamantha.wordpress.com/tag/fijian-funeral-ceremonies/ (accessed Jul. 25, 2018).
Lorimer Fison, "Notes on Fijian Burial Customs," *Journal of the Anthropological Institute of Great Britain and Ireland* Vol. 10, 1881.

217 Nawee, "Traditional Tongan Funerals," *Nawee*, Dec. 3, 2013, https://nauwee.wordpress.com/2013/12/03/traditional-tongan-funerals/ (accessed Jul. 26, 2018).

Storytelling in Samoa

Sailing northeast to Samoa, storytelling is the interconnecting thread that strings the island's death traditions together. Upon death, a family member is selected to be the *tulafale* (chief funerary orator) who is responsible for communicating the somber news to all friends and family as well as organizing and conducting all gatherings during the mourning period.

The tulafale also acts as the administrator charged with funeral director-esque duties of arranging the funeral and getting the surviving family to come to a consensus of what should be done for the funeral and disposition of the body (unless the deceased planned ahead and had a death plan). Most importantly, though, the tulafale's most prestigious duty is leading the funerary speeches, reciting the genealogy, and preparing the ceremonial kava (an entheogenic plant drunk to enhance the spirituality of the occasion).[218]

Them Bones in Hawai'i

Up in the northernmost vertex of the Polynesian triangle, the state of Hawai'i (though still disputed by many native Hawaiians to be a prolonged military occupation due to the unscrupulous way the US acquired the Hawaiian Islands), there is a pervasive concept of inherent spiritual power called *mana*. Everyone has mana, though great and high-ranking people are believed to have more of it, which helps them achieve even more out of life. In particular, human bones (*iwi*) are thought to contain large concentrations of a person's mana. This meant the native Hawaiians held a special reverence for the bones of the dead.

Generally, the corpse was traditionally interred in the earth or in caves, which were useful in allowing nature to do the dirty work of reducing the body down to its bones. Having possession of someone's bones was believed to give the possessor the living mana of the deceased. It didn't

218 Zoë Byrne, "The Tulafale's Role: Samoan Oratorial Traditions for Death and Funeral," Apr. 3, 2014, http://blog.sevenponds.com/cultural-perspectives/the-tulafales-role-samoan-oratorial-traditions-for-death-and-funeral (accessed Jul. 26, 2018).

matter if you were a good or wicked person; mana has no morality and can be equally found in great heroes and in monstrous villains. A notable example of this was when Captain James Cook was killed on the Big Island of Hawai'i. Though relations between the Hawaiians and the captain had soured (resulting in him being killed on the beach), the captain's bones were preserved and divided between the chiefs of the Big Island because they recognized the great amount of mana their enemy had despite their contempt for him.[219]

Though, before it could be reduced to bones, taking care of the dead body was a difficult family affair. The dead body was seen as unclean both spiritually and hygienically, and so those relatives who took care of the cadaver until a burial ritual could be performed were seen as tainted. They couldn't enter anyone else's house, they couldn't eat food that they didn't personally cook, they couldn't make physical contact with anyone, and they were forbidden from working. After the burial, these familial under-takers had to purify themselves in ocean waters and receive a communal blessing to cleanse the aura of death from them.[220]

Lei'd to Rest

Crossing over into mainland mainstream popular culture, the native Hawaiian tradition of the funeral lei has been adopted by a multitude of faiths and secularists. Associated with the spirit of *aloha,* leis are used as iconic gifts of loving welcome and departure. In native Hawaiian fashion, funeral leis are nowadays draped atop a casket, placed around a framed picture of the deceased, worn by grieving family members, and used to mark the site of a burial, fatal accident, or memorial.

Traditionally, these funeral leis are to be left at their memorial sites or with the body during burial/cremation, and if not, then they're to be

---

219 Betty Fullard-Leo, "Sacred Burial Practices," *Coffee Times,* Feb. 1998, http://www.coffeetimes.com/feb98.htm (accessed Jul. 26, 2018).

220 Ryan Lynn, "Traditional Hawaiian Funeral Rituals," *University of Alaska Anchorage Department of Anthropology,* 2015, http://anthreligion.commons.uaa .alaska.edu/funerary-rituals/traditional-hawaiian-funerary-rituals/ (accessed Jul 26, 2018).

thrown into the ocean in memoriam of the dead. While there's no wrong choice of plant from which to fashion a funeral lei, the most appropriate funeral leis are usually made from maile (*Alyxia oliviformis*) leaves and flowers (though do note that maile are not exclusive to funeral leis, so don't start making grim assumptions should you see someone wearing a maile lei).

Polynesian Takeaway:
HOLDING THE DEAD ACCOUNTABLE

When someone dies, we have a strange habit of beatifying them into icons of goodness. No matter who the person was in life, how they treated others, or how people truly felt about them, the deceased is suddenly remembered as "the kindest, most generous, loving, funny, (insert lauded adjective here) human being ever." If you want your sins washed away, it seems like all you have to do is die, and then no one will remember them anymore (or at least will downplay them and make excuses for them).

When it comes to remembering the dead, the Māori of New Zealand keep it real. They hold the dead accountable, they don't overlook or try to minimize their faults, and they will publicly let the community know what was wrong with the deceased at their funeral. Respect for the dead is great, but if the person wasn't worthy of respect while alive, they surely don't suddenly become worthy of it just because they died.

If you've seen the '80s cult classic *Heathers*, you'll remember how well that film parodies this warped postmortem perception we have of the dead. In it, a stuck-up, selfish, vile, belittling teenage bully dies, but after hearing of her death, her school's entire student body elevates her memory to that of the ideal student, friend, and human being. They rationalize away all the hateful things she did and go through a lot of mental gymnastics to perceive them as elaborate cries of help.

No! She was just an awful human being, and there are awful human beings in real life, too. If your mom was nice to you but was a nasty homophobic racist to everyone else...if your brother was always there to give you a ride somewhere but went around burglarizing homes for drug money...if your grandparents were sweet to you but used to go on drunken stupors and beat their own kids back in the day... if anyone consistently contributed to human misery while alive (even though they also had some redeeming qualities), then their death doesn't make all that disappear. Your Polynesian takeaway challenge is to hold the dead accountable and don't let your grief romanticize the deceased as people they weren't. Someone dying doesn't mean that the truth has to die with them.

Deities & Legends

DEGEI

Degei is the supreme god in Fijian mythology. He hatched the egg from which all human life originated, he created the world, he judges and rules over the dead, and he's the cause of destructive natural phenomena such as earthquakes, tidal waves, storms, rain, and seasons. His appearance is that of a serpent, and he's considered a capriciously wrathful deity who causes mass death and starvation via the elements.

Being death specific, there are two caves by which Fijian souls would enter the underworld: Cibaciba and Drakulu. Inside these caves awaits Degei and a large lake. If Degei deems the soul to have been wicked or just average and lacking noteworthy goodness, then he offers them a boat with which to cross the lake. However, the boat always capsizes and the souls sink down to Murimuria, a place of on-and-off punishment. If the soul was notably good while alive, Degei would tell them about a secret route around the lake that would take them to the paradisiac realm of Burotu, where they could have a happy afterlife.[221]

---

221 A. W. Reed, and Inez Hames, *Myths & Legends of Fiji & Rotuma* (New York: Literary Productions, Inc, 1997).
Sir James George Frazer, *The Belief in Immortality and the Worship of the Dead* (London: Macmillan, 1913).

HINE-NUI-TE-PŌ

In Māori mythology, Hine-nui-te-pō is the goddess of death, nighttime, and queen of the underworld. According to legends, Hine-nui-te-pō suffered a traumatic psychological shock (à la Evelyn Mulwray in *Chinatown*) when she discovered that her husband was actually her father (apparently her husband knew she was his daughter the whole time, but never told her so as to prevent this very reaction from her).

Feeling disgusted, lied to, and supremely violated, she ran off into the darkness of the underworld. Her husband/father eventually went to retrieve her, but during her time in the darkness, she became self-actualized, assertive, and confidently independent. She refused to ever return to him but offered to take shared custody of their children (all human beings) wherein he would have them while alive, and she would have them after death.[222]

KANALOA

In Hawaiian mythology, Kanaloa is one of the four major Hawaiian deities that rule the whole pantheon. As an aquatic god of water, he has a squid-like appearance, and fishermen often sought his protection from the dangers of the sea. In legends, he is often mentioned in relation to another major Hawaiian deity, Kāne (the sun/sky god and divine creator). Together, the two represent equal but opposite forces of nature (akin to the yin-yang in Taoism). Kāne represented warmth, creativity, and light, while Kanaloa represented coldness, destruction, and darkness.

Over time, Christian missionaries aligned Kanaloa as a Satanic figure who embodied pure evil. They even went so far as to work a *Paradise Lost* story arc into the native Hawaiian mythology wherein Kanaloa and his demonic underlings declared a war against the "good" deities. Kanaloa and his forces were defeated, and they were sent down to live in the underworld as punishment. The missionaries had such an impact on rewriting

---

222 Anthony Alpers, *Maori Myths and Tribal Legends* (Auckland: Longman Paul, 1964).

the Hawaiians' mythological past that Kanaloa's modern position as god of death, the underworld, and magic (which the missionaries saw as sinful) all stem from Christianity's forceful influence over the centuries and not from traditional beliefs native to the islands.[223]

MILU

The traditional Hawaiian deity of death (before Christian missionaries gave that title to Kanaloa) was Milu. Milu was a mythic human and the great chieftain of Waipio on the Big Island. According to legend, he was advised to get lots of bedrest after barely surviving an attack on his life. As a man of action, however, his sedentary recovery bothered him to no end, and it didn't help that the most spectacular surfing waves ever seen were currently being enjoyed on Waipio's beaches by his people. He couldn't resist and went out surfing, but after a gnarly crash, his poor health prevented him from being able to swim back up to the surface.

Milu drowned, but he was given rulership over the underworld (*Lua-o-Milu*) named in his honor. He ruled much in the same charismatic manner as he did while alive, and the spirits of the dead enjoyed playing games, learning new hobbies/skills, squabbling with one another, and feasting. In this way, aside from being dead, the afterlife really wasn't much different from the living life on the Hawaiian Islands.[224]

WHIRO

Whiro is the Māori god of darkness and the embodiment of all evil. From his abode in the underworld, he schemes how to harm humans, and all earthly ills are believed to originate from him. As legends have it, Whiro gets his power from eating the buried bodies of the deceased (thus

223 Martha Beckwith, "Kane and Kanaloa," *Hawaiian Mythology*, 1940, http://www.sacred-texts.com/pac/hm/hm07.htm (accessed Jul. 31, 2018).
Ophvedius, "Satan's historical presence in other cultures: Kanaloa," *Modern Church of Satan*, Nov. 11, 2008, http://www.modernchurchofsatan.com/grotto/viewtopic.php?f=16&t=3455 (accessed Oct. 6, 2018)

224 W. D. Westervelt, "How Milu Became the King of Ghosts," *Hawaiian Legends of Ghosts and Ghost-Gods* (Boston: Ellis Press, 1916) http://www.sacred-texts.com/pac/hlog/hlog17.htm (accessed Jul. 31, 2018).

explaining decomposition). Out of fear that the never-ending supply of dead humans would one day make Whiro so powerful that he would be able to destroy all of existence, cremation had sometimes been tradition-ally used by the Māori as a way to mitigate Whiro's food source.[225]

225 Michael Brookes, "Drabbles of the Gods—Whiro," *The Cult of Me*, Apr. 1, 2015, http://thecultofme.blogspot.com/2015/04/drabbles-of-gods-whiro .html (accessed Jul 27, 2018).

"Whiro," *Encyclopedia Mythica*, Mar. 3, 1997, https://pantheon.org/articles/w/ whiro2.html (accessed Jul. 27, 2018).

21
OCEANIC MAGICAL COMMUNITY

LEARNING FROM THE LAND DOWN UNDER

Graciously taking time out of his busy schedule to visit us while we're here in Oceania is my friend Andrés Engracia. He learned of death quite early on in his life, not too long after moving to Australia at the age of three. Since then, he's become an author, past-life spiritual regression therapist, spiritual practitioner, and facilitator of sacred workshops and creative sessions for aspiring writers down in Sydney. You can find out more about him on his website, www.mrengracia.com, but be sure to check out his *Saints & Mystics Reading Cards* if you love the mix of history and mysticism as much as I do.

Andrés, like many of us, is not a *true* native of the land in which he lives. Nevertheless, the place in which we grow up profoundly affects us and shapes our worldview. More than just our language and accent, each space of land carries with it its own magic, mysticism, and ancient ways that we subconsciously accept as just how life is since we know no place else. Not until we travel do we really see how uniquely magic the traditions of the place we grew up in and call home can be. Andrés had such an upbringing down in Australia, where the legends and rituals of the aboriginal peoples helped shape the way he mourns the dead.

My first experience and real initiation to mortality and dying unfurled when I was ten years old when my mother passed away of cervical cancer just suddenly within a year of diagnosis. I remember my mother stopped wearing colours and began to dress only in white as her days to death grew fewer. Even though she tried her best to protect me from realising the inevitability of what was to come, I understood that she was preparing her mind and spirit toward transition.

The moment my mom passed, my body felt like a void with nowhere to go. I was numb of emotion, feeling, and expression, and the only time the emptiness broke was when my brother forgot his written speech at her church funeral and I thought how my mother would have laughed at the silly mishap. That small instance of an unplanned mistake reminded me of the crafty, simple, silly joys life humours us with. The wounds that cracked my heart turned to gold, and my heart began to reglue itself.

When my mother moved us to Australia from Spain, I was just shy of three years old, and in those early years growing up, my first introduction to the indigenous aboriginal cultures took place in my school. There, I was told of the beautiful story of the Dreamtime creation where the spirits became part of the land, taking shape and form in the flora and fauna, man and woman, rocks and earth. This story of reality resonated deeply within me, but it wasn't until much later in life I learnt of its interplay in Australia's sacred rituals of death and dying, and only much further in life until I discovered how instrumental these practices are in offering powerful devotions of repayment to the energies of the land and the life we lived.

Today, most modern indigenous peoples of Australia mix a modern funeral with traditional elements. A friend and colleague of mine, Rhian-

non, once shared with me that at the indigenous memorial ceremony of one of her cousins, the person officiating briefly mentioned seeing her cousin's totem animal, which signified that she was at peace now. This made me realise that even with the assistance of funeral directors who provide modern forms of burial rites, there is a power in bringing back old traditional rituals from the land in which we live and in how interconnected we always are with the local earth, nature, and animals … even in death.

Here are three of the most powerful ceremonies that I undertake during mourning that were inspired by the land and aboriginal peoples of my home here in Australia and that I hope may bring comfort and peace to you as well:

1. Break the grief by sharing together in community. Laughter, tears, reflection, or even silent moments all help to dismantle the barriers and masks restricting our emotions long enough to allow the real, gritty pains to pour out. Do not stay alone. Life is for living and loving with people.

2. Gather some found leaves and flower petals, find a river stream or ocean where you can sit quietly, and begin a deep meditation on your loved one. Remember their presence and certain memories. Bring through all the emotions and let them pour into the gathered collection. Once you reach the point of yearning or tears, release the leaves and petals into the water and let it all go. Sometimes we carry too much burden and pain, and this ritual allows us to release those dense ties in a soulful and healing way.

3. A powerful way to remember our connections to the Earth Mother of the land that we live on, especially during mourning, is to go to a tree in your garden and on nontoxic recyclable paper gift tags, write wishes and small letters to your deceased loved one before tying them to the branches. Let the tree become the conduit for the love to be sent and after a time, take those tags down and place them in the compost, or burn them safely in a fireproof container. By earth or fire, either will carry the messages deep across space and time to those in all planes of the Dreamtime.

—ANDRÉS ENGRACIA

DANCE OF DEATH

Dancing is a time honored and sacred tradition throughout Polynesia, and it has endured to modern times. Though many Polynesian dances nowadays are put out there on display with the end goal of entertaining tourists and promoting the marketable "mystique" of the Pacific Islands, that doesn't make them any less sacred or magical. These sacred dances can be fluid and sensual like the Hawaiian hula, or they can be forceful and intimidating like the Māori haka. And their range of symbolic, spiritual meanings is just as vast.

The other community member whom you were to meet here in Oceania was going to choreograph for you a funerary hula. It was to be based on a mix of traditional mourning steps and modern free-form interpretive dance. This native Hawaiian choreographer had insisted on mixing the interpretive with the traditional since it was best representative of how we all grieve in our own way. The traditional steps in honor of continuing the past legacy of grief known to all our ancestors. The spur-of-the-moment unrehearsed movements in honor of the unpredictability and personal journey of each person's own individual grief.

However, this dance of death remains (possibly appropriately) incomplete. You see, our native Hawaiian community member was choreographing a mourning hula for us based on the one that she had choreographed for herself after the loss of her own child. I didn't push for details, but she revealed that dancing the hula was her life, so when her son died unexpectedly while still very young, she knew no other way to grieve but to dive into her passion of dance. In honor of her son and as a cathartic release, she performed a mourning hula at the funeral.

Knowing about this, I reached out to her to see if she'd be willing to share this dance with us, and she was thrilled. She said she wouldn't share her own dance, but would create a new, generalized one for all of us. However, the choreographing of this new hula brought back sad memories, almost a déjà vu of preparing for her own son's funeral. She thought she had completely overcome that grief, but like an unstoppable deluge, the tears and feelings of loss came flooding on back. In the end, she apologetically informed me that she just couldn't bring herself to do it. I assured her it was alright, and that she didn't let me down.

Aside from the obvious symbolism of "Death interrupts our preset plans, forcing us to continue on in a new way," the reoccurrence of grief experienced by my friend is a powerful thing to remember and a lesson in its own right. Grief never goes away completely; we just learn to adjust. When you love someone very much, you'll always be aware of their absence, and never will there be a time when you're forever perfectly okay with them not being in the physical world anymore. One day you'll hear a certain song, see a particular film, or have a flashback memory that'll bring you to your knees with renewed grief even if it has been years since your loved one's passing, and sometimes it'll happen out of the blue for no discernable reason at all. Your recovery time from these waves of grief will be faster as time goes by, but there'll always be a bit of grief inside of you that'll never go away.

Our choreographer friend from Hawai'i was so sure that she had already gotten past the worst of it in grieving for her child. It surprised her just how fresh everything became again, years after the incident, and she was wise enough to know not to ignore it or suppress her feelings. She needed space and time to grieve again and, in an act of self-care, let me know that she just couldn't choreograph a new dance at this time as she had promised.

Something similar will probably (most likely) happen to you in the future, and when it does, be as wise and self-nurturing as our Hawaiian friend and acknowledge your grief, no matter how long ago the loss was. If you need to take a minute and ride through a wave of tears and sorrow, allow yourself to do so. And if someone you know begins to grieve, seemingly out of nowhere, for someone long past, don't dismiss their feelings. Don't force them to "suck it up" or "get over it." Be there for them, help them out, and respect their grief. A little respect goes a long way.

PART 7

THE AMERICAS

The evolution from happiness to
habit is one of death's best weapons.
JULIO CORTÁZAR

When people think about death rituals and a devotion toward the macabre, the cultures of the Americas are often some of the first to come to mind. In addition to the African diasporic cultures in Brazil and the Caribbean, the thoroughly native cultures throughout North and South America are well associated with death and the afterlife. The Aztecs and their infamous human sacrifices to literally bloodthirsty deities. The Maya and their complex underworld of adventures. The often-studied corpse-eating tribes of the Amazon jungle. The Native American shamans who can travel into the spiritual realms to aid their people. The spine-chilling ghost stories from the horrors of European colonialism. And more.

For our morbid travels across the New World, we'll go from pole to pole. Starting in southern Patagonia of Argentina, we'll ride northward all the way to the frozen shores of the Arctic Sea. It's a lot of ground to cover, and this last leg of our journey may be the darkest. So stay close, and take care with the information you are about to learn and see. The worship of Death has always been and still is very much alive and well here in the Western Hemisphere.

22
LATIN AMERICA

Cultural

Patagonian Tattoos

Down here at the southern edge of Argentina and Chile live the Aóni-kenk people (commonly known to outsiders as the Tehuelche). A nomadic people famous for their cave art, the Aónikenk have historically lived in continuous travel across the harsh landscape of Patagonia. Though an arduous lifestyle, the mix of their unforgiving environment and being constantly on the move prevented European colonizers from wanting to settle in their homeland or permanently subdue them. Thus their cosmology was preserved intact, as was their view of the afterlife: belief in a dual underground/celestial dichotomy of experiences.

The Aónikenk believe that the spirits of the dead reside in a magical cavern with many passageways forming an intricate labyrinth. The sky is another place the spirit could reside, and it's believed that all the stars in the night sky are deceased ancestors. However, the death goddess Seécho Sésom would determine if you were even allowed an afterlife at all.

Fortunately, she isn't picky. All that's necessary is for her to see the tribe's distinctive tattoo on your body's left arm (parallel lines inside of which there'd be an upside-down triangle whose apex balanced on the apex of a right-side-up triangle), and you'd be good. Not having that tattoo meant you were not part of the tribe and thus denied an afterlife by being thrown into the sea. Aónikenk burial rites mimic this belief in that corpses without the distinctive tattoo are simply tossed into a body of water.[226]

Cemetery Werewolves

Riding the rails across the expanse of the Pampas to the northeastern edge of Argentina, the landscape becomes subtropical. This is the historical territory of the Guaraní people, which stretches over a large swath of land covering northern Argentina, Uruguay, Brazil, and Paraguay, and in this territory exists el Luisón. El Luisón is believed to be a werewolf-like canine demon who rules over the night and resides exclusively in cemeteries and burial grounds.

El Luisón (which is a derivative of *lobizón,* the Argentine Spanish word for "werewolf," since the hellhound's original Guaraní name is lost to history) was closely associated with death in Guaraní culture. He even feasted upon the rotting flesh and bones of the dead. Humans could turn into a lesser luisón if el Luisón passed through a person's legs, but because el Luisón was confined to burial grounds, only those who entered a cemetery would be in danger.

---

226 Chris Moss, *Patagonia: A Cultural History* (Oxford: Signal Books Ltd., 2008).
     Austin Whittall, "More on the Patagonian Labrys, Phoenicians and Cretans,"
     Patagonian Monsters, Nov. 5, 2013, http://patagoniamonsters.blogspot
     .com/2013/11/more-on-patagonian-labrys-phoenicians.html (accessed
     Aug. 6, 2018).

Modern psychologists and Guaraní poets believe that el Luisón is the Guaraní's way of explaining grief-related post-traumatic stress disorder (PTSD). The logic is that if a person suffered a psychotic break from losing a loved one, then they would most likely experience bouts of PTSD around reminders of their loved one's death. So, the cemetery itself acts as a trigger. Also, before modern cemeteries, burial grounds were common haunts for hungry, sickly dogs who dug up the shallow dead for food; thus it would make sense from a premodern perspective that a wild dog of the cemetery would be blamed for inducing psychoses in people who we would now label as grief-PTSD sufferers who were already on edge and emotionally triggered by the burial site of their loved ones.[227]

Threatening the Saints

The other Guaraní death deity is San La Muerte (not to be confused with la Santa Muerte, whom we'll talk about once we reach Mexico). San La Muerte is beloved throughout northern Argentina and Paraguay. He's a folk saint born from the mix of the Guaraní's veneration of their ancestors' bones and the Jesuit Catholic missionaries' teachings on sainthood. Because he looks exactly like the Grim Reaper, except with his cloak (usually, but not always) open to show his skeletal frame, the Vatican has formally denounced his following as "pagan" (which it partly is, but that doesn't make it a bad thing, right?).[228]

While most devotees of San La Muerte consider themselves Catholic, their relationship with him isn't typical of Catholicism's supplicant-granter power balance when usually dealing with the saints. You see, devotees don't petition favors from San La Muerte, they *threaten* him for them (via his

227 Susan Smith Nash, "Folklore and the Horrors of War: 'El Luison' and Cadaver-Eating Dogs," *E-Learning Queen*, Apr. 9, 2005, http://elearnqueen .blogspot.com/2005/04/folklore-and-horrors-of-war-el-luison.html (accessed Aug. 6, 2018).

228 "¿Qué es San La Muerte, el polémico culto que se relaciona con el crimen?" *El Observador*, Apr. 17, 2012, https://www.elobservador.com.uy/que-es-san -la-muerte-el-polemico-culto-que-se-relaciona-el-crimen-n276645 (accessed Aug. 6, 2018).

statue) until he grants them what they want. Methods vary from hanging him upside down, burying him, or leaving him outside exposed to the elements until your wishes are met.

After a prayer is answered in your favor, though, it is paramount to reward him with offerings of common luxuries (cigars, alcohol, flowers, spare money, etc.). Because he can be physically persuaded to answer prayers, he doesn't have a moral compass, and so he is often the favorite go-to saint for immoral or unethical desires.[229]

Dark Delicacies of the Amazon

Further north in the jungles of the Amazon rainforest, one of the greatest societal and macabre taboos is still practiced as a time-honored funerary ritual: mortuary cannibalism. Although technically mortuary cannibalism can be found in many cultures on every continent (except you, Antarctica), the most well-known and studied are those we saw in New Guinea and those here in the Amazonian tropics where the Wari' people are the most well-known to practice this culinary taboo. Though they haven't practiced it since the 1960s (due to external pressure and disgust from Christian missionaries), eating their deceased tribespeople was once regarded as an honor of extreme difficulty. Anthropologists have popularly labeled it "compassionate cannibalism."[230]

You see, the Wari' people practiced two kinds of cannibalism, exocannibalism and endocannibalism. Exocannibalism involved eating outsiders (prisoners of war, unlucky anthropologists, etc.) whom the Wari' didn't see as people. Only Wari' were considered "people"; outsiders were animals that could ethically be treated as any other pieces of meat. Endocannibalism, however, was the eating of one's own tribespeople, and though they dreaded having to do it, they practiced endocannibalism in order to save the soul from loneliness.

---

229 "Cómo es el culto a San La Muerte," *La Nación*, Apr. 17, 2014, https://www
     .lanacion.com.ar/1683079-como-es-el-culto-a-san-la-muerte (accessed Aug.
     6, 2018).
230 Beth A. Conklin, *Consuming Grief: Compassionate Cannibalism in Amazonian Society*
     (Austin: University of Texas Press, 2001).

It was believed that once a Wari' died, the soul would be released from the body as soon as the corpse's flesh had rotted away. If the body was left out to rot in the jungle, then the soul would wander the earth alone for all eternity (or be trapped underground if they were buried). To prevent this, tribe members who were not blood relatives would eat the flesh of the deceased so that the soul would stay within the tribe (literally and figuratively) for ever and ever. However, the hot, moist environment of a tropical rainforest is perfect for accelerating putrefaction, and so by the time the tribe could be rounded up and all the preritual ceremonies performed, the corpse could often be fully bloated, discolored, actively rotting, and infested with maggots. No matter the condition, though, the flesh had to be eaten to save the soul, and though the rotted flesh was cooked, it was never a pleasant ordeal.[231]

A Place in the Inca Sun

Straight outta the rainforest and over the Andes, we find evidence of the mighty Inca, who once ruled supreme. Most impressively, they built their empire (which they referred to as *Tawantinsuyu*, roughly translated to "The Four United Regions") and astoundingly ruled over it without the use of writing, iron, the wheel, and beasts of burden to pull a plough. Still, their influence spread over much of the Andes to what is now Peru, Bolivia, Chile, Argentina, Ecuador, and even a bit of Colombia. Though they no longer exist, their legacy of morbid practices and beliefs still echoes on in the modern-day cultures of these regions.

When talking about death, the Inca were heavy proponents of reincarnation. Now, this isn't the same kind of earthly reincarnation found in Hinduism and Buddhism, but rather a bodily assumption (à la the Virgin Mary in Catholicism) into a heavenly afterlife. Being literal sun worshippers (they

---

231　Beth A. Conklin, "'Thus Are Our Bodies, Thus Was Our Custom': Mortuary Cannibalism in an Amazonian Society," *American Ethnologist* 22:1, Feb. 1995. Alice Robb, "Will Overpopulation and Resource Scarcity Drive Cannibalism?" *The New Republic*, Jun. 19, 2014, https://newrepublic.com/article/118252/cannibalism-and-overpopulation-how-amazon-tribe-ate-their-dead (accessed Aug. 6, 2018).

believed themselves to be children descended from the sun), the most blissful place one could be was in the loving warmth of the sun, and so the sun
was the ideal reincarnation destination. However, in order to be reincarnated
at all, a person had to observe the Inca moral code: *ama suwa, ama llulla, ama
quella* (don't steal, don't lie, don't be lazy). If the person was a thief, liar, or
unproductive member of society, their spirit would exist forever in the cold
ground, where no loving sunlight could ever reach them.[232]

South American Mummies

The practice of mummification is, perhaps, the most famous of all Inca
burial rituals. The majority of mummies were in either fetal or seated positions, and their preserved corpses were venerated in rituals and magical
ceremonies. These often served as figureheads of the ancestors and presided over weddings, harvests, or farewell celebrations to troops off to
battle.

To create the mummies, the body fluids would be drained, organs
removed, salt stuffed inside the body, preserving alcohol (maize beer)
poured in and on the cadaver, and the body left alone to essentially freeze-
dry in the ultra-arid high-altitude regions of the empire. Notoriously, in
addition to ancestor veneration, sacrificial victims (including children)
were mummified and positioned at sacred shrines around the empire,
believed to be a way the Inca asserted psychological control over their conquered subjects.[233]

The Underworld of the Maya

Of all the civilizations in pre-Columbian Latin America, the Maya were
unique in that they had a developed writing system. Because of this, we
know a lot about their life and beliefs from authentic, firsthand sources

---

232 "Inca Civilization," *New World Encyclopedia,* http://www.newworldencyclopedia
.org/entry/Inca_Civilization#Religion (accessed Aug. 7, 2018).

233 Tom D. Dillehay, "Incan Religion," *Encyclopedia of Death and Dying,* http://www
.deathreference.com/Ho-Ka/Incan-Religion.html (accessed Aug. 7, 2018).
Mark Cartwright, "Inca Mummies," *Ancient History Encyclopedia,* Jun. 16, 2014,
https://www.ancient.eu/article/699/inca-mummies/ (accessed Aug. 7, 2018).

and aren't as reliant on biased secondhand accounts from Spanish soldiers and missionaries. For all of us fascinated with the morbid and the macabre, that means we have quite an extensive library of information on their funerary practices and afterlife beliefs.

This is especially true with stories regarding the Maya underworld of Xibalba, which was an unhappy, dark, dismal place that everyone ultimately went to and was ruled by a number of fearsome gods who had names like "Blood Gatherer," "Pus Master," and "Skull Scepter." Xibalba was also filled with demons who were ambivalent to the humans arriving daily. They helped sometimes, they harmed sometimes, and sometimes they often did a bit of both. The only way to avoid Xibalba was to have your cause of death be a violent death, often as a warrior in battle (which included the "battlefield" of a sports game). For everyone else, though, Xibalba was an inevitability. Rich, poor, good, bad, old, young—none of it mattered; everyone went to Xibalba.[234]

Preparations for Xibalba

We'll get more into the horrors of Xibalba in the "Deities & Legends" section coming up, but for now, we'll stay above ground and focus on the physical. The body was left behind and either buried or cremated with tremendous ceremony. Maize kernels were placed in the mouth of the deceased as a symbol of new life (albeit a new life in Xibalba). More gruesomely, people from the lower classes were sacrificed upon the death of a member of the ruling aristocracy so that the wealthy could have an entourage of people to help them when enduring Xibalba. The actual cadavers themselves were sprinkled with cinnabar shavings as a way to help the deceased look more demonic in the afterlife and blend in with the demons of Xibalba so as to avoid being a target (red being the color of death).

The living could (and often did) interact with the dead, and the most magical tool for necromancy was a mirror. Of course, these aren't the same kind of mirrors that are common today, but rather polished stones that had

234 Mark Cartwright, "Xibalba," *Ancient History Encyclopedia*, Oct. 21, 2014, https://www.ancient.eu/Xibalba/ (accessed Dec. 16, 2018).

a concave, reflective surface. This meant that the reflected image would appear a bit distorted, thus making the image seem somehow demonic or otherworldly.

The dead were also very apt to help out the living. Traditionally, the Maya believed that everyone had multiple souls, and while the main, conscious soul went to Xibalba, other souls would ethereally remain around to do various tasks, including aide the living. On the flip side, the best way the living could aid the dead would be to give offerings at their resting place to help ease their burdens in Xibalba.[235]

Aztec Blood Debt

The Aztec Empire (which is a modern name given to the ruling indigenous people who called themselves the "Mexica") is probably the most morbidly notorious in Mesoamerica to us nowadays because of their penchant for human sacrifice. Granted, many cultures throughout Latin America (and elsewhere) participated in human sacrifice, but the Aztecs just took it to a whole other level due to the supreme importance they placed on it as a necessity for the world to even function. You see, in Aztec mythology, death is the precursor to life. Mankind is the result of the gods sacrificing themselves, and because of this, humans were forever indebted to the gods on a primal level.

So, following the gods' cosmic lead, it was believed that something had to die in order for something else to be given life, and this was exemplified in their human sacrifices. Since human beings were seen as the epitome of life on earth, a human sacrifice was the epitome of all sacrifices that one could give to the gods. These were complex affairs that required lots of preplanning, selecting the perfect sacrifice, getting them in commune with the deity to whom they would be sacrificed, choosing an auspicious day/

---

235 Yurina Fernández Noa, "The Maya: Funeral Rituals," *Yucatán Today*, http://yucatantoday.com/mayas-funeral-rituals/?lang=en (accessed Aug. 8, 2018). Woolf, *Ancient Civilizations: The Illustrated Guide to Belief, Mythology, and Art.*

time, etc. Usually, the sacrifices were warriors (slaves every now and then, but the more honorable the person, the more honorable the sacrifice).[236]

Blood was seen as the liquid of life, and by spilling human blood in a carefully arranged sacrifice, the universe was able to keep on going. Sacrificial blood helped the plants grow, the seasons change, the sun rise, and so on. A blood offering, however, didn't always have to be a grand affair; it could be a personal and private low-key ritual in the same way someone could privately say a prayer. Supposing the petition wasn't something major, it was often acceptable for people to offer up their own blood in a self-directed mini ceremony (think less of a droplet of blood from a pinprick, and more of a torrent of blood from running a barbed rope through your tongue). The frequent shedding of blood and human sacrifices intertwined into the social expectations of Aztec citizens and influenced daily life outside these sanguine ceremonies.[237]

These Sides of Paradise

Being sacrificed to the gods wasn't all bad, though. It had a lot of positive postmortem perks in the afterlife. Like the Maya, the Aztecs believed that your cause of death influenced where your soul would go. It didn't matter your morality, ethics, age, wealth, status, or anything else; the absolute only thing that determined your afterlife realm was how you died.

The best of all possible deaths would be a heroic death. In addition to dying on the battlefield or from battle injuries, heroic deaths included being a sacrifice to the gods and dying while (or through complications from) giving birth (pregnant women were seen as soldiers in the battle of childbirth). The reward for such a heroic death would be that your soul would join Huitzilopochtli (supreme god of the sun and war) near the glory and warmth of the sun for four years, and then you'd transform into a hummingbird (Huitzilopochtli's symbolic animal).

---

236 Diego Durán, *Historia de las Indias de Nueva-España y islas de Tierra Firme* (London: Forgotten Books, 2018).

237 Fray Diego de Landa, *Relación de las cosas de Yucatán* (Mexico City: Miguel Ángel Porrúa, 1982).

If not a heroic death, the next best option was an aquatic death. This included deaths from drowning, floods, storms, being struck by lightning (associated with storms), and waterborne diseases (cholera, dysentery, typhoid fever, etc.). These people's souls were thought to travel to Tlalocán, ruled over by the rain god Tláloc. Tlalocán was a verdant paradise of leisure, and because of the uniqueness of aquatic deaths, it was believed that the gods specifically selected these people to gain entry into Tlalocán by killing them in such a unique way. The really touching part about Tlalocán, though, was that, aside from a watery death, the physically deformed and those with mental retardation all got a free pass into this happy afterlife. The thought was that this was divine compensation for having to be forced to endure such a difficult and limited existence while alive and that they never got a fair shot at possibly having a heroic death.

However, the vast majority of Aztecs went to the underworld of Mictlán. Mictlán was a nine-layered, intricate underworld full of torturous dangers and general unpleasantness. According to legends, the soul would have to travel to the ninth and deepest level of Mictlán (which usually took about four earth years) by crossing razor-studded mountains, rivers of blood, savage jaguars, and more (and if the obstacles were too tough, then too bad; you had no option but to keep on trying to get past each obstacle for all eternity until you finally succeeded to the next one). Once on the ninth level, the soul would come face-to-face with the skeletal lady and lord of the underworld, Mictecacíhuatl and Mictlantecuhtli, by whom they would be torn to shreds in entombed darkness.[238]

---

238 Dr. Susan G. Gillespie, "What Did Ordinary People Turn Into in the Afterlife?" *Mexico Lore*, May 2013, http://www.mexicolore.co.uk/aztecs/ask-experts/what -did-ordinary-people-turn-into-in-the-afterlife (accessed Aug. 9, 2018).

Silvia Trejo, "Tlalocan: 'Recinto de Tláloc,'" *Arqueología Mexicana* Vol. 64, Nov. 2003.

Luz Espinosa, "Mictlán: el lugar de los muertos," *Cultura Colectiva*, Sept. 23, 2014, https://culturacolectiva.com/letras/mictlan-el-lugar-de-los-muertos/ (accessed Aug. 9, 2018).

Melissa Bjordal, "Ancient Aztec Perspectives on Death and the Afterlife," *The Christi Center*, Feb. 11, 2013, http://christicenter.org/2013/02/ancient-aztec -perspective-on-death-and-afterlife/ (accessed Aug. 9, 2018).

Underworld Royalty

Together, Mictecacíhuatl and Mictlantecuhtli rule Mictlán. They reside in the ninth and lowest level of Mictlán and receive the souls of the dead who finally made it all the way through the underworld. Mictecacíhuatl, appropriate for queen of the dead, has a skeletal, defleshed physique with mouth agape like a corpse (which she uses to swallow the stars before day-break). She held particular dominion over the bones and remains of the dead, as well as acting as the mistress of ceremonies who presided over funerary and death-related events (like *Día de Muertos*).[239]

As king of the dead, Mictlantecuhtli also had a skeletal appearance, except he was usually depicted as being splattered with blood, having eye-balls in his eye sockets, giving a toothy grin, and accessorizing with large gauges in his ears (which were the only fleshy parts on him). He also wore a headdress of owl feathers (owls being the bestial symbols of death) and a necklace of corpse eyes. In temperament, he was very shrewd and was one of the main opponents against creating the human race, since it meant utilizing the remains of dead gods that were in his realm. His modus operandi would be to tear human souls to shreds once they made it to his presence.[240]

Día de Muertos

Of course, no morbid trek through Mexico would be complete without mentioning the world famous "Day of the Dead" celebration. Falling on November 2 (All Souls' Day in the Catholic calendar), Día de Muertos (more popularly called "Día de los Muertos" by Spanish speakers outside of Mexico) is a large public holiday focused on getting in touch with one's ancestors and remembering the dead so that they live on in the minds of the living.

---

239 Adela Fernández, *Dioses prehispánicos de México: mitos y deidades del panteón nahuatl* (Mexico City: Panorama, 1996).

240 Eduardo Matos Moctezuma, and Felipe Solís Olguín, *Aztecs* (London: Royal Academy of Arts, 2002).
Mary Miller, and Karl Taube, *An Illustrated Dictionary of the Gods and Symbols of Ancient Mexico and the Maya* (London: Thames & Hudson, 2003).

Similar to the Qingming Festival we saw in China, Día de Muertos is celebrated by families traveling to the cemeteries in which their loved ones are buried and spending time near the corpse. These macabre visits can be all-day affairs with cleaning and routine maintenance of the graves in the morning, picnic lunches and storytelling in the afternoon, and a communal celebration with music, candles, and revelry with fellow cemetery-goers throughout the night.

If it's impossible to actually travel to the gravesite (illness, distance, cremation, etc.), then a temporary shrine altar set up in the home becomes the focus. In addition to a photo of the deceased, their favorite foods, drinks, brands of cigarettes, candies, and other treats are offered, while their favorite music is played. Aztec marigolds are common universal offerings due to their association with death in Aztec mythology.

The modern festivities are a mix of pre-Columbian and Catholic beliefs, but the origins of Día de Muertos are pure Aztec. Originally, it was the celebration day for Mictecacíhuatl and because she has a skeletal appearance, faces and bodies were painted to resemble skeletons in honor of her and of human mortality. As protectress of bones and human remains, this Aztec celebration for Mictecacíhuatl inevitably involved celebration of deceased ancestors and rituals at gravesites where their bones lay at rest.

When Spain's Catholic missionaries arrived, they saw all this ancestor worship as something that had to be stamped out. However, it was too ingrained and beloved by the people to be fully eradicated. So, the missionaries did the next best thing by co-opting the festival and melding it with something more Catholic. The closest thing to an "ancestor worship day" in Catholicism is November 2's All Souls' Day (a solemn day in remembrance of all deceased souls), and so the Aztec celebration in honor of Mictecacíhuatl moved to November (it was originally in August), became known as "Día de Muertos," and ever after became a Church-sanctioned way to celebrate All Souls' Day despite its obvious pagan underpinnings.[241]

Latin American Takeaway:
THE JOY OF NECROMANCY

Usually when people think of necromancy, they think of solemn, dark, somber affairs of communicating with the dead for them to assist in a dire endeavor. Yeah, there's a time and place for that, but who says it *has to* be like that? Why not engage in necromancy just to have a good time and casually connect with our dearly departed like in Mexico's Día de Muertos festivities?

Don't be that friend/relative who only contacts people when you have a problem or when you need something from them. No one likes those people. A true bond is having a relationship with someone without *needing* them. And since you don't want to be that person to your living friends/family, why are you going be like that to those on the other side? So, for your Latin American takeaway challenge, do a bit of necromancy just for the joy of it or to just stay in touch, not just when you need something.

And if you're daring, take it a step further. You can use this perspective to find humor in dark subject matter. Just because something has associations with darkness, death, and the macabre doesn't mean it's all doom and gloom. There is a meditative peace in cemeteries. There is a healing in the shadows. There is a universal oneness in decomposition. The next time you encounter something "dark," look for the joy that can be celebrated in it. It's all a question of attitude.

---

241 John D. Morgan, and Pittu Laungani, *Death and Bereavement Around the World: Death and Bereavement in the Americas* Vol. 2 (New York: Routledge, 2003).
Randy Cordova, "Day of the Dead history: Ritual dates back 3,000 years and is still evolving," *Arizona Central*, Oct. 24, 2017, https://www.azcentral.com/story/entertainment/holidays/day-of-the-dead/2014/09/24/day-of-the-dead-history/16174911/ (accessed Aug. 10, 2018).
"Historia," *Día de los Muertos*, http://diadelosmuertos.yaia.com/historia.html (accessed Aug. 10, 2018).

Deities & Legends

THE MAYA HERO TWINS

Of all the Maya legends, the adventure of the Hero Twins (Hunahpu and Xbalanque) is the most epic, with a story line equal to a Hollywood film. The tale revolves around their journey to the underworld of Xibalba wherein they challenge the death gods to the most intense sports show-down ever written by an ancient civilization. The full story with all its detail and plot twists can be found in the ancient Maya text of the *Popol Vuh*, but for our brief time here, we'll learn the basic story of what happened … in two acts.

ACT 1: Dead Ringers

The twins' father and uncle were well-known as the best ballplayers in existence (the Maya ball game was like a mix of basketball and hacky sack wherein the objective was to get a rubber ball through a raised vertical ring by only using your hip, elbow, and knee and without letting the ball hit the ground).[242] Envious, the top two ranking underworld gods (known as the Lords of Death) challenged them to a two-on-two game in the under-world of Xibalba, but the twins' father and uncle never returned and were assumed dead. Eventually, the twins grew up to be equally talented ball-players. So, the Lords of Death challenged them to a game in the under-world, too, and the twins accepted so they could avenge their relatives who were presumed to be murdered in Xibalba by the Lords.

They ventured through the underworld and its many deadly hazards until they reached the court of the Lords of Death. The Lords, however, required the twins to pass the Dark House test to see if they were truly worthy to play ball against them. If the twins could survive for an entire night inside the Dark House (a house that was pitch dark inside, the dan-ger being one's own paranoid imagination in the blindness), then they could challenge the Lords; if they failed, they would die. The twins sur-

---

242 Gerhard Blümchen, "The Maya ball game: Comparison of the physical load with modern ball games," *Cardiology* 113:4, 2009.

vived this first test and competed against the Lords in a ball game. However, the twins purposely lost.

Consequently, the twins were given another all-night house challenge. If they survived, they'd get a rematch; if they lost, they'd get another all-night house challenge (with the Lords' plan being that the twins would never win a match and just eventually die during one of these house challenges).

This second challenge was the Razor House (a house filled with razors). The twins survived, had a rematch, and lost again on purpose. The same happened after they survived the Cold House (a house of freezing cold) and the Jaguar House (a house filled with hungry jaguars). All the while, though, they gained a sort of underdog following in Xibalba as persistent and scrappy survivors unlike anything the underworld demons and souls of the dead had ever seen.

Alas, things suddenly changed in the Bat House (a house filled with hungry bats) when Hunahpu was decapitated by one of the bats. Since Xbalanque survived, he competed in a two-on-one rematch (by himself) against the Lords, who used Hunahpu's severed head as the ball. During the game, Xbalanque retrieved the head, reattached it to his brother's corpse to even the teams, and together they beat the Lords of Death.

Being sore losers, the Lords killed the surviving twin anyway. This unprecedented act of unsportsmanlike conduct caused a rift among the spirits and demons in Xibalba; some supported the Lords, and some saw the Lords as unjust tyrants who didn't keep their word to the fan-favorite *real* winners.

ACT 2: *The Greatest Show Unearthed*

Now officially dead, the twins resided in Xibalba but were able to avoid further persecution from the Lords. This was thanks to disguises given to them by the loyal fans they had amassed through their underdog rematches against the Lords. Thus their plan was working, since this slow buildup of an underworld following is why they kept purposely losing all initial matches.

Some of their demon fans eventually taught them the magic of resurrection from the second death. (According to legend, if a dead soul died a second time, they would cease to exist altogether and spend eternity in a void of oblivion.) Supposedly, this magic could bring a person back from the void. So, the disguised twins began to travel throughout Xibalba doing street performances of this magic act in which they'd kill a volunteer and then resurrect them back from the void.

It was a hit. Their traveling sideshow grew in popularity until the buzz reached the Lords, who invited the entertainers to do a performance for them at their court. The twins obliged, and as they suspected, the Lords volunteered themselves to be the show's resurrected stars. So, the twins killed them... but never resurrected them. The brothers' long and intricate plan of revenge had finally been achieved. However, with the ruling Lords gone, Xibalba descended into chaos as individuals and factions battled for power to be the new rulers of the underworld.

The twins' quest for vengeance had finally been fulfilled, but they hadn't realized that they painted themselves into a corner. Their magic could only resurrect a person from second death, not first death, and so despite avenging their father and uncle, they were stuck in Xibalba for all eternity. Nevertheless, for all their heroism, the gods decided to reward the twins by transforming one into the sun and the other into the moon, having them reside in the heavens from then on, banishing the darkness of the world with their light.[243]

LA LLORONA

La Llorona (literally, "The Weeping Woman") is one of the most famous morbid legends in Mexico and among Mexican communities throughout the world. She is a boogeyman (boogeywoman?) type of ghost who preys on children with the intent of killing them. Belief in her is still fiercely upheld in parts of Mexico, and in addition to being a scare tactic for chil-

---

243 Dennis Tedlock, *Popol Vuh* (New York: Simon & Schuster, 1996).
"Maya Hero Twins," *History on the Net*, https://www.historyonthenet.com/maya-hero-twins/ (accessed Aug. 16, 2018).

dren to behave, alleged spectral sightings of her still occur and tend to be almost always at night and near a body of water.

Though the specifics of her legend vary, the general folktale is that a beautiful woman (usually named María since it's a generic "any-woman" name in Latinx culture) living in a poor village catches the eye of a wealthy aristocrat traveling through town, and the two marry. She gives birth to two of his children, but her husband's constant business traveling sparks tension. At first, she was upset that he was being a bad father to their babies since he was constantly absent, but then the resentment became more personal as each time he would return home, she noticed that he'd only spend time with the kids and never her. In time, he stopped returning altogether.

Years later when the babies had grown into young children and their father's abandonment had left María impoverished, she took her kids out to play in the local river. It was then that María spotted her estranged husband riding by in a posh carriage with a younger woman. In that moment, she had a nervous breakdown and saw her children as the reason her husband left her. She drowned them in the river. When she regained her senses, she began weeping profusely as only a mother who regrets murdering her own children could do. Minutes later, she drowned herself in that same river.

It's said that her ghost wanders the earth, still weeping with profound sorrow. Hearing her wailing is known as a bad omen of misfortune to come, and children are told to be careful of her since she would try to kill them too (out of residual resentment or confusing them for her own kids).[244]

244 Christine Delsol, "Mexico's legend of La Llorona continues to terrify," *San Francisco Gate*, Oct. 9, 2012, https://www.sfgate.com/mexico/mexicomix/ article/Mexico-s-legend-of-La-Llorona-continues-to-3933072.php (accessed Aug. 15, 2018).

Joe Hayes, *La Llorona: The Weeping Woman* (El Paso: Cinco Puntos Press, 2006).

LA SANTA MUERTE

Now, I've actually already written an entire, separate book all about this Mexican folk deity of death, so if you're extra curious, you can check out *La Santa Muerte: Unearthing the Magic & Mysticism of Death*. But for our time here, I'll show you some of the basics about why she is such a growing phenomenon in Mexican communities here in Mexico and abroad.

At her core, la Santa Muerte (whose name is Spanish for "Holy Death") is literally the personification of death, often visualized as a female Grim Reaper. Her devotion originated in Mexico, and though there's speculation that it could've predated the arrival of the Spanish, belief in her was a well-kept secret among the faithful until the 1990s when it started to enter mainstream consciousness. La Santa Muerte's devotees (past and present) usually come from groups who are ostracized and maligned by traditional Mexican Catholic society. These often include criminals, prostitutes, the working poor, self-empowered women, and the LGBT+ community.

Not feeling like they belong in the Catholic Church yet still culturally raised in a Catholic tradition, they believe themselves to be Catholic through and through yet unworthy of God's favor (because of their "sins"). Instead, they ask la Santa Muerte to advocate to Him on their behalf. Essentially, it's Mexican Catholicism with the cult of Our Lady of Guadalupe substituted with the cult of Lady Death.

Why death, though? It's because death doesn't judge. Death accepts all people equally regardless of their morality, goodness, intentions, or past actions. To the outcasts of the world, la Santa Muerte's total nonjudgment is a much-needed refuge in a world where they are hated by society for reasons often beyond their control. God, the Virgin Mary, and all the saints in Heaven may judge them, but death is the one supernatural force that they know will never do such a thing.

The flip side is that la Santa Muerte's total nonjudgment is also why she gets a lot of bad press. Since she will not judge anyone's petitions no matter what they are, a good number of her devotees often ask for morally ambiguous or downright wicked things. Drug cartels frequently petition her to help move some product. Prostitutes petition for a safe and profitable night. Assassins petition that their bullets find their mark. And so on. Whether out of pure malicious intent or because they are victims of circumstance with no other avenues to financially support themselves and their loved one, they know that God would *never* help with such petitions, but because la Santa Muerte is death (and death doesn't have a moral compass), they know she'll help them with any and all such favors.

EL TÍO

El Tío (literally, "The Uncle"… a name that came about by the natives' mispronunciation of *Dios*, Spanish for "God") [245] is an interesting folk demon still very much believed in around the Bolivian mining town of Potosí, specifically in the mines of Cerro Rico. You see, during colonial times, Potosí was the nerve center of the Spanish Empire's silver extraction from the New World, and the cost of human (read "native") lives it took to mine all that silver was staggering. Due to the sheer quantity of death and ever-hellish conditions, the mines in and around Potosí were believed to be haunted. Even today, the mines here are still in operation and still unbelievably dangerous (around fourteen deaths each month) due to the nature of the work, low safety standards, and all the toxic dust in the air down there. That's where el Tío comes into the picture.

El Tío is the spiritual entity of the mines, who looks a lot like a cartoonish, Pan-inspired devil (except less whimsy and more fright). Since the underground (and thus all mines) is his domain, he's believed to have the power to decide whether you'll return to the surface alive or not. To appease him and curry favor, miners erect effigy shrines to him near the aboveground entrances and leave offerings of cigarettes, alcohol, and coca leaves (a native plant used as a stimulant and for alleviation of altitude sickness… as well as the base ingredient for cocaine). When on break or

245 José Miguel Redondo, "En las entrañas de las minas de Potosí, la puerta del infierno," *El Rincón de Sele*, Mar. 31, 2014, https://www.elrincondesele .com/en-las-entranas-de-las-minas-de-potosi-bolivia-la-puerta-del-infierno/ (accessed Sept. 18, 2018).

not on duty, they hang out with him at these makeshift shrines and keep him company.

The complicated part of all this is that these miners are virtually all devout Catholics. Yet despite official condemnation from the Vatican, these locals still hold true to their traditional animistic belief in spirits residing in natural things and places (such as mines and mountains). The practice of "separate but equal" is how the miners balance out their two simultaneous yet opposing religious beliefs. The deal is that el Tío is *never* brought out of the mines or talked about aboveground (except for his unofficial feast day of August 1, when the locals sacrifice a llama to him in a big ceremony), and, in turn, any talk of Christianity is *never* uttered while underground in his realm. And thus both God and el Tío are kept appeased.[246]

---

246 "The Devil's Miner," *Public Broadcasting Corporation,* http://www.pbs.org/independentlens/devilsminer/mountain.html (accessed Aug. 10, 2018). Harry Stewart, "Meet El Tio: The Devil Who Rules the Underworld of Bolivia's Mines," *Culture Trip,* Oct. 20, 2017, https://theculturetrip.com/south-america/bolivia/articles/meet-el-tio-the-devil-who-rules-the-underworld-of-bolivias-mines/ (accessed Aug. 10, 2018).

23
NATIVE NORTH AMERICA

Cultural

While technically Mexico and Mesoamerica are part of North America, the last leg of our global trek around the world is here in the US/Canadian parts of this continent. Of course, before there was a "US" or a "Canada" there were the native peoples of these lands comprising many, many varying tribes. Each tribe has their own culture, customs, and beliefs that intersect with regional similarities yet are still distinctly their own. As with everywhere else we've been, the breadth of human cultures here is much too vast for our fast-paced worldwide tour, and so we'll be unable to visit the morbid traditions of every single native tribe. Nevertheless, we'll be sure to visit as many as we can along our route before reaching our final destination up along the frozen shores of the Arctic Sea.

Of Horses and Men

As we ride the train over the border from Mexico, our first stop takes us into Comanche territory. The Comanche (known amongst themselves as the Nʉmʉnʉʉ people) are renowned for their horsemanship, and it's their equestrian abilities that allowed them to control much of what is now Texas, New Mexico, Oklahoma, and Kansas. In their funerary rituals, horses were sacrificed in honor of the deceased (and the higher the status, the more horses were slaughtered).

Wherever the death occurred, the body of a Comanche would be buried on the western edge of camp (so the soul could follow the setting sun into the hunting fields of the afterlife), but not before a lariat was used to tie the knees to be bent up to the stomach and the body was wrapped in a blanket. Naturally, the corpse would be put on a horse en route to the gravesite for the deceased's last ride into the sunset.[247]

Skin-Walkers

Westward into Arizona, New Mexico, and bits of Utah is the Navajo Nation. Known more authentically as the Diné people, they have some of the most startling and macabre folklore in all the Americas, particularly in regard to the skin-walkers. It must be noted, though, that in-depth talk of the skin-walkers to people who are not Diné is extremely taboo. Thorough storytelling about or involving skin-walkers is seen as dangerous and as the opening of a Pandora's box that'll unleash malevolence unto the world by people who do not truly understand the cultural context of these evil ones. (Not even J. K. Rowling is immune to this taboo, receiving severe

---

247 Fritz Zimmerman, "The Comanche Indians Mortuary Practices," *American Indians History*, Jul. 31, 2011, https://americanindianshistory.blogspot .com/2011/07/mortuary-customs-of-native-americans.html (accessed Aug. 13, 2018).
Daniel J. Gelo, "Comanche," *Encyclopedia.com*, 2002, https://www. encyclopedia.com/history/united-states-and-canada/north-american -indigenous-peoples/comanche (accessed Aug. 13, 2018).

backlash for talking about and culturally appropriating skin-walkers into YA novel baddies).[248]

I know, it's a bit of a tease to tell you that there is this evil morbid folklore and then say we cannot really go in-depth about it, but there is a bit we *can* learn without crossing the line into learning *too* much. From authentic sources that are Diné-approved as low-grade information, we outsiders can safely know the skin-walkers are essentially Diné magic workers who have been corrupted by their own power and turned evil. They are shape-shifters who can appear as various animals and can even possess the bodies of living animals and people by locking eyes with them. Ultimately, skin-walkers proactively bring about misery to all beings via sickness, death, famine, insanity, and implementation of dark urges within people. Though many a magic worker can go bad, it's rumored that only those who murder a blood relative can become a full-fledged skin-walker.[249]

Desert Cry

Riding along northwestward into Nevada, we enter the high desert that the Paiute tribes call home. Officially, there are three main tribes (Northern Paiute, Owens Valley Paiute, and Southern Paiute), but the Owens Valley and Southern Paiute were the two to practice the unique funerary tradition of the Cry Ceremony (*yaxape*). In the nights between death and burial, the community would come together for the Cry Ceremony to honor the dead through the singing of the Bird Songs (musical creation stories and

248 Douglas Perry, "J.K. Rowling embraces skinwalkers; Native Americans slam her for 'lies and misperceptions'," *The Oregonian*, Mar. 10, 2016, https://www .oregonlive.com/entertainment/index.ssf/2016/03/jk_rowling_embraces _skinwalker.html (accessed Aug. 13, 2018).

249 Joanne Teller, and Norman Blackwater, *The Navajo Skinwalker, Witchcraft, & Related Spiritual Phenomena: Spiritual Clues: Orientation to the Evolution of the Circle* (Conshohocken, Infinity Publishing, 1997).
Cory Daniel, "Skinwalkers," *The Phoenix Enigma*, Dec. 17, 2015, http:// thephoenixenigma.com/skinwalkers/ (accessed Aug. 13, 2018).

myths)[250] and the traditional 142 Salt Songs (sacred songs about spiritual and physical landscapes that transcend life and death as well as musically map out historic locations of valuable resources such as salt).[251]

Following these emphatic eulogies came the distribution of the deceased's valuables to the community. Occasionally, there is a grand Cry Ceremony wherein all members of the entire tribe get together to celebrate all those who died in the previous year. To this day, it is still one of the largest celebrations of the Paiute people, though it is becoming less and less common as the years go by.[252]

Corpse Canoes

Up further northwest along the Columbia River that divides Oregon and Washington, the Chinook people are known for their canoe burials done to assist the deceased in the afterlife. Upon death, the body is adorned by relatives with dentalium shells and then placed in their canoe. The canoe is then filled with items symbolic to the deceased's trade, but it's never set out to sea. Rather, the corpse decomposes in the canoe, out of reach of scavenger animals thanks to being wrapped in mats and suspended on stilts. Meanwhile, the family members of the deceased cut off their own hair and change their names, helping to signify the death of that persona they had in the deceased's living years and the birth of a new persona they now must have without the deceased in their lives, an acknowledgment of how death permanently changes us.

250 Chris Clarke, "Native Singers Keep Bird Songs Alive," *KCET*, Nov. 2, 2011, https://www.kcet.org/socal-focus/native-singers-keep-bird-songs-alive (accessed Nov. 1, 2018).

251 Frederic Murray, "Shifting Boundaries: Violence, Representation, and the Salt Songs of the Great Basin Peoples," *Southeastern Oklahoma State University*, 2011, http://www.se.edu/nas/files/2013/03/NAS-2011-Proceedings-Murray.pdf (accessed Nov. 1, 2018).

252 Richard C. Hanes, and Laurie Collier Hillstrom, "Paiutes," *Countries and Their Cultures*, http://www.everyculture.com/multi/Le-Pa/Paiutes.html (accessed Aug. 13, 2018).
Joëlle Clark, "Southern Paiute Cultural History Curriculum Guide," *National Park Service*, Sept. 2010, https://www.nps.gov/para/learn/education/upload/total-final-curriculum.pdf (accessed Aug. 13, 2018).

With wise foresight, the Chinook also reflect on their own mortality while alive and preplan for the distribution of their possessions. It's not uncommon for members of the tribe to publicly decree who will get what upon their death, and this includes spouses. If a married person is dying, he or she will decree the people who are eligible to be the widow(er)'s new spouse (through societal expectations, though, the deceased's brother/sister is usually the designated replacement so as to keep the bond between the in-laws intact). Regardless, after death, the widow(er) must choose a new partner from only those whom their now-dead spouse decreed as eligible.[253]

Dead or Alive

When it comes to reincarnation, belief in it is widespread among many North American tribes though it's markedly different from the kind we've seen in Asia and Latin America. One example of Native American reincarnation takes us up into the northern parts of British Columbia where the Gitxsan tribe's idea of death and reincarnation transcends time itself.

In a nutshell, their belief is that the dead can travel into the present and the future, and all people who are alive now can visit the past, thus blurring the cosmic timeline down to the very definition of what it means to be dead or alive. They also believe animals can do this, too, and countless are the Native American tribes who believe in the incarnation of animals. This can be seen in the widespread practice of thanking the spirit of an animal who had just been killed for food. The hope is that the animal will hold no ill will in its next reincarnation and offer itself as food again or refrain from revenge.[254]

253 Franz Boas, "Chinook Texts," *Sacred-Texts*, 1894, http://www.sacred-texts
     .com/nam/nw/chinook/cht30.htm (accessed Aug. 13, 2018).
     Gary R. Varner, *Ghosts, Spirits & the Afterlife in Native American Folklore and
     Religion* (Raleigh: OakChylde/Lulu Press, 2010).
254 Ojibwa, "Traditional Native Concepts of Death," *Native American Netroots*,
     Sept. 1, 2014, https://nativeamericannetroots.net/diary/1726 (accessed
     Aug. 13, 2018).

Reincarnation was also a major belief to tribes on the Atlantic Sea-board, notably among the Lenni Lenape peoples of Delaware, New Jersey, eastern Pennsylvania, and southern New York. The female elders of this tribe would be tasked with finding out the past lives of each new child. To do this, the female elders examined the infant's body for any marks or tell-tale signs followed by presenting the baby with objects, words, and sounds associated with certain people, things, and places.[255]

Matrilineal Mourning Wars

Death took a slightly different approach in matrilineal tribes, though, especially among the Iroquois, whose confederacy of Mohawk, Oneida, Onondaga, Seneca, Cayuga, and Tuscarora tribes lived on the vast swath of land around the Great Lakes from Illinois and Kentucky to New York and Québec. If anyone was at fault for the death of a fellow tribesperson, the price would be ten strings of wampum (decorative shell-bead belts) for a male victim and twenty wampum for a female victim (women were seen as more valuable since they could create and house new life). But if someone outside the community was at fault, a Mourning War would be declared.

A Mourning War would commence when the matriarch of the victim's family requested her tribe's warriors kidnap someone from the offender's family. With the kidnapped person in her possession, the matriarch would then judge the level of grief the hostage had toward what his/her family had done. If the grief was deemed inadequate or insincere, then each tribe-sperson would individually torture the hostage, after which the hostage would be forcibly adopted into the matriarch's family (effectively replacing the deceased victim in reparation). However, if the grief was considered adequate and sincere, then they would forego the torture and welcome the new person into their tribe. Either way, there was no return for the kidnapped.[256]

---

255 Ojibwa, *Native American Netroots*, 2014.

256 Michele Meleen, "Native American Death Rituals," *Love To Know*, https://dying.lovetoknow.com/native-american-death-rituals (accessed Aug. 13, 2018).

Soul Solidarity

One of the largest Native American ethnic groups had their territory just north of the Iroquois in what is now Ontario, Manitoba, Minnesota, Wisconsin, Michigan, and portions of Saskatchewan. These are the Ojibwe people (commonly known as the Chippewa), and they held the belief that the spirit didn't exit the body immediately upon death, but only after a four-day resting period in the buried corpse. During these crucial four days, a fire would be lit at the head of the grave each night to show solidarity with the trapped spirit.

On the fourth day, a medicine man would preside over a great feast in celebration of the soul finally being able to be released and at peace. After the meal, each celebrant would receive one of the deceased's earthly possessions, and in exchange, the recipient had to give an unworn piece of clothing to the deceased's closest living relative. Throughout the following years, that relative would then distribute the new clothes to people whom they deemed worthy.

The only personal possession not up for exchange was the deceased's food bowl. For a whole year, the closest living relative would bring this bowl to every meal he/she attended and have it filled each time as a sign of remembrance. If this relative was a widow, then she would be expected to not adorn herself and keep ungroomed during that year lest she attract sexual or romantic attention.[257]

Arctic Senicide

And here we've arrived at our last stop, the final station on our global trek, the Arctic taiga and tundra of Canada, Alaska, and Greenland. Here in this perennially cold climate, the Inuit peoples have adopted unique funerary rituals and beliefs for their unforgiving environment. One of the biggest morbid rumors is that the Inuit used to set their elderly relatives adrift on an ice floe to die once they'd become a burden. The reasoning was that life

257 Sister M. Inez Hilger, "Chippewa Burial and Mourning Customs," *American Anthropologist* 46:2, 1944, https://anthrosource.onlinelibrary.wiley.com/doi/pdf/10.1525/aa.1944.46.4.02a00240 (accessed Aug. 13, 2018).

here in the Arctic north was very difficult and supporting people who could no longer contribute to survival was a detriment to the greater good of the community.

In truth, though, while this *was* practiced a long time ago, it was only done during rare times of mass famine and only as a last resort (not just because of some *Logan's Run*-esque timeline on perceived human usefulness). Moreover, the elderly person him-/herself would choose this suicidal fate of their own volition to help the greater good of the younger generations. It was not forced upon them.

As the ritual went, the elderly person would announce their decision for suicide (usually via hanging, not freezing on an ice floe) and everyone would be expected to persuade them not to do it (regardless of their true feelings on the decision). Still, once the announcement was made, non-fulfillment of the deed was believed to result in all sorts of misfortune befalling the community. Those who helped assist in the suicide were ritually shunned for a time, but the community deeply empathized with them because everyone knew it was a tough task that no one wanted.[258]

Ending on a Light Note

Before we go, we must see one of the most visually stunning morbid beliefs here in the Arctic north. To do this, we have to look upward at one of the most awe-inspiring and well-known phenomena of these cold lands, the aurora borealis (aka the "northern lights"). Though a cosmic-magnetic array of dancing colors in the dark sky brings to mind the positivity of a nighttime rainbow of sorts, the Inuit associated this phenomenon with death.

They believed that the aurora was their ancestors getting back in touch with them, and that the living could communicate back via whistling. In Greenland, the northern lights were specifically the spirits of all those who

---

258 Alexander H. Leighton, and Charles C. Hughes, "Notes on Eskimo Patterns of Suicide," *Southwestern Journal of Anthropology* 11:4, 1955, https://ethicsofsuicide.lib.utah.edu/tradition/indigenous-cultures/arctic-cultures/saint-lawrence-eskimo/ (accessed Aug. 15, 2018).

died as children. In northern Alaska, however, it was a physical manifestation of evil, and tribes carried knives as a safety precaution when the aurora was out. To most Inuit tribes, though, this colorful phenomenon was simply a window into knowing that their ancestors were enjoying the afterlife and having a really good time.[259]

Native North American Takeaway:
GIVING SPACE TO GRIEF

The Paiute tribes in Nevada teach a great lesson on loss, and that is the sacredness of giving space to grief. Through their Cry Ceremonies, they create a mental and temporal space to allow themselves to feel grief. They give themselves permission to feel sad, to feel joyful for their loved one's new adventures in the great beyond, and to feel a mix of anything and everything in between. Everyone grieves differently depending on their history with the deceased as well as their own life experiences and worldview.

The problem with many of us in the industrialized West (well, *one* of the problems at least) is that we feel pressured to grieve a certain way for a specified amount of time. We psych ourselves into thinking we have to fit in a certain mold of grief expression, and if we aren't sad enough or if we're able to move on too quickly, it'll seem like we didn't care.

And then that makes us question if we really did care as much as we thought, and the descent down the rabbit hole of "correct amounts of displayed compassion" takes us further and further into confusing darkness. Conversely, if we grieve more than is "appropriate" or long past when others have been able to move on, then we also think something is wrong with us, adding more pressure onto the already crushing overwhelm of grief.

By giving space to grief like the Paiute tribes, we can avoid these added-on psychological pressures. Just knowing that there is no "universally

259 M. Boyanova, "Aurora Borealis—The Northern Lights," *Study English Today*, http://www.studyenglishtoday.net/aurora_borealis.html (accessed Aug. 15, 2018).

correct" way or amount of time to grieve relieves a lot of pressure in and of itself.

So, for your Native North American takeaway challenge, let go of your expectations on grief and ignore the expectations of those around you. Even if you've experienced loss before, each death hits us differently because each personal connection was different, and we're different people than who we once were back then during a previous loss. So be gentle with yourself and give space to grief the next time you lose someone close to you.

Deities & Legends

MUUT

Among the Cahuilla people of Southern California (around modern Palm Springs and the Salton Sea), Muut is both the deity of death and the personification of death itself. Visually, he looks like an owl, and thus the hooting of an owl is understood as an ominous sign that someone will soon die or has just died.

Muut was specifically made by the creator god Mukat as a way to protect the earth. You see, despite creating humans, Mukat was pretty ambivalent toward them. At times he'd help them, and at times he'd go out of his way to mess with them (explaining the unpredictability and seemingly random nature of life). In one of his more misanthropic moods, he believed that too many humans at one time would destroy the earth by overpopulating it and demanding of it more than it could adequately and equitably give to everyone. Thus, he created Muut as a way to safeguard the greater good of the planet and make sure that there are never too many of these humans around at any given time.[260]

---

260 Walter Feller, "Religion—Worldview," *Desert Gazette*, http://mojavedesert.net/cahuilla-indians/03.html (accessed Aug. 17, 2018).
Lowell John Bean, *Mukat's People: The Cahuilla Indians of Southern California* (Berkeley: University of California Press, 1974).

THE DEMON BABIES AND CURSED MERMAID OF PYRAMID LAKE

Up in the arid desert of the Great Basin, a few good miles north of Reno is Pyramid Lake, home to the Pyramid Lake Paiute tribe of northern Nevada. The lake and tribe get their names from the iconic, large, pyramid-shaped limestone formations that jut upward from the waterline. Out in the barren middle of nowhere, this large 350-foot deep lake is a phenomenal sight, which is made eerie by the fact that it's also alleged to be the portal to the watery abyss of demonic babies and a vengeful mermaid.

The geographic nature of the lake itself already has perceived death associations since it's where the water from nearby Lake Tahoe (via the Truckee River) flows, pools, and essentially comes to die (evaporate). Many people also (still to this day) drown in the lake every year, and their bodies are often never recovered. Depending on which legend you believe, the reason for this is either the demon water babies or the wicked mermaid within its depths.

The water babies legend is based on the rumored infanticides carried out by the Paiute there. According to the rumors, the lake was the disposal place where deformed, premature, sickly, and miscarried babies were tossed away. Their tortured souls are believed to still haunt the lake and drag people down into its abyss to play with them and keep them company. Urban legend has it that their cries and laughter can still be heard, and the dead babies themselves can still be seen near the lake in the blackness of nighttime in the desert.

The Paiute, however, vehemently deny this history of infanticide, claiming it to be a hit-piece fabrication by colonizers to dehumanize them (and modern scholarly research agrees with them[261]). Even still, the Paiute's own legend of Pyramid Lake is one of death and sorrow. In this native version, a mermaid from the lake and a young man from the tribe fell in love

---

261 Simi Linton, *Claiming Disability: Knowledge and Identity* (New York: NYU Press, 1998).
Don D. Fowler, and Catherine S. Fowler, "Stephen Powers' 'The Life and Culture of the Washo and Paiutes'," *Ethnohistory* 17:3-4, 1970.

with each other, but their love was balked at, teased, and outright rejected by the tribe.

Tribespeople harassed the mermaid and demanded that she return to the lake and not seduce any of their able men (...*sigh*...blaming the woman...). Hurt, heartbroken, and enraged, the mermaid cursed the lake and the people who lived near it, and she would sometimes return to land so that she could eat Paiute babies, surreptitiously transform into the now-dead baby, and attack the unsuspecting mothers. Soon after the curse was placed is supposedly when the white man arrived to the land and the ensuing wars with these colonizers began, leaving some to still believe that the mermaid of Pyramid Lake was the supernatural cause for their tribe's downfall and subjugation to the US military.[262]

SEDNA

Sedna is the Inuit goddess of sea animals, hunting, heaven, destiny, life, and death. There are many myths associated with her, but the one about how she became the Arctic deity of death is one of the most interesting. According to this myth, Sedna is sexually uninterested in men and dismissive of all the suitors that her father (the creator god Anguta) brings to her. As the rebellious daughter she is, Sedna jokingly marries a dog, an act that enrages her father to the point that he attempts to kill her and dump her body in a lake during a boat ride (à la *The Godfather: Part II*). Ever after that incident, she lives in the depths of the ocean with a lesbian lover, controlling the life and death of humans by providing and/or withholding from them the bounty of the sea (the Inuit people's main food source).

---

262 Eric Grundhauser, "Pyramid Lake," *Atlas Obscura*, https://www.atlasobscura .com/places/pyramid-lake (accessed Aug. 17, 2018).
Phyllis Doyle Burns, "Pyramid Lake Mysteries, Legends and Hauntings," *The Creative Exiles*, Apr. 27, 2017, https://www.creativeexiles.com/2017/04/ pyramid-lake-mysteries-legends-hauntings/ (accessed Aug. 17, 2018).
Mychelle Blake, "This Lake In Nevada Has A Dark History That Will Never Be Forgotten," *Only In Your State*, Oct. 24, 2016, https://www.onlyinyourstate .com/nevada/lake-in-nv-dark-history/ (accessed Aug. 17, 2018).

After his daughter becomes the official death goddess, Anguta gains the role of psychopomp, whereby he ferries the souls of the dead to the middle of the icy sea (like he did to his daughter) and tosses them into the freezing depths so they can sink down into Sedna's realm, which lies beneath the bottom of the seafloor. Her realm is called Adlivun (often depicted as a frozen wasteland), and souls stay there for a whole year to be purified. Once fully purified, they then ascend to the moon, where they can finally be in eternal peace.[263]

263 Penczak, *Gay Witchcraft: Empowering the Tribe*, 2003.
"Inuit Mythology Submitted Names," *Behind the Name*, https://www
.behindthename.com/submit/names/usage/inuit-mythology (accessed
Aug. 18, 2018).
Franz Boas, *The Central Eskimo* (Washington, D.C.: Government Printing
Office, 1888), https://www.gutenberg.org/files/42084/42084-h/42084
-h.htm (accessed Aug. 18, 2018).

24
AMERICAN MAGICAL COMMUNITY

THE SCOURGE OF GOD

"The Scourge of God" was an epithet used to describe Attila the Hun. He and his murderous riders would descend upon a village like a bat out of hell and cause horrific levels of wanton destruction and death in their wake. According to legend, when asked why he caused such atrocities, he mockingly responded that he was just the scourge that their God had sent down to earth to punish them.

In the modern world, this seems brutal and extreme. "Civilized" etiquette dictates that we allow karma to dispense punishment upon the wicked, not that we become spiritual vigilantes giving people their comeuppance before its due time. However, sometimes we want to expedite karma just a bit and see our enemies squirm here and now rather than trusting that the universe will bring it about someday somehow.

In working with la Santa Muerte, many of her devotees have no qualms with taking it upon themselves to be the conduit that speeds up the due karma to their enemies and making sure those who've wronged them get their comeuppance much sooner rather than later, via the harmful magic of hexes.

With us now is Steven Bragg, a devotee of la Santa Muerte since 2011. He has over two decades of experience working with various spiritual and magical systems and has written two small instructional booklets on la Santa Muerte (*La Santisima Muerte: Devotional Guide of the Most Holy Death* and *La Santisima Muerte: Working with Her Robes*). You can find more of his stuff at The Vodou Store (vodoustore.com), but today he's paying us a visit here to, if we so dare, help us partner with la Santa Muerte to punish and hex those whom we feel deserve it.

Upon completion of this payback spell, your enemies' karma (whether actually justified or as perceived from your own pettiness) from wronging you will hit them fast and hit them hard, effectively causing them to suffer and causing you, like Attila the Hun, to become the conduit scourge with which God shall punish them.

> *Beginning on a Saturday or Monday night, gather all the items listed below and go in front of your altar for Santa Muerte. Have an image or statue of La Negra (the black-robed Santa Muerte) in the center of the altar. Light black candles and incense, and say whatever opening prayers you normally say.*
>
> *Take a recent photo with the enemy's name written nine times on the back and crossed with a large black "X." Place a magnet or lodestone in the middle of the photo and sprinkle iron filings or magnetic sand over it to feed it. Add some yellow mustard seeds and red pepper flakes to give this part of the working heat, and include some dry brown rice, also to feed this part of the working.*
>
> *Fold the photo away from you, turning and folding counterclockwise until there is a small packet holding all the items inside. Take black string*

and wind it away from you nine times; turn the packet counterclockwise, and wind the string nine more times, forming a cross on both sides of the packet. Tie the string with at least three knots, saying, "In the name of the Father, the Son, and the Holy Spirit," incorporating the Catholic influences in your work with her. Pass this packet through the incense smoke and blow tobacco smoke on it, either from a cigar or cigarette. Bless or baptize this packet as the enemy by using Holy Water or water gathered from a cemetery. The packet now becomes the heart of your working.

Place the packet inside a glass jar. Add in small amounts of cemetery dirt, sulfur, yellow mustard seeds, red pepper flakes, whisky, thorns, pins, broken glass, and fill the jar the rest of the way with a dark vinegar. These items keep the target agitated, soured, and drunk, making it difficult to think clearly and opening the door for the person to make mistakes and bad decisions.

Place the lid tightly on the jar, and seal it with wax from a black taper candle. Once sealed, place the jar on a plate, fix the taper candle to the top of the jar, and begin to speak to la Santa Muerte of the black robe, telling her all about how this person has wronged or hurt either you or someone you care about. Let your emotions rise to show her how much pain you feel because of this person and to feed this working. When you begin to feel the emotional wave recede, give thanks to la Santa Muerte and say your closing prayers. Allow the black taper to burn down completely.

The next night, light up your altar and say your opening prayers. Light another black taper and fix it to the top of the jar. Speak to la Santa Muerte again like you did the night before, and when finished close up and allow the taper to burn down. Repeat this seven more nights, for a total of nine nights.

When this is done, place the jar, all leftover wax from the candles, and nine coins in a brown paper bag. As soon as you can, take this to a cemetery and bury it somewhere on the grounds, making sure to pay three coins at the entrance to the cemetery and not exposing the jar to sunlight. As soon as you return home from the cemetery, take an already prepared cleansing bath made with salt, rosemary, mint, rue, basil, and Holy Water (or some other type of blessed water.)

*When la Santa Muerte has completed the working, pay her with
flowers, tequila, cigarettes,or breads, and surround her image or statue
with twelve small taper candles of alternating red, white, and black colors.
Light up her altar and the twelve candles, say your opening prayers, and
give her thanks for completing the work you asked of her. Sit with her for
a while before closing and allow the candles to burn down.*

—*Steven Bragg*

INTRANQUIL SPIRITS

You might remember our friend Anthony Lucero from way back when
we were trekking through ancient Greece, but now he's come to share
with us something different, something dangerous. Arguably the crème
de la crème of forbidden and risky magic of the macabre, Anthony is going
to show us how to summon an Intranquil Spirit. Now a warning: Unless
you're a seasoned, trained professional in the dark arts, absolutely, positively do not try this at home. This infamous bit of Tex-Mex magic is
supremely powerful, but woe to the one who realizes too late that they've
unleashed a power that will destroy them.

*I just want to start off by saying I do not encourage undertaking this work
unless you are an experienced magickal practitioner, nor do I claim liability
for those who undertake this work or the results thereof. The Intranquil
Spirit is not actually one specific spirit as some may think; the Intranquil
Spirit can be seen as an umbrella term for a group of restless spirits who
reside in "Hell." The common approach to this working is for reconciliation, but it's not limited to just that. The Intranquil Spirit can also be
called upon to torment another person into submitting to your will, and
similar workings are common in various forms of Latin and North American folk magick.*

*I first encountered this practice when I began studying magickal prac-
tices within my Hispanic culture. This is a very intense form of controlling
work that may easily be accomplished by other avenues of magickal work.
When you undertake work with the Intranquil Spirit, numerous events
can transpire: some may experience what the target of the spell is experi-*

encing (restlessness, anxiety, fear, etc.), while others may experience no such things, and yet others may experience poltergeist activity. This can be dependent on the type of spirit you call up. When calling on an Intranquil Spirit, you may end up with the spirit of someone who was executed, who committed suicide, who was a murderer, etc. Once rapport is established, you may call upon a specific spirit who is in Hell.

Prior to the work, I recommend performing uncrossing work and establishing protections upon yourself.

Tools:
- *Graveyard dirt*
- *Poppet of your target*
- *Black arts oil*
- *Controlling oil*
- *Controlling powder*
- *Necromancy incense*
- *Black candle*
- *Black-tipped pens*

Perform your regular opening rituals, baptize the poppet, and call to the spirit of the target. Light the incense and perform an invocation to a deity of death from your practiced pantheon while holding the graveyard dirt in your hands. Use this as a base for the spell to be placed upon.

Light a candle predressed in the oils and offer water to the spirits. Put powder into the poppet; pin each of their body parts when mentioned in the following prayer:

Spirits who suffer in the infernal reaches of the afterlife, hear me! Come forth and manifest my desires. Like the bugs that crawl restlessly and unceasingly, torment the spirit of [name] in this manner so that [name] will be obedient and submit to my will! Encircle the spirit of [name] so their sight and drive be only to fulfilling my will of [your desire]! Grasp their hands so that [name]

only reaches out to complete my will. Pierce their feet so
they move only to be humbled and defeated before me.
Pierce their ears so [name] thoughts be only to me and
my desires. Pierce and torment their nose and mouth
so that [name] yearns and hungers only to submit to
my will and kneel before me.

*Make a promise of offerings (food and drink or flowers) that you will
give once the work is completed. Repeat the spell for nine nights when the
moon is waning.*

—ANTHONY LUCERO

SPIRITUAL INTRUSIONS

Like the living, not all spirits of the dead have good intentions. Some
of them like to play creepy tricks for amusement, and some like to purposely harm you because they get off on being sadistic. And still some are
working to haunt you on the behalf of a human enemy utilizing harmful
magic. Brian Simpson has come here as the final community member on
our journey to help give us a ritual for when the spirits of the dead can
get out of hand. A member of the Diné (Navajo) tribe, Brian grew up
on the reservation, encountering all sorts of spirits. Nowadays, he uses
his spiritual insight as a cofounder of the magic store Toad and Broom
(toadandbroom.com).

Regardless of your spiritual tradition, though, you can use this ritual to
cleanse unwanted spiritual intrusions. Who knows? It may even save your
life one day.

*I had set up my ceremonial tools in front of me while the woman who owned
the house we were in sat next to me with her teenage children. They watched
as I pulled a crystal the size of a tennis ball out of its protective pouch and
smudged it with burning sage, waving my hawk wing fan in each direction.
I had been called by the mother, who had said there was something in her
home and it was scaring her children.*

Growing up around medicine men on the reservation, having to get up and go to help someone like this was not uncommon. When I was younger and under the tutelage of a medicine man, he would often call at odd hours for me to accompany him to some undisclosed location to help with a traditional healing ceremony that varied from person to person.

In this case, it was not a healing ceremony, which I soon found out. As smoke surrounded the crystal in the dimly lit room, I heard, "Look outside her bedroom window." I looked around the room to see if anyone else had heard that, but no one did. I asked the woman to go outside with me and to bring a flashlight as it was after 8 p.m. and dark out.

As we went outside, I heard the voice again. "Here … Here …" With the woman behind me shining the light in front of me so I didn't trip, I walked in the direction I heard the voice, and suddenly I heard, "Stop." This time the woman looked at me and asked if I said that. I said I didn't.

We happened to be under her daughter's bedroom window, and as she shined the light on the ground, we saw a little makeshift poppet half-buried in the ground. It was made of cloth stuffed with dirt, herbs, and other stuff we couldn't identify. We dismantled the doll and cleansed the material, and as we did this we heard the house make a loud creak sound. We looked at each other, finished the ceremony, and went back inside. Her kids said they heard the house creak all of a sudden as the object was destroyed. To make sure they didn't have any future issues, I had her follow up with the following cleansing.

Here's a simple way of clearing off potential spiritual intrusions whether they be human curses like in that buried poppet example, or spirits from beyond who are acting of their own volition, or even just extra negative energy in the area. (This can be adapted according to your personal spiritual paradigm; below is just a framework).

Tools:
- *Sage*
- *Glass of Water*
- *Rosemary*

- *Cedar*
- *Charcoal*

Burn a bit of sage in a previously cleansed space and place a clear glass of water in front of you. Take some of the sage and mix it with the rosemary and cedar. Break up the bits of herbs and say a prayer or incantation for spiritual cleansing and to be free of the negativity that is affecting you.

Reserve a bit of the herbs to burn later and mix the other parts into the water. Stir the water with your finger or some other magick tool and say a prayer again that it will purify you and cleanse you as well as the space you are in. After a few moments of reflection on this, take the herbs that you set aside and put some onto a lit charcoal. The herbs should be loose enough that they can catch fire and smolder to burn for a bit. If you use a lighter or match on it be careful not to burn yourself. (Essential oils can be substituted with some creativity).

Imagining an equal-armed cross lying in front of you, pass the water mixture to the east-facing arm and back to the center, then to the south-facing arm and back to the center, then to the west-facing arm and back to the center, and finally to the north-facing arm and back to the center.

Holding the glass over the smoldering incense, state again your petition. Next, dip your hands into the mixture and dress yourself with the mixture from head to toe, brushing in a downward motion as if brushing off dust. Make sure your hands are fully damp with the liquid as you do this.

Say a prayer that you will be free of all negativity that has affected your life and that all envy and negativity that is tormenting you or has been cast on you by others will be removed and no longer affect you.

Once done, sprinkle the rest of the mixture around your home and save the herbs so you can sprinkle them in front of your door to help reinforce the protective and cleansing aspects as well as to filter off any negativity that may be on you or any others who enter your home.

—BRIAN SIMPSON

END OF THE LINE

*Alas, poor Yorick! How surprised he would
be to see how his counterpart [corpse] of
today is whisked off to a funeral parlor and
is in short order sprayed, sliced, pierced,
pickled, trussed, trimmed, creamed,
waxed, painted, rouged and neatly
dressed—transformed from a common
corpse into a Beautiful Memory Picture.*
JESSICA MITFORD (THE AMERICAN
WAY OF DEATH REVISITED)

And so it has come to this. Here we are, at the end of the line. Our global trek around the world, exploring the morbid and the macabre within cultures throughout the ages, has been far too quick. It seems like we just hopped aboard our journey not too long ago, doesn't it? But then, life's like that, huh? It goes by in the blink of an eye.

One day you're teaching your kids their ABCs, and before you know it, you're all ordering off the senior discount menu together for lunch when they come visit you (which isn't as often as you'd like, but you understand they're busy). One moment you're with your fiancé(e) signing the marriage certificate together, and then just like that—*snap*—you're signing the paperwork to take them off life support and planning their funeral.

Everything just goes by so fast. The good times whiz past like a blur, like they've always just been a memory. The bad times tend to linger, like they'll never go away. And all the other times just seem to act as filler while we look forward to more good times and dread the inevitable bad ones.

Because no one knows what happens to us after death, most of us tend to classify it as something bad, but then again, the unknown is always assumed to be something bad, even if it turns out not to be. Ruled by fear, we force ourselves to live a certain self-limiting way in the belief that by doing so we'll avoid something bad happening to us in the afterlife. But what if we're wrong, and we've denied ourselves the fullness of life because of this fear of this unknown of what happens on the other side?

One beautiful discussion of this that I'll never forget happened my sophomore year at university. I was living in a three-bedroom house with seven other roommates (oh, college), and we all somehow got into this late-night discussion of death and the afterlife. Asking each other what we believed would happen after death, some of us recited our religion's scripted outcomes, and others admitted to not knowing what'll happen, but Jane was the only one who outright stated that there is no afterlife. Nothing happens; we just cease to exist.

None of us could wrap our minds around no afterlife. An eternity of oblivion, existing in a void of black nothingness forever and ever? Jane, however (in that way of hers where she could correct you while still being endearing), reminded us that in order for the afterlife to be a void of eternal nothingness, that would still count as existence of an afterlife because we would have to still exist (in some way) for us to experience and perceive the nothingness. The reality is, everything just stops. Without a form of consciousness, nothing can happen after death. Everything just ends.

Needless to say, our minds were blown, and we began asking her that fundamental human question: "But if nothing happens after death, what prevents you from just doing whatever you want? Doesn't that scare you? You're so nice; what keeps you morally in check?"

And her answer was simple: "Yeah, it scares me sometimes, but it makes me happy to be a good person, and if this one lifetime is all that I'll ever have for all eternity, I want to be happy during it."

To this day, Jane's affirmation impacts me. When someone is a good person who also believes that no afterlife reward will come from their goodness nor punishment from their lack of it, *that* is the ultimate sign of a good person. All of us who are good because we believe in rewards and punishment after death are just being self-serving, and our goodness is just a means to an end.

Of course, I can't leave you here at the station without talking about one more thing: life after the death of a loved one. As the maxim goes, "Death is harder for the living than it is for the dead." Whatever happens in the afterlife, we'll find out soon enough, but what is definitely well-known here and now is the pain, emptiness, and unbearable loneliness of losing a loved one.

And I know we've talked about grief a number of times on our world tour and have seen it through a number of cultural lenses, but the truth of the matter is that there is no secret way to get over grief. The advice, wisdom, and examples given to you along our travels may help to ease the pain, but it'll never go away completely. Ironically, the best way to soften grief is knowing that it will stay with you forever.

Think of it this way. Imagine yourself by the banks of a small lake. The water is peaceful, serene, and perfectly still, allowing it to perfectly reflect the beauty all around it. Now grab a large stone and hurl it into the lake. A splash of noise is created, and the water becomes turbulent with waves of the impact rippling to all edges of the lake. The surface is now distorted, unable to reflect anything recognizable. Nothing can be done to stop the churning of the water; attempts to do so will just cause more waves. The lake just has to ride it out, and in time, the water will calm.

And when the lake is once again peaceful, serene, and reflecting the beauty of the world, onlookers will say that the lake is back to how it was before that large stone was thrown into it and caused all that chaos. But the truth is, it's not. The lake has been forever changed. That stone is still down there. It lies at the base of the lake and has fundamentally altered the landscape deep down inside. Although no one can visibly see it, that stone will always be down there, and despite the surface's return to normalcy, the inside of the lake will never be the same again.

That's how grief is. Like the stone, a death will impact your life, leaving chaos and confusion in its wake. If you try to force yourself to stop your emotions, you'll just make things worse. Only time will calm things down and bring peace back into your life. And, of course, when you're back to "normal," everyone will think you're back to exactly the way you were before the death. But you know things can never be the way they were. That stone of grief is forever inside you. It may not affect you like it once did when it first impacted you, but it's still there, make no mistake about it. You just learn to live with it and go on.

So, now that we're about to head our separate ways, be sure to live your best life. Tomorrow is not guaranteed, and old age (even with all its inconveniences) is a gift denied to many. You're alive now, and isn't that reason enough to celebrate and be happy? And when death does come, will you look back with amazement at all the things you've done or with regret at all the things you prevented yourself from doing? Until then, though, be easy on yourself. Cry when you're sad. Mourn when there's a death, and know that grief is the medicine, not the impediment, for healing from a loss. And if still none of this makes any sense to you, don't worry; it will someday.

BIBLIOGRAPHY

Aayush. "Lord Chitragupta—Who Helps Lord Yamaraj to Maintain Karmic Accounts." Detechter. https://detechter.com/lord -chitragupta-who-helps-lord-yamaraj-to-maintain-karmic -accounts/ (accessed Jun. 6, 2018).

Abel, Ernest L. *Death Gods: An Encyclopedia of the Rulers, Evil Spirits, and Geographies of the Dead.* Westport, CT: Greenwood Press, 2009.

Alpers, Anthony. *Maori Myths and Tribal Legends.* Auckland, NZ: Longman Paul, 1964.

American-Israeli Cooperative Enterprise. "Angel of Death." Jewish Virtual Library. http://www.jewishvirtuallibrary.org/angel-of -death (accessed May 14, 2018).

Anderson, Allan. "African Religions." *Encyclopedia of Death and Dying.* http://www.deathreference.com/A-Bi/African-Religions.html (accessed May 29, 2018).

Associated Press. "Vatican Issues New Rules on Catholic Cremation." *Canadian Broadcasting Corporation.* October 25, 2016. http://www .cbc.ca/news/world/vatican-catholic-cremation-1.3820336 (accessed May 25, 2018).

Baines, Wesley. "The Symbolism of the Cherry Blossom." Beliefnet. http://www.beliefnet.com/inspiration/the-symbolism-of-the -cherry-blossom.aspx (accessed Jun. 25, 2018).

Baker, Heather D., Eleanor Robson, and Gabor Zolyomi. *Your Praise Is Sweet: A Memorial Volume for Jeremy Black from Students, Colleagues and Friends.* London: British Institute for the Study of Iraq, 2010.

Barrow, Richard. "What to Expect If You Are Invited to a Thai Funeral." *Buddhism in Thailand*. August 5, 2011. http://www. thaibuddhist.com/what-to-expect-if-you-are-invited-to-a-thai-funeral/ (accessed Jun. 7, 2018). No longer available online.

Baumann, Benjamin. "The Khmer Witch Project." *Ghost Movies in Southeast Asia and Beyond: Narratives, Cultural Contexts, Audiences.* Edited by Peter J. Bräunlein and Andrea Lauser. Boston: Brill Academic Publishers, 2016.

Bean, Lowell John. *Mukat's People: The Cahuilla Indians of Southern California*. Berkeley, CA: University of California Press, 1974.

Beckwith, Martha. "Kane and Kanaloa." *Hawaiian Mythology*. 1940. http://www.sacred-texts.com/pac/hm/hm07.htm (accessed Jul. 31, 2018).

Bhikkhu, Nanamoli, and Bodhi Bhikkhu. *The Middle Length Discourses of the Buddha: A Translation of the Majjhima Nikaya*. Boston: Wisdom Publications, 2001.

Bichell, Rae Ellen. "When People Ate People, A Strange Disease Emerged." *NPR*. September 6, 2016. https://www.npr.org/sections/thesalt/2016/09/06/482952588/when-people-ate-people-a-strange-disease-emerged (accessed Jul. 2, 2018).

Biddle, Nicholas, and Francis Markham. "Census 2016: What's Changed for Indigenous Australians?" *The Conversation*. June 27, 2017. https://theconversation.com/census-2016-whats-changed-for-indigenous-australians-79836 (accessed Jul. 10, 2018).

Bjordal, Melissa. "Ancient Aztec Perspectives on Death and the Afterlife." The Christi Center. February 11, 2013. http://christicenter.org/2013/02/ancient-aztec-perspective-on-death-and-afterlife/ (accessed Aug. 9, 2018).

Blake, Mychelle. "This Lake in Nevada Has a Dark History that Will Never Be Forgotten." Only In Your State. October 24, 2016. https://www.onlyinyourstate.com/nevada/lake-in-nv-dark-history/ (accessed Aug. 17, 2018).

BIBLIOGRAPHY

Blümchen, Gerhard. "The Maya Ball Game: Comparison of the Physical Load with Modern Ball Games." *Cardiology* 113, no. 4 (2009): 231–5.

Boas, Franz. *The Central Eskimo*. Washington, DC: Government Printing Office, 1888. https://www.gutenberg.org/files/42084/ 42084-h/42084-h.htm (accessed Aug. 18, 2018).

———. "Chinook Texts." Sacred-Texts. 1894. http://www.sacred-texts .com/nam/nw/chinook/cht30.htm (accessed Aug. 13, 2018).

Bodiford, William M. "Zen in the Art of Funerals: Ritual Salvation in Japanese Buddhism." *History of Religions* 32, no. 2 (1992).

Boyanova, M. "Aurora Borealis—The Northern Lights." *Study English Today*. http://www.studyenglishtoday.net/aurora_borealis.html (accessed Aug. 15, 2018).

Brookes, Michael. "Drabbles of the Gods—Whiro." *The Cult of Me*. April 1, 2015. http://thecultofme.blogspot.com/2015/04/drabbles -of-gods-whiro.html (accessed Jul 27, 2018).

Brown, Michael. "What Really Happens When You Die?" *The Guardian*. February 15, 2008. https://www.theguardian.com/ lifeandstyle/2008/feb/16/healthandwellbeing.weekend2 (accessed Jun. 22, 2018).

Browne, Edward G. *A Year amongst the Persians: Impressions as to the Life, Character, and Thought of the People of Persia, Received During Twelve Month's Residence in that Country in the Years 1887-8*. London, Adam and Charles Black, 1893.

Bryant, Clifton D., and Dennis L. Peck. *Encyclopedia of Death and the Human Experience*. Thousand Oaks, CA: SAGE Publications, 2009.

Burnakov, V. A. "Erlik Khan in the Traditional Worldview of the Khakas." *Archaeology, Ethnology and Anthropology of Eurasia* 39, no. 1 (March 2011).

Burns, Phyllis Doyle. "Pyramid Lake Mysteries, Legends and Hauntings." The Creative Exiles. April 27, 2017. https://www .creativeexiles.com/2017/04/pyramid-lake-mysteries-legends -hauntings/ (accessed Aug. 17, 2018).

Bygott, Robert. *Kuru: The Science and the Sorcery*. 2010; Mt. Lawley, Western Australia: Siamese Films.

Byrne, Zoë. "The Tulafale's Role: Samoan Oratorial Traditions for Death and Funeral." April 3, 2014. http://blog.sevenponds.com/ cultural-perspectives/the-tulafales-role-samoan-oratorial-traditions -for-death-and-funeral (accessed Jul. 26, 2018).

Capano, Kristen. "Tangihanga: A Look Into a Traditional Maori Funeral." *Seven Pounds*. May 25, 2017. http://blog.sevenponds.com/ cultural-perspectives/tangihanga-look-traditional-maori-funeral (accessed Jul 25).

Carelli, Francesco. "The Book of Death: Weighing Your Heart." *London Journal of Primary Care* 4, no. 1 (2011). https://www.ncbi.nlm.nih .gov/pmc/articles/PMC3960665/ (accessed Oct. 24, 2018).

Clark, Joëlle. "Southern Paiute Cultural History Curriculum Guide." National Park Service. September 2010. https://www.nps.gov/ para/learn/education/upload/total-final-curriculum.pdf (accessed Aug. 13, 2018).

Clarke, Chris. "Native Singers Keep Bird Songs Alive." *KCET*. November 2, 2011. https://www.kcet.org/socal-focus/native -singers-keep-bird-songs-alive (accessed Nov. 1, 2018).

Collier, Mark, and Bill Manley. *How to Read Egyptian Hieroglyphs: A Step-by-Step Guide to Teach Yourself*. Berkeley: University of California Press, 2003.

Conklin, Beth A. *Consuming Grief: Compassionate Cannibalism in Amazonian Society*. Austin, TX: University of Texas Press, 2001.

———. "'Thus Are Our Bodies, Thus Was Our Custom': Mortuary Cannibalism in an Amazonian Society." *American Ethnologist* 22, no. 1 (February 1995).

Cordova, Randy. "Day of the Dead History: Ritual Dates Back 3,000 Years and Is Still Evolving." Arizona Central. October 24, 2017. https://www.azcentral.com/story/entertainment/holidays/day -of-the-dead/2014/09/24/day-of-the-dead-history/16174911/ (accessed Aug. 10, 2018).

Coulter, Charles Russell, and Patricia Turner. *Encyclopedia of Ancient Deities*. New York: Routledge, 2000.

Dallapiccola, Anna L. *Dictionary of Hindu Lore and Legend*. New York: Thomas & Hudson, 2004.

Daniel, Cory. "Skinwalkers." *The Phoenix Enigma*. December 17, 2015. http://thephoenixenigma.com/skinwalkers/ (accessed Aug. 13, 2018).

Davidson, Baruch S. "Do Jews Bury the Dead in a Specific Direction?" *Chabad*. January 2017. https://www.chabad.org/library/article_cdo/ aid/1672031/jewish/Are-Bodies-Buried-in-a-Specific-Direction.htm (accessed May 14, 2018).

Davisson, Zack. "Katabira no Tsuji—The Crossroad of Corpses." Hayakumonogatari Kaidankai. October 31, 2013. https:// hyakumonogatari.com/2013/10/31/katabira-no-tsuji-the -crossroad-of-corpses/ (accessed Nov. 19, 2018).

Dayrell, Elphinstone. *Folk Stories from Southern Nigeria, West Africa*. London: Longmans, Green, and Company, 1910.

Delsol, Christine. "Mexico's Legend of La Llorona Continues to Terrify." *San Francisco Gate*. October 9, 2012. https://www.sfgate .com/mexico/mexicomix/article/Mexico-s-legend-of-La-Llorona -continues-to-3933072.php (accessed Aug. 15, 2018).

Dillehay, Tom D. "Incan Religion." *Encyclopedia of Death and Dying*. http://www.deathreference.com/Ho-Ka/Incan-Religion.html (accessed Aug. 7, 2018).

Doniger, Wendy. *The Rig Veda*. New York: Penguin Classics, 2005.

Donnison, Alexandra. *The Appropriation of Death in Classical Athens*. Wellington: Victoria University of Wellington, 2009. http://researcharchive.vuw.ac.nz/xmlui/bitstream/handle/10063/1153/thesis.pdf?sequence=1 (accessed May 16, 2018).

Doughty, Caitlin. *From Here to Eternity: Traveling the World to Find the Good Death* (New York: W. W. Norton & Company, 2017).

———. "Let's Talk FUNERAL STRIPPERS." Ask A Mortician. March 23, 2018. https://www.youtube.com/watch?v=bFM_w_tN2B4 (accessed Jun. 14, 2018).

———. "The Self Mummified Monks." Ask A Mortician. March 24, 2017. https://www.youtube.com/watch?v=FlmMtZ4J3qQ (accessed Jun. 28, 2018).

———. *Smoke Gets in Your Eyes: And Other Lessons from the Crematory* (New York: W. W. Norton & Company, 2015).

———. "TOMB SWEEPING DAY!!!" Ask A Mortician. April 4, 2017. https://www.youtube.com/watch?v=WVFr7ynB8s8 (accessed Jun. 14, 2018).

———. "Wherein I Mercilessly Slaughter Your Dreams of a Viking Funeral." The Order of the Good Death. October 22, 2012. http://www.orderofthegooddeath.com/wherein-i-mercilessly-slaughter-your-dreams-of-a-viking-funeral (accessed May 2, 2018).

Durán, Diego. *Historia de las Indias de Nueva-España y islas de Tierra Firme*. London: Forgotten Books, 2018.

Dyer, Charles G. *Abatwa: A Little African Mythology*. Seattle: CreateSpace Independent Publishing, 2013.

Edwards, Rosy. "New Orleans Jazz Funerals: Where Life Is Celebrated through the Joy of Music." *Metro*. October 8, 2017. https://metro.co.uk/2017/10/08/new-orleans-jazz-funerals-where-life-is-celebrated-through-the-joy-of-music-6965499/ (accessed Jun. 4, 2018).

Ellis, Hilda Roderick. *The Road to Hel: A Study of the Conception of the Dead in Old Norse Literature*. Santa Barbara, CA: Praeger, 1968.

Espinosa, Luz. "Mictlán: el Lugar de los Muertos." Cultura Colectiva. September 23, 2014. https://culturacolectiva.com/letras/mictlan -el-lugar-de-los-muertos/ (accessed Aug. 9, 2018).

Evslin, Bernard. *Gods, Demigods and Demons: A Handbook of Greek Mythology*. New York: I.B. Tauris, 2007.

Faulkner, Dr. Raymond O. *The Egyptian Book of the Dead: The Book of Going forth by Day*. San Francisco: Chronicle Books, 1994.

Faure, Bernard. *The Rhetoric of Immediacy: A Cultural Critique of Chan/Zen Buddhism*. Princeton: Princeton University Press, 1991.

Feller, Walter. "Religion—Worldview." Desert Gazette. http:// mojavedesert.net/cahuilla-indians/03.html (accessed Aug. 17, 2018).

Fernández, Adela. *Dioses Prehispánicos de México: Mitos y Deidades del Panteón Nahuatl*. Mexico City: Panorama, 1996.

Fernández Noa, Yurina. "The Maya: Funeral Rituals." Yucatán Today. http://yucatantoday.com/mayas-funeral-rituals/?lang=en (accessed Aug. 8, 2018).

Fife, Steven. "The Roman Funeral." In *Ancient History Encyclopedia*. January 18, 2012. https://www.ancient.eu/article/96/the-roman -funeral/ (accessed May 21, 2018).

Figula, M. Sentia. "Pagan Funeral Rites." Neo Polytheist. November 8, 2015. http://romanpagan.blogspot.com/2015/11/pagan-funeral -rites_8.html (accessed May 22, 2018).

Fison, Lorimer. "Notes on Fijian Burial Customs." *Journal of the Anthropological Institute of Great Britain and Ireland*. Vol. 10, 1881.

Foundation of the Hellenic World. "Burial Customs." Mycenean Greece. 1999. http://www.fhw.gr/chronos/02/mainland/en/ mg/society/burials/index.html (accessed May 16, 2018).

Fowler, Don D., and Catherine S. Fowler. "Stephen Powers' 'The Life and Culture of the Washo and Paiutes'." *Ethnohistory*. 17, no. 3–4 (1970).

Frankel, Dr. Neil A. "Facts and Figures." *The Atlantic Slave Trade and Slavery in America*. June 13, 2009. http://www.slaverysite.com/Body/facts%20and%20figures.htm (accessed May 31, 2018).

Frazer, Sir James George. *The Belief in Immortality and the Worship of the Dead*. London: Macmillan, 1913.

Freedman, David Noel. *Eerdmans Dictionary of the Bible*. Grand Rapids: William B. Eerdmans Publishing Company, 2000.

Friedman, Amy, and Meredith Johnson. "Tell Me a Story: Searching for Death (A West African Tale)." *UExpress*. April 1, 1999. https://www.uexpress.com/tell-me-a-story/1999/4/1/searching-for-death-a-west-african (accessed Oct. 5, 2018).

Fullard-Leo, Betty. "Sacred Burial Practices." *Coffee Times*. February 1998. http://www.coffeetimes.com/feb98.htm (accessed Jul. 26, 2018).

Gadalla, Moustafa. *Egyptian Divinities: The All Who Are THE ONE*. 2nd ed. Greensboro: Tehuti Research Foundation, 2001.

Geels, Anton. *Subud and the Javanese Mystical Tradition*. New York: Routledge, 1996.

Geller. "Mara." *Mythology.net*. October 23, 2016. https://mythology.net/demons/mara/ (accessed Jun. 11, 2018).

———. "Shinigami." *Mythology.net*. October 28, 2016. https://mythology.net/japanese/japanese-gods/shinigami/ (accessed Jun. 28, 2018).

Gelo, Daniel J. "Comanche." *Encyclopedia.com*. 2002. https://www.encyclopedia.com/history/united-states-and-canada/north-american-indigenous-peoples/comanche (accessed Aug. 13, 2018).

Gillespie, Dr. Susan G. "What Did Ordinary People Turn Into in the Afterlife?" *Mexico Lore*. May 2013. http://www.mexicolore.co.uk/aztecs/ask-experts/what-did-ordinary-people-turn-into-in-the-afterlife (accessed Aug. 9, 2018).

Goldade, Jenny. "Cultural Spotlight: Cambodian Funeral Traditions." Frazer Consultants. July 21, 2017. http://www.frazerconsultants .com/2017/07/cultural-spotlight-cambodian-funeral-traditions/ (accessed Jun. 8, 2018).

———. "Cultural Spotlight: Chinese Taoist." *Frazer Consultants*. August 11, 2017. https://www.frazerconsultants.com/2017/08/cultural -spotlight-chinese-taoist-funeral-traditions/ (accessed Jun. 12, 2018).

———. "Cultural Spotlight: Mongolia." *Frazer Consultants*. November 10, 2017. http://www.frazerconsultants.com/2017/11/cultural -spotlight-mongolian-funeral-traditions/ (accessed Jun. 15, 2018).

———. "Cultural Spotlight: South Korea." *Frazer Consultants*. October 6, 2017. https://www.frazerconsultants.com/2017/10/ 201710201710cultural-spotlight-south-korean-funeral -traditions/ (accessed Jun. 19, 2018).

———. "Cultural Spotlight: Vietnamese Funeral Traditions." *Frazer Consultants*. December 1, 2017. http://www.frazerconsultants .com/2017/11/cultural-spotlight-vietnamese-funeral-traditions/ (accessed Jun. 8, 2018).

———. "Cultural Spotlight: Viking Funeral Traditions." *Frazer Consultants*. March 24, 2017. http://www.frazerconsultants .com/2017/03/cultural-spotlight-viking-funeral-traditions/ (accessed May 23, 2018).

Greater Lansing. "Chevra Kadisha." *Timeline for Jewish Traditions in Death and Mourning*. March 28, 2004. http://kehillatisrael.net/docs/ chevra_timeline.htm (accessed May 14, 2018).

Grundhauser, Eric. "Pyramid Lake." *Atlas Obscura*. https://www. atlasobscura.com/places/pyramid-lake (accessed Aug. 17, 2018).

Guthke, Karl Siegfried Guthke. *The Gender of Death: A Cultural History in Art and Literature*. New York: Cambridge University Press, 1999.

Hackett, Conrad, and David McClendon. "Christians Remain World's Largest Religious Group, but They Are Declining in Europe." Pew Research Center. April 5, 2017. http://www.pewresearch.org/fact -tank/2017/04/05/christians-remain-worlds-largest-religious -group-but-they-are-declining-in-europe/ (accessed May 25, 2018).

Hammer, Rabbi Jill. "Lilith, Lady Flying in Darkness." My Jewish Learning. https://www.myjewishlearning.com/article/lilith-lady -flying-in-darkness/ (accessed Nov. 6, 2018).

Hanes, Richard C., and Laurie Collier Hillstrom. "Paiutes." Countries and Their Cultures. http://www.everyculture.com/multi/Le-Pa/ Paiutes.html (accessed Aug. 13, 2018).

Harris, Tim. "Druid Doc with a Bee in His Bonnet." The Age. September 16, 2002. https://www.theage.com.au/articles/ 2002/09/15/1032054710047.html?oneclick=true (accessed May 22, 2018).

Hart, George. *A Dictionary of Egyptian Gods & Goddesses*. New York: Routledge, 1986.

Hayes, Joe. *La Llorona: The Weeping Woman*. El Paso, TX: Cinco Puntos Press, 2006.

Hayes, Lynn. "Lucifer: Satan or Venus?" Beliefnet. http://www .beliefnet.com/columnists/astrologicalmusings/2009/07/ lucifer-satan-or-venus.html (accessed May 28, 2018).

Hays, Jeffrey. "Egyptian Book of the Dead and Ancient Egyptian Views of the Afterlife." Facts and Details. 2012. http://factsanddetails .com/world/cat56/sub364/item1949.html (accessed May 8, 2018).

Herodotus. "Herodotus on Burial in Egypt." In *Ancient Hitory Encyclopedia*. January, 2012. https://www.ancient.eu/article/ 89/herodotus-on-burial-in-egypt/ (accessed May 9, 2018).

Herold, Andre Ferdinand. "The Life of Buddha." Translated by Paul C. Blum. Sacred-Texts. 1927. http://www.sacred-texts.com/bud/lob/ index.htm (accessed Jun. 7, 2018).

Higgins, Rawinia. "Tangihanga—Death Customs." In *Te Ara - the Encyclopedia of New Zealand*. Wellington: Manatū Taonga Ministry for Culture and Heritage, 2011. https://teara.govt.nz/en/tangihanga -death-customs (accessed Jul. 25, 2018).

Hilger, Sister M. Inez. "Chippewa Burial and Mourning Customs." *American Anthropologist* 46, no. 2 (1944). https://anthrosource. onlinelibrary.wiley.com/doi/pdf/10.1525/aa.1944.46.4.02a00240 (accessed Aug. 13, 2018).

Holzman, Donald. "The Cold Food Festival in Early Medieval China." *Harvard Journal of Asiatic Studies* 46, no. 1 (June 1986).

Homer. *Iliad*. Translated by Robert Fagles. New York: Penguin Classics, 1991.

Hopler, Whitney. "Archangel Azrael." ThoughtCo. August 25, 2018. https://www.thoughtco.com/meet-archangel-azrael-124093 (accessed Oct. 26, 2018).

Hori, Ichiro. "Self-Mummified Buddhas in Japan. An Aspect of the Shugen-Dô ('Mountain Asceticism') Sect." *History of Religions* 1, no. 2 (1962).

Hovanec, Kyle. "Korea Haunt: The Most Famous Korean Ghosts." SeoulSync. http://seoulsync.com/culture/traditional/famous -korean-ghosts (accessed Jun. 20, 2018).

Hungarian Research Institute of Canada. "The Visigoths and the Marosszentanna Culture." History of Transylvania. March 15, 2001. http://mek.oszk.hu/03400/03407/html/24.html (accessed May 22, 2018).

Ibn al-Hajjaj, Imam Muslim. *Sahih Muslim*. https://sunnah.com/ muslim (accessed May 16, 2018).

Insaidoo, Kwame A. *Moral Lessons in African Folktales*. Bloomington, IN: AuthorHouse, 2011.

Isaac, Ali. "Donn, the Mysterious Irish Lord of the Dead." Irish Central. June 27, 2017. https://www.irishcentral.com/roots/history/donn-the-mysterious-irish-lord-of-the-dead (accessed May 25, 2018).

Iyá, Dr. Eñi Achó. "When a Santero/a Dies…" About Santería. January 19, 2014. http://www.aboutsanteria.com/santeras-blog/when-a-santeroa-dies (accessed Jun. 1, 2018).

Jaffe, Rabbi Howard. "In Judaism what is believed to happen to someone after they die? Is there some idea of an afterlife, or is that purely a Christian invention?" ReformJudaism.org. https://reformjudaism.org/judaism-what-believed-happen-someone-after-they-die (accessed May 14, 2018).

Jaide, Don. "Ani the Mother of the Igbos: The Many Manifestations of Isthar." Rasta Livewire. April 7, 2012. https://www.africaresource.com/rasta/sesostris-the-great-the-egyptian-hercules/ani-the-mother-of-the-igbos-the-many-manifestations-of-ishtar/ (accessed May 31, 2018).

Jarus, Owen. "Mummy Brain: Gray Matter-Removal Tool Found In Ancient Egyptian Skull." *Huffington Post*. December 15, 2012. https://www.huffingtonpost.com/2012/12/15/mummy-brain-removal-tool-egyptian_n_2301802.html (accessed May 9, 2018).

Jellison, Ashley. "Necrophilia in Ancient and Modern Times." *Out Front*. January 16, 2017. https://www.outfrontmagazine.com/trending/culture/necrophilia-ancient-modern-times/ (accessed Oct. 2, 2018).

Jochim, Christian. "Chinese Beliefs." *Encyclopedia of Death and Dying*. http://www.deathreference.com/Ce-Da/Chinese-Beliefs.html (accessed Jun. 13, 2018).

Johnson, Honor. "Morrigan." The Order of Bards, Ovates & Druids. https://www.druidry.org/library/gods-goddesses/morrigan (accessed May 24, 2018).

Johnston, Sarah Iles. *Religions of the Ancient World: A Guide*. Cambridge: Belknap Press, 2004.

Jordan, Prof. David K. "The Jade Guidebook: A Visitor's Guide to Hell." UC San Diego Department of Anthropology. January 30, 2009. http://pages.ucsd.edu/~dkjordan/chin/yuhlih/yuhlih-intro.html (accessed Jun 15, 2018).

Joyce, P. W. *A Social History of Ancient Ireland: Treating of the Government, Military System, and Law; Religion, Learning, and Art; Trades, Industries, and Commerce; Manners, Customs, and Domestic Life, of the Ancient Irish People*. Provo, UT: Repressed Publishing, 2014. (original edition: New York: Longsman, Green, and Co., 1903).

Kaduce, Candy. "Creation and Islam." Neptune Society. October 13, 2015. https://www.neptunesociety.com/cremation-information-articles/cremation-and-islam (accessed May 15, 2018).

Kaleem, Jaweed. "Home Funerals Grow as Americans Skip the Mortician for Do-It-Yourself After-Death Care." *Huffington Post*. December 6, 2017. https://www.huffingtonpost.com/2013/01/25/home-funerals-death-mortician_n_2534934.html (accessed Oct. 25, 2018).

Kenny, Elizabeth. "Shintō Mortuary Rites in Contemporary Japan." *Cahiers d'Extrême-Asie* vol. 9 (1996). https://www.persee.fr/doc/asie_0766-1177_1996_num_9_1_1124 (accessed Jun. 22, 2018).

Kingsley, Danny. "World's Oldest Burial Redated to 40,000 Years." *Australian Broadcasting Corporation*. February 20, 2003. http://www.abc.net.au/science/articles/2003/02/20/788032.htm (accessed Dec. 11, 218).

Kisala, R. "Japanese Religions." *Nanzan Guide to Japanese Religions*. ed. by P Swanson, and C. Chilson. Honolulu: University of Hawaii Press, 2005.

Koidde, Oshun. "El Ituto: La Ceremonia Posterior a la Mmuerte del Santero." Iwaros. December 21, 2017. https://iworos.com/ osha/2017/12/721/el-ituto-la-ceremonia-posterior-a-la-muerte -del-santero/ (accessed Jun. 1, 2018).

Kǒng Fūzǐ, *The Analects of Confucius: A Philosophical Translation*, translated by Roger T. Ames, and Henry Rosemont, Jr. New York: Ballantine Books, 1999.

Korean Embassy. "Funeral Rites." AsianInfo.org. 2000. http://www .asianinfo.org/asianinfo/korea/cel/funeral_rites.htm (accessed Jun. 19, 2018).

Korff, Jens. "Mourning an Aboriginal Death." Creative Spirits. https:// www.creativespirits.info/aboriginalculture/people/mourning-an -aboriginal-death (accessed Jul. 10, 2018).

Kosloski, Philip. "Why Is Satan Depicted with Horns, Red Tights and a Pitchfork?" Aleteia. October 17, 2017. https://aleteia. org/2017/10/17/why-is-satan-depicted-with-horns-red-tights -and-a-pitchfork/ (accessed Oct. 27, 2018).

Kramer, Kenneth P. "Hinduism." *Encyclopedia of Death and Dying*. http:// www.deathreference.com/Gi-Ho/Hinduism.html (accessed Jun. 5, 2018).

Kvam. Kristen E., Linda S. Schearing, and Valarie H. Ziegler. *Eve and Adam: Jewish, Christian, and Muslim Readings on Genesis and Gender*. Bloomington, Indiana: University Press, 1999.

Kwekudee. "Afro-Brazilian Boa Morte Festival: A Unique Testament of Strength and Endurance of African Women in Diaspora." Trip Down Memory Lane. September 21, 2012. https://kwekudee -tripdownmemorylane.blogspot.com/2012/09/afro-brazilian -boa-morte-festival.html (accessed Jun. 1, 2018).

Kwon, Heonik. *Ghosts of War in Vietnam*. Cambridge: Cambridge University Press, 2008.

Ladner, Mimsie. "Who's Who: Korean Ghosts, Goblins, and Gumiho." Seoul Searching. http://www.myseoulsearching.com/2013/10/korean-ghosts-goblins-gumiho.html (accessed Jun. 20, 2018).

———. "On Death, Dying, and Funerals in Korea." Seoul Searching. http://www.myseoulsearching.com/2013/02/korean-funeral.html (accessed Jun. 19, 2018).

Laing, Karen. "Can You Organise a Funeral Yourself?" Lady Anne Funerals. April 7, 2016. https://www.ladyannefunerals.com.au/blog/do-it-yourself-diy-funerals (accessed Oct. 25, 2018).

de Landa, Fray Diego. *Relación de las Cosas de Yucatán.* Mexico City: Miguel Ángel Porrúa, 1982.

Landtman, Gunner. *The Kiwai Papuans of British New Guinea.* London: Macmillan, 1927.

Le Bohec, Yann. *The Imperial Roman Army.* New York: Routledge, 2000.

Lee, Je Son. "In North Korea, sometimes the dead come back." *NK News.* September 22, 2015. https://www.nknews.org/2015/09/in-north-korea-sometimes-the-dead-come-back/ (accessed Jun. 19, 2018).

Leighton, Alexander H., and Charles C. Hughes. "Notes on Eskimo Patterns of Suicide." *Southwestern Journal of Anthropology* 11, no. 4 (1955). https://ethicsofsuicide.lib.utah.edu/tradition/indigenous-cultures/arctic-cultures/saint-lawrence-eskimo/ (accessed Aug. 15, 2018).

Leong, Harry. "King Yama." The Jade Turtle Records. February 10, 2011. http://jadeturtlerecords.blogspot.com/2011/02/king-yama_10.html (accessed Jun. 15, 2018).

Light, Richard A. *Guides for Performing Tahara.* May 2005. http://jewish-funerals.org/sites/default/files/spiritweb/cknm.pdf (accessed May 14, 2018).

Lincoln, Rabbi David H. *The Use of Mausoleums for Jewish Burial*. June 7, 1983. https://www.rabbinicalassembly.org/sites/default/files/public/halakhah/teshuvot/20012004/21.pdf (accessed May 14, 2018).

Linton, Simi. *Claiming Disability: Knowledge and Identity* .New York: NYU Press, 1998.

Luangrath, Julia. "Krasue." Pseudoparanormal. March 20, 2012. http://www.pseudoparanormal.com/2012/03/krasue.html (accessed Jun. 8, 2018).

Luck, Annemarie. "Suicide in Japan: the Reasons, the Statistics, and the TELL Support." Tokyo Weekender. August 18, 2017. https://www.tokyoweekender.com/2017/08/suicide-in-japan-the-reasons-the-statistics-and-the-tell-support/ (accessed Jun. 27, 2018).

Lynch, Patricia Ann. *African Mythology A to Z*. 2nd ed. New York: Chelsea House Publishers, 2010.

Lynn, Ryan. "Traditional Hawaiian Funeral Rituals." University of Alaska Anchorage Department of Anthropology. 2015. http://anthreligion.commons.uaa.alaska.edu/funerary-rituals/traditional-hawaiian-funerary-rituals/ (accessed Jul 26, 2018).

M.J.L. "Do Jews Believe in Satan?" My Jewish Learning. https://www.myjewishlearning.com/article/satan-the-adversary/ (accessed May 28, 2018).

MacDonnell, A. A. *Vedic Mythology*. Strasburg: Von Karl J. Trübner, 1897.

MacFarland, Amanda. "Death In Haiti." The Crudem Foundation. http://crudem.org/death-haiti/ (accessed Jun. 1, 2018).

MacKenzie, Donald A. MacKenzie. *Myths of Babylonia and Assyria*. Los Angeles: HardPress Publishing, 2006.

Mackie, Timothy. "The Book of Job: What's Going On Here?" The Bible Project. https://thebibleproject.com/blog/book-job-whats-going/ (accessed May 28, 2018).

Maniapoto, Moana. "Tangihanga—A Dying Tradition." E-Tangata. August 15, 2015. https://e-tangata.co.nz/reflections/tangihanga -a-dying-tradition/ (accessed Jul 25, 2018).

Manning, Scott. "Spartan Burial Practices and Honoring Fallen Soldiers." Historian on the Warpath. April 11, 2011. https:// scottmanning.com/content/spartan-burial-practices/ (accessed May 16, 2018).

Mariotti, Valentina, Silvana Condemi, and Maria Giovanna Belcastro. "Iberomaurusian Funerary Customs: New Evidence from Unpublished Records of the 1950s Excavations of the Taforalt Necropolis (Morocco)." *Journal of Archaeological Science* 49 (2014).

Mark, Joshua J. "Burial." In *Ancient History Encyclopedia*. September 2, 2009. https://www.ancient.eu/burial/ (accessed May 5, 2018).

———. "Ereshkigal." In *Ancient History Encyclopedia*. January 11, 2017. https://www.ancient.eu/Nergal/ (accessed May 13, 2018).

———. "Inanna's Descent: A Sumerian Tale of Injustice." In *Ancient History Encyclopedia*. February 23, 2011. https://www.ancient.eu/ article/215/inannas-descent-a-sumerian-tale-of-injustice/ (accessed Nov. 6, 2018).

———. "Nergal." In *Ancient History Encyclopedia*. January 17, 2017. https://www.ancient.eu/Nergal/ (accessed May 11, 2018).

Martin, Richard. "Japanese Cremation Ashes Rituals: Kotsuage and Bunkotsu." Scattering Ashes. June 21, 2013. https://scattering -ashes.co.uk/different-cultures/japanese-cremation-ashes-rituals -kotsuage-bunkotsu/ (accessed Jun. 22, 2018).

Martin, Rochelle. "The Handling and Transfer of the Deceased in Ontario." Community Deathcare Canada. March 27, 2016. https:// www.communitydeathcare.ca/handling-transfer-deceased-ontario/ (accessed Oct. 25, 2018).

Maspero, Henri. *Le Taoïsme et les Religions Chinoises*. Paris: Éditions Gallimard, 1971.

Mather, Rev. Cotton. "Of Beelzebub and His Plot." Original Sources. 1693. http://originalsources.com/Document. aspx?DocID=5DDGZ6LDDLS5NMR (accessed May 28, 2018).

Mazi, Adah. "African Gods: Igbo Deities." Nairaland. June 6, 2017. http://www.nairaland.com/3844529/african-gods-igbo-deities (accessed May 31, 2018).

McCurry, Justin. "Japan: Robot Dogs Get Solemn Buddhist Send-off at Funerals." *The Guardian*. May 3, 2018. https://www.theguardian .com/world/2018/may/03/japan-robot-dogs-get-solemn-buddhist -send-off-at-funerals (accessed Jun 25, 2018).

Mead, Simon; Whitfield, Jerome; Poulter, Mark; Shah, Paresh; Uphill, James; Campbell, Tracy; Al-Dujaily, Huda; Hummerich, Holger; Beck, Jon. "A Novel Protective Prion Protein Variant that Colocalizes with Kuru Exposure." *New England Journal of Medicine* 361, no. 21 (November 19, 2009).

Meas, Roth, "Crocodile Flags, a Rite of Death." *The Phnom Penh Post*. August 17, 2012. https://www.phnompenhpost.com/7days/ crocodile-flags-rite-death (accessed Jun. 8, 2018).

Meleen, Michele. "Native American Death Rituals." Love To Know. https://dying.lovetoknow.com/native-american-death-rituals (accessed Aug. 13, 2018).

Meow, Jordy. "Japan's Suicide Forest: Aokigahara." Offbeat Japan. June 6, 2018. https://offbeatjapan.org/aokigahara-the-suicide-forest/ (accessed Nov. 19, 2018).

Miller, Mary, and Karl Taube. *An Illustrated Dictionary of the Gods and Symbols of Ancient Mexico and the Maya*. London: Thames & Hudson, 2003.

Mirza, Sumair, and Jason Tsang. "The Romans and Their Dead." Classics Unveiled. http://www.classicsunveiled.com/rome1/ html/romedead.html (accessed May 21, 2018).

Mitcalfe, Barry. "Te Rerenga Wairua: Leaping Place of the Spirits." *Te Ao Hou*. Vol. 35. June, 1961, http://teaohou.natlib.govt.nz/journals/ teaohou/issue/Mao35TeA/c20.html (accessed Jul. 25, 2018).

Mitford, Jessica. *The American Way of Death Revisited*. New York: Knopf Doubleday Publishing Group, 1998.

Moctezuma, Eduardo Matos, and Felipe Solís Olguín. *Aztecs*. London: Royal Academy of Arts, 2002.

Monroe, M. H. "The Afterlife in Aboriginal Australia." Australia: The Land Where Time Began. Apil. 15, 2013. http://austhrutime.com/ afterlife.htm (accessed Jul. 11, 2018).

Morgan, John D., and Pittu Laungani. *Death and Bereavement Around the World: Death and Bereavement in the Americas*. Vol. 2. New York: Routledge, 2003.

Moss, Aaron. "Organ Donation." *Chabad*. May 2008. https://www .chabad.org/library/article_cdo/aid/635401/jewish/Organ -Donation.htm (accessed May 11, 2018).

Moss, Chris. *Patagonia: A Cultural History*. Oxford: Signal Books Ltd., 2008.

Mufti, Imam Kamil. "Belief in Life After Death." The Religion of Islam. January 4, 2015. https://www.islamreligion.com/articles/38/belief -in-life-after-death/ (accessed May 15, 2018).

Muhumuza, Rodney. "Africa Slowly Turning to Cremations, though Long Taboo." *Associated Press*. May 26, 2018. https://www.apnews. com/e4d90cbae6b84d2d95e74e357f2b8c16 (accessed Nov. 14, 2018).

Murray, Frederic. "Shifting Boundaries: Violence, Representation, and the Salt Songs of the Great Basin Peoples." Southeastern Oklahoma State University. 2011. http://www.se.edu/nas/files/2013/03/ NAS-2011-Proceedings-Murray.pdf (accessed Nov. 1, 2018).

Nash, Jesse W., and Elizabeth Trinh Nguyen. *Romance, Gender, and Religion in a Vietnamese-American Community: Tales of God and Beautiful Women*. New York: Edwin Mellen Press, 1995.

Näsström, Britt-Mari. *Freyja: The Great Goddess of the North*, 2nd ed. Harwich Port, MA: Clock & Rose Press, 2003.

National Conference of Commissioners on Uniform State Laws. Uniform Determination of Death Act. August 1, 1980. http://www .lchc.ucsd.edu/cogn_150/Readings/death_act.pdf (accessed May 11, 2018).

Nawee. "Traditional Tongan Funerals." Nawee. December 3, 2013. https://nauwee.wordpress.com/2013/12/03/traditional-tongan -funerals/ (accessed Jul. 26, 2018).

Nedelman, Michael. "Inside Japan's 'Suicide Forest'." *CNN*. January 4, 2018. https://www.cnn.com/2018/01/03/health/japan-suicide -forest-intl/index.html (accessed Nov. 19, 2018).

Newton, Paula. "The Long Goodbye: Why Funerals Are Big Business in Ghana." *CNN*. March 11, 2014. http://www.cnn. com/2014/03/11/world/africa/on-the-road-ghana-funerals/index. html (accessed May 29, 2018).

Ng, Heidi. "Hong Kong's Taoist Funerals: The Superstition, Symbolism and How to Stop Your Soul Being Dragged into the Coffin." *South China Morning Post*. July 19, 2017. http://www.scmp.com/lifestyle/ article/2102955/hong-kongs-taoist-funerals-superstition -symbolism-and-how-stop-your-soul (accessed Jun. 12, 2018).

Niziolomski, J., J. Rickson, N. Marquez-Grant, and M. Pawlett. "Soil Science Related to the Human Body after Death." The Corpse Project. March 2016. http://www.thecorpseproject.net/wp-content/ uploads/2016/06/Corpse-and-Soils-literature-review-March -2016.pdf (accessed Jun. 1, 2018).

Nobel, Justin. "Christmas and Death in North Korea." Funeralwise. December 24, 2015. https://www.funeralwise.com/digital-dying/ christmas-and-death-in-north-korea/ (accessed Jun. 19, 2018).

Northern Sydney Local Health District. *Death and Dying in Aboriginal and Torres Strait Islander Culture: Sorry Business*. August 2015. https://www.nslhd.health.nsw.gov.au/Services/Directory/Documents/Death%20and%20Dying%20in%20Aboriginal%20and%20Torres%20Strait%20Islander%20Culture_Sorry%20Business.pdf (accessed Jul 10, 2018).

Ó hÓgáin, Dáithí. *Myth, Legend & Romance: An Encyclopaedia of the Irish Folk Tradition*. Upper Saddle River: Prentice Hall General, 1991.

Ojibwa. "Traditional Native Concepts of Death." Native American Netroots. September 1, 2014. https://nativeamericannetroots.net/diary/1726 (accessed Aug. 13, 2018).

Oliver, Douglas L. *Oceania: The Native Cultures of Australia and the Pacific Islands*. Vol 1. Honolulu: University of Hawaii Press, 1989.

Oliver, Leaman. *The Qu'ran: An Encyclopedia*. New York: Routledge, 2005.

Olivier. "Child Suicide in Japan: The Leading Cause of Death in Children." Humanium. February 27, 2017. https://www.humanium.org/en/child-suicide-in-japan-the-leading-cause-of-death-in-children/ (accessed Oct. 31, 2018).

Ophvedius. "Satan's Historical Presence in Other Cultures: Kanaloa." Modern Church of Satan. November 11, 2008. http://www.modernchurchofsatan.com/grotto/viewtopic.php?f=16&t=3455 (accessed Oct. 6, 2018)

Osborne, Samuel. "China Vows to Crack Down On Funeral Strippers." *Independent*. February 21, 2018. https://www.independent.co.uk/news/world/asia/china-funeral-strippers-crack-down-rural-attract-mourners-death-a8220866.html (accessed Jun. 14, 2018).

Paley, Rachel Tepper. "Animals Dropped Dead Inside Roman 'Gate to Hell.' Scientists Just Figured Out Why." *Time.com*. February 22, 2018. http://time.com/5171047/turkey-gate-to-hell-pamukkale-hierapolis/ (accessed May 21, 2018).

Penczak, Christopher. *Gay Witchcraft: Empowering the Tribe*. San Francisco: Red Wheel/Weiser, 2003.

Perry, Douglas. "J.K. Rowling Embraces Skinwalkers; Native Americans Slam Her for 'Lies and Misperceptions'." *The Oregonian*. March 10, 2016. https://www.oregonlive.com/entertainment/index.ssf/2016/03/jk_rowling_embraces_skinwalker.html (accessed Aug. 13, 2018).

Perry, Yvonne. "Haitian Vodoun Perspectives on Death and Dying." *Ezine Articles*. October 28, 2009. http://ezinearticles.com/?Haitian-Vodoun-Perspectives-on-Death-and-Dying&id=3172822 (accessed Jun. 1, 2018).

Persons, Larry S. *The Way Thais Lead: Face as Social Capital*. Chiang Mai: Silkworm Books, 2016.

Pike, Matthew. "The Fanfare of Vietnam's Funerals." Culture Trip. January 12, 2018. https://theculturetrip.com/asia/vietnam/articles/the-fanfare-of-vietnams-funerals/ (Jun. 8, 2018).

Prower, Tomás. *La Santa Muerte: Unearthing the Magic and Mysticism of Death*. Woodbury, MN: Llewellyn Worldwide, 2015.

———. *Queer Magic: LGBT+ Spirituality and Culture from Around the World*. Woodbury, MN: Llewellyn Worldwide, 2018.

Rabiipour, Nick. "What Do Catholics Really Believe About Purgatory?" The Catholic Company. November 1, 2017. https://www.catholiccompany.com/getfed/what-catholics-really-believe-purgatory/ (accessed May 27, 2018).

Radez, Wes. "How to Celebrate the Qingming Festival." Chinese American Family. October 2, 2018. http://www.chineseamericanfamily.com/qingming-festival/ (accessed Nov. 24, 2018).

Raffaele, Paul. "Sleeping with Cannibals." *Smithsonian Magazine*. September 2006. https://www.smithsonianmag.com/travel/sleeping-with-cannibals-128958913/ (accessed Jul. 2, 2018).

Redondo, José Miguel. "En las Entrañas de las Minas de Potosí, la Puerta del Infierno." El Rincón de Sele. March 31, 2014. https://www.elrincondesele.com/en-las-entranas-de-las-minas-de-potosi-bolivia-la-puerta-del-infierno/ (accessed Sept. 18, 2018).

Reed, A. W., and Inez Hames. *Myths & Legends of Fiji & Rotuma*. New York: Literary Productions, Inc. 1997.

Reis, João José. *Death Is a Festival: Funeral Rites and Rebellion in Nineteenth Century Brazil*. Translated by H. Sabrina Gledhill. Chapel Hill, NC: University of North Carolina Press, 2003.

Rhodios, Apollonios. *The Argonautika*. Translated by Peter Green. Berkeley, CA: University of California Press, 2007.

Rider, Pantera. "Sumerian Burial Practices/Beliefs." Burial Practices of the Ancient World. April 17, 2012. http://ancientworldburialpractices.blogspot.com/2012/04/sumerian-burial-practicesbeliefs.html (accessed May 8, 2018).

Riggs, Christina. *The Beautiful Burial in Roman Egypt: Art, Identity, and Funerary Religion*. New York, Oxford University Press, 2005.

Robb, Alice. "Will Overpopulation and Resource Scarcity Drive Cannibalism?" *The New Republic*. June 19, 2014. https://newrepublic.com/article/118252/cannibalism-and-overpopulation-how-amazon-tribe-ate-their-dead (accessed Aug. 6, 2018).

Romero, Juan. "African Golden Jackals Are Actually Golden Wolves." *Science Magazine*. July 30, 2015. http://www.sciencemag.org/news/2015/07/african-golden-jackals-are-actually-golden-wolves (accessed May 10, 2018).

Roy, Janmajit. *Theory of Avatāra and Divinity of Chaitanya*. New Dehli: Atlantic Publishers & Distributors, 2002.

Ruddock, Dr. Vilma. "Death Rituals in Africa." LoveToKnow. https://dying.lovetoknow.com/Death_Rituals_in_Africa (accessed May 29, 2018).

Ruhlmann, Sandrine. "Objects and Substances of Funeral Mediation in Mongolia: Coffin, Miniature Yurt and Food Offerings." Material Religions. April 8, 2015. http://materialreligions.blogspot .com/2015/04/objects-and-substances-of-funeral.html (accessed Jun. 15, 2018).

Russell, Samantha. "Two Funerals and a Baby." From Mushrooms to Mangoes. April 24, 2012. https://bulasamantha.wordpress.com/ tag/fijian-funeral-ceremonies/ (accessed Jul. 25, 2018).

Saalih al-Munajjid, Shaykh Muhammad. "Authentic Descriptions of Munkar and Nakeer." Islam Question and Answer. July 29, 2005. https://islamqa.info/en/72400 (accessed May 16, 2018).

———. "Name of the Angel of Death." *Islam Question and Answer*. July 13, 2003. https://islamqa.info/en/answers/40671/name-of-the -angel-of-death (accessed Oct. 26, 2018).

Sadgrove, Jones, and Greatrex. "Isolation and characterisation of (-)-genifuranal: the principal antimicrobial component in traditional smoking applications of Eremophila longifolia (Scrophulariaceae) by Australian aboriginal peoples." *Journal of Ethnopharmacology* 154, no. 3 (July 3, 2014).

Saint-Lot, Marie José Alcide. *Vodou, a Sacred Theatre: The African Heritage in Haiti*. Pompano Beach, FL: Educa Vision, 2004.

Saleem, Shehzad. "The Social Directives of Islam: Distinctive Aspects of Ghamidi's Interpretation." *Renaissance Islamic Journal*. April 3, 2017. https://web.archive.org/web/20070403024603/http://www .renaissance.com.pk/Marislaw2y4.html (accessed May, 15, 2018).

Sanders, Fr. William. "The Process of Becoming a Saint." Catholic Education Resource Center. https://www.catholiceducation.org/ en/culture/catholic-contributions/the-process-of-becoming-a-saint .html (accessed Sept. 30, 2018).

Sang-Hun, Choe. "South Koreans, Seeking New Zest for Life, Experience Their Own Funerals." *New York Times*. October 26, 2016. https://www.nytimes.com/2016/10/27/world/what-in-the-world/korea-mock-funeral-coffin.html (accessed Jun. 19, 2018).

Seetharaman, G. "Seven Decades After Independence, Mmany Small Languages in India Face Extinction Threat." *Economic Times*. August 13, 2017. https://economictimes.indiatimes.com/news/politics-and-nation/seven-decades-after-independence-many-small-languages-in-india-facing-extinction-threat/articleshow/60038323.cms (accessed Jun. 29, 2018).

Sheng Yen. *Orthodox Chinese Buddhism: A Contemporary Chan Master's Answers to Common Questions*. Translated by Douglas Gildow and Otto Chang. Berkeley, CA: North Atlantic Books, 2007.

Siddiqui, Dr. Mona. "Ibrahim—the Muslim View of Abraham." *BBC.com*. September 4, 2009. http://www.bbc.co.uk/religion/religions/islam/history/ibrahim.shtml (accessed May 15, 2018).

Silberberg, Naftali. "Why Does Jewish Law Forbid Cremation?" Chabad. April 2017. https://www.chabad.org/library/article_cdo/aid/510874/jewish/Why-Does-Jewish-Law-Forbid-Cremation.htm#footnote1a510874 (accessed May 11, 2018).

Simek, Rudolf. *Dictionary of Northern Mythology*. Translated by Angela Hall. Rochester, NY: Boydell & Brewer, 2008.

Singer, Isidore. *The Jewish Encyclopedia*. New York: Funk & Wagnalls Company, 1901. https://www.studylight.org/encyclopedias/tje/s/samael.html (accessed May 14, 2018).

Smith Nash, Susan. "Folklore and the Horrors of War: 'El Luison' and Cadaver-Eating Dogs." E-Learning Queen. April 9, 2005. http://elearnqueen.blogspot.com/2005/04/folklore-and-horrors-of-war-el-luison.html (accessed Aug. 6, 2018).

Stacey, Aisha. "Funeral Rites in Islam." The Religion of Islam. January 2, 2012. https://www.islamreligion.com/articles/4946/viewall/funeral-rites-in-islam/ (accessed May 15, 2018).

Stan, M. "Omolu." UCR Panda Blog. May 7, 2009. http://ucrpandas. blogspot.com/2009/05/omolu.html (accessed Jun. 4, 2018).

Starr, Mirabai. *Saint Michael the Archangel: Devotion, Prayers & Living Wisdom*. Surry Hills: ReadHowYouWant, 2012.

Stefon, Matt. *Islamic Beliefs and Practices*. ed. by Hope Lourie Killcoyne. New York: Rosen Publishing Group, 2009.

Steinsland, Gro, and Preben Meulengracht Sørensen. *Humans and Powers in the Viking World*. Stockholm: Ordfront, 1998.

Stewart, Cameron. "Naming Taboo Often Ignored in Breaking News." *The Australian*. July 13, 2013. https://www.theaustralian.com.au/ business/media/naming-taboo-often-ignored-in-breaking-news/ news-story/5ea91f685d3a866f87c48a26061ce7e1 (accessed Dec. 11, 2018).

Stewart, Harry. "Meet El Tio: The Devil Who Rules the Underworld of Bolivia's Mines." Culture Trip. October 20, 2017. https:// theculturetrip.com/south-america/bolivia/articles/meet-el -tio-the-devil-who-rules-the-underworld-of-bolivias-mines/ (accessed Aug. 10, 2018).

Story, Karen. "A Burial in West Africa." The Order of the Good Death. April 20, 2016. http://www.orderofthegooddeath.com/a-burial-in -west-africa (accessed May 29, 2018).

Sturluson, Snorri. *The Poetic Edda*. Translated by Lee M. Hollander. Austin, TX: University of Texas Press, 1986.

———. *The Prose Edda*. Translated by Jesse Byock. New York: Penguin Books, 2006.

———. *Ynglinga Saga*, 1225. (via The medieval & Classical Literature Library). http://mcllibrary.org/Heimskringla/ynglinga.html (accessed May 22, 2018).

Switzer, John. "What Do Catholics Believe about the Devil?" U.S. Catholic. September 2014. http://www.uscatholic.org/ articles/201408/what-do-catholics-believe-about-devil-29310 (accessed May 28, 2018).

Tan, Yvette. "Why Do Some Chinese Funerals Involve Strippers?" *British Broadcasting Corporation.* February 24, 2018. https://www.bbc. com/news/world-asia-china-43137005 (accessed Jun. 14, 2018).

Tedlock, Dennis. *Popol Vuh.* New York: Simon & Schuster, 1996.

Teller, Joanne, and Norman Blackwater. *The Navajo Skinwalker, Witchcraft, & Related Spiritual Phenomena: Spiritual Clues: Orientation to the Evolution of the Circle.* Conshohocken: Infinity Publishing, 1997.

Tembo, Ph.D., Mwizenge S. "Funeral and Burial Customs in Zambia." Bridgewater College Wordpress. https://wp.bridgewater.edu/ mtembo/culture-of-zambia/funerals-and-burials/ (accessed May 29, 2018).

Thacker, Eugene. "Black Illumination: Zen and the Poetry of Death." *The Japan Times.* July 2, 2016. https://www.japantimes.co.jp/ culture/2016/07/02/books/black-illumination-zen-poetry -death/#.WzFgfKdKhPY (accessed Jun. 25, 2018).

Thakur, Pallavi. "How Did Lord Buddha Die?" SpeakingTree. May 26, 2017. https://www.speakingtree.in/allslides/how-did-lord-buddha -die (accessed Jun. 7, 2018).

Thavis, John. "Vatican Commission: Limbo Reflects 'Restrictive View of Salvation'." Catholic News Service. April 20, 2007. http:// webarchive.loc.gov/all/20070508193238/http://www.catholicnews .com/data/stories/cns/0702216.htm (accessed May 27, 2018).

Toohey, Peter. "Death and Burial in the Ancient World." In *The Oxford Encyclopedia of Ancient Greece and Rome.* Oxford: Oxford University Press, 2010.

Traverso, Vittoria. "In China, Ghosts Demand the Finer Things in Life." Atlas Obscura. October 19, 2017, https://www.atlasobscura. com/articles/china-ghost-festival-burning-money (accessed Jun. 14, 2018).

Than, Ker. "Neanderthal Burials Confirmed as Ancient Ritual."
  National Geographic. December 16, 2013. https://news
  .nationalgeographic.com/news/2013/12/131216-la-chapelle
  -neanderthal-burials-graves/ (accessed May 5, 2018).

Taylor, John H. *Journey Through the Afterlife: Ancient Egyptian Book
  of the Dead.* Cambridge, MA: Harvard University Press, 2013.

Telban, Borut, and Daniela Vávrová. "Ringing the Living and the
  Dead: Mobile Phones in a Sepik Society." *The Australian Journal
  of Anthropology* 25, no. 2 (2014).

Thepbamrung, Nattha. "Soaring Cost of Dying." *Bangkok Post.*
  December 15, 2013. https://www.bangkokpost.com/news/special
  -reports/384890/soaring-cost-of-dying (accessed Jun. 7, 2018).

Theuws, Frans. "Grave Goods, Ethnicity, and the Rhetoric of Burial
  Rites in Late Antique Northern Gaul." *Ethnic Constructs in Antiquity:
  The Role of Power and Tradition,* edited by Ton Derks and Nico
  Roymans. Amsterdam: Amsterdam University Press, 2009.

Tomorad, Mladen. "Ancient Egyptian Funerary Practices from the First
  Millenium BC to the Arab Conquest of Egypt (c. 1069 BC-642
  AD)." *The Heritage of Egypt.* Vol. 2. Cairo: Al-Hadara Publishing.
  May 2009. http://www.egyptologyforum.org/THOE/Heritage_of_
  Egypt_5_English.pdf (accessed May 9, 2018).

Toynbee, J. M. C. *Death and Burial in the Roman World.* Baltimore: Johns
  Hopkins University Press, 1996.

Trejo, Silvia. "Tlalocan: 'Recinto de Tláloc.'" *Arqueología Mexicana* Vol.
  64. November 2003.

Trungpa, Chogyam, and Francesca Fremantle. *The Tibetan Book of the
  Dead: The Great Liberation Through Hearing in the Bardo.* Boulder, CO:
  Shambhala Publications, 2000.

U.S. Catholic Conference. *Catechism of the Catholic Church,* 2nd ed. New
  York: Doubleday, 2003.

Uttal, William R. *Dualism: The Original Sin of Cognitivism.* New York:
  Routledge, 2013.

V., Jayaram. "Concept of Death, Hell and Afterlife in Hinduism." Hinduwebsite. http://www.hinduwebsite.com/hinduism/death .asp (accessed Jun. 5, 2018).

———. "Death and Afterlife in Hinduism." Hinduwebsite. http:// www.hinduwebsite.com/hinduism/h_death.asp (accessed Jun. 5, 2018).

Van Huygen, Meg. "Give My Body to the Birds: The Practice of Sky Burial." Atlas Obscura. March 11, 2014. https://www.atlasobscura .com/articles/sky-burial (accessed Jun. 7, 2018).

Varner, Gary R. *Ghosts, Spirits & the Afterlife in Native American Folklore and Religion.* Raleigh: OakChylde/Lulu Press, 2010.

Viet Nam National Administration of Tourism. "Funeral Ceremony." Viet Nam Tourism. http://www.vietnamtourism.com/en/index .php/about/items/2450 (accessed Jun. 8, 2018).

Wang, Peter. "Top 20 Ancient Chinese Inventions." China Whisper. November 21, 2012. http://www.chinawhisper.com/top-20 -ancient-chinese-inventions/ (accessed Jun. 12, 2018).

Welton, Benjamin. "10 Monstrosities From Korean Folklore." The Trebuchet. June 27, 2016. http://literarytrebuchet.blogspot .com/2016/06/10-monstrosities-from-korean-folklore.html (accessed Jun. 20, 2018).

Westcott, Ben. "Socialism with Chinese Characteristics? Beijing's Propaganda Explained." *CNN.* March 10, 2018. https://www.cnn .com/2018/03/10/asia/china-npc-communist-party-phrases-intl/ index.html (accessed Nov. 16, 2018).

Westervelt, W. D. "How Milu Became the King of Ghosts." *Hawaiian Legends of Ghosts and Ghost-Gods.* Boston: Ellis Press, 1916. http:// www.sacred-texts.com/pac/hlog/hlog17.htm (accessed Jul. 31, 2018).

White, Claire, Daniel M. T. Fessler, and Pablo S. Gomez. "The effects of corpse viewing and corpse condition on vigilance for deceased loved ones." *Evolution and Human Behavior* 37, no. 6 (2016).

Whittall, Austin. "More on the Patagonian Labrys, Phoenicians and Cretans." Patagonian Monsters. November 5, 2013. http://patagoniamonsters.blogspot.com/2013/11/more-on-patagonian-labrys-phoenicians.html (accessed Aug. 6, 2018).

Wilkinson, Toby A. H. *Early Dynastic Egypt*. New York: Routledge, 2001.

Wilton, David. *Word Myths: Debunking Linguistic Urban Legends*. New York: Oxford University Press, 2008.

Wise, Caroline. "Maman Brigitte She Comes from Angletere: Thoughts of a Brighid Devotee on the Earthquake in Haiti." Mirror of Isis. https://mirrorofisis.freeyellow.com/id523.html (accessed Jun. 4, 2018).

Woolf, Greg. *Ancient Civilizations: The Illustrated Guide to Belief, Mythology, and Art*. San Diego: Thunder Bay Press, 2005.

Xiuzhong Xu, Vicky, and Bang Xiao. "Ghost Marriages: A 3,000-Year-Old Tradition of Wedding the Dead Is Still Thriving In Rural China." *Australian Broadcasting Corporation*. May 2, 2018. https://www.abc.net.au/news/2018-04-07/ghost-marriages-in-rural-china-continue-to-thrive/9608624 (accessed Oct. 30, 2018).

Yoon, Mina. "What Happens When You Die in North Korea? A Funeral System Explained." *NK News*. April 4, 2014. https://www.nknews.org/2014/04/what-happens-when-you-die-in-north-korea-a-funeral-system-explained/ (accessed Jun. 19, 2018).

Yunajjam, Amr-Athtar. "Mythology and Religion of Pre-Islamic Arabia: Deities, Spirits, Figures and Locations." Arabian Paganism. November 9, 2011. http://wathanism.blogspot.com/2011/11/deities-beings-and-figures-in-arabian.html (May 16, 2018).

Zimmerman, Fritz. "The Comanche Indians Mortuary Practices." American Indians History. July 31, 2011. https://americanindianshistory.blogspot.com/2011/07/mortuary-customs-of-native-americans.html (accessed Aug. 13, 2018).

ONLINE WEB PAGE SOURCES

Academy for Ancient Texts: http://www.ancienttexts.org/

Age UK: https://www.ageuk.org.uk/

Ancient History Encyclopedia: https://www.ancient.eu/

Ask A Mortician: https://www.youtube.com/user/
OrderoftheGoodDeath

Behind the Name: https://www.behindthename.com/

Biography.com: https://www.biography.com/people/buddha-9230587

British Broadcasting Corporation: http://www.bbc.com/

Burial Practices of the Ancient World:
http://ancientworldburialpractices.blogspot.com/
2012/04/sumerian-burial-practicesbeliefs.html

Catholic News Agency: https://www.catholicnewsagency.com/

Catholic Online: https://www.catholic.org/

China Underground: https://china-underground.com/

Church of Candomblé: http://churchofcandomble.com/

Common Ground: https://www.commonground.org.au/

Cremationpedia: http://www.cremationpedia.org/index.html

CubaYoruba: https://cubayoruba.blogspot.com/

The Daoist Encyclopedia: http://en.daoinfo.org/wiki/Main_Page

Deities Daily: http://deitiesdaily.tumblr.com/

Día de los Muertos: http://diadelosmuertos.yaia.com/

Divine Moon: http://divinemoonblog.org/

The Druid Network: https://druidnetwork.org/

eCondolence.com: http://www.econdolence.com/

The Economist: https://www.economist.com/

EcuRed Enciclopedia: https://www.ecured.cu/
EcuRed:Enciclopedia_cubana

Encyclopædia Britannica: https://www.britannica.com/

Encyclopedia.com: https://www.encyclopedia.com/

Encyclopedia Mythica: https://pantheon.org/

Flower Leis: https://www.flowerleis.com/

Funeral Consumers Alliance: https://funerals.org/

Funeralwise: https://www.funeralwise.com/

Greek Mythology: https://www.greekmythology.com/

Le Grenier de Clio: https://mythologica.fr/index.html

Haiti Observer: http://www.haitiobserver.com/

History.com: https://www.history.com/

History on the Net: https://www.historyonthenet.com/

In the Light Urns: https://www.inthelighturns.com/
   funeral-information/

iTravel NZ: http://www.itravelnz.com/

Jewish Virtual Library: https://www.jewishvirtuallibrary.org/

Mechon Mamre: https://www.mechon-mamre.org/

Mesoamerica Blog: https://mesoamericablog.wordpress.com/

Muslim Funeral Services Ltd.: https://www.mfs.asn.au/

The Mystica: https://www.themystica.com/

La Nación: https://www.lanacion.com.ar/

National Geographic: https://news.nationalgeographic.com/news/
   2013/12/131216-la-chapelle-neanderthal-burials-graves/

New World Encyclopedia: http://www.newworldencyclopedia.org/
   entry/Info:Main_Page

The Noble Qu'ran: https://quran.com/

El Observador: https://www.elobservador.com.uy/

Online Etymology Dictionary: https://www.etymonline.com/

Oxford Classical Mythology Online: https://web.archive.org/web/
   20110629173245/http://www.oup.com/us/companion.websites/
   0195153448/studentresources/chapters/ch25/?view=usa

Pew Research Center: http://www.pewresearch.org/

Prehistoric Wildlife: http://www.prehistoric-wildlife.com/index.html

Public Broadcasting Corporation: https://www.pbs.org/

Religión y Santería: https://religionysanteria.blogspot.com/

Theoi Greek Mythology: http://www.theoi.com/

Toltec Civilization: https://www.sites.google.com/site/
   tolteccivilization/Home

United States Conference of Catholic Bishops: http://www.usccb.org/

World Bank Group: http://www.worldbank.org/

INDEX

A

B

C

TO WRITE TO THE AUTHOR

If you wish to contact the author or would like more information about this book, please write to the author in care of Llewellyn Worldwide and we will forward your request. Both the author and the publisher appreciate hearing from you and learning of your enjoyment of this book and how it has helped you. Llewellyn Worldwide cannot guarantee that every letter written to the author can be answered, but all will be forwarded.

Please write to:

Tomás Prower

℅ Llewellyn Worldwide

2143 Wooddale Drive

Woodbury, MN 55125-2989

Please enclose a self-addressed stamped envelope for reply
or $1.00 to cover costs. If outside the USA, enclose
an international postal reply coupon.

Many of Llewellyn's authors have websites with additional information and resources. For more information, please visit our website:

LLEWELLYN.COM